Afro-American Literature in the Twentieth Century

Afro-American Literature in the Twentieth Century

The Achievement of Intimacy

MICHAEL G. COOKE

Yale University Press
New Haven and London

Designed by James J. Johnson
and set in Caledonia type.
Printed in the United States of America by
Murray Printing Company, Westford, Massachusetts.

Library of Congress Cataloging in Publication Data

Cooke, Michael G.
  Afro-American literature in the twentieth century.

  Bibliography: p.
  Includes index.
  1. American literature—Afro-American authors—History and criticism.
2. American literature—20th century—History and criticism.   3. Afro-Americans in
literature. I. Title.
PS153.N5C67   1984   810′.9′896073   84-5066
ISBN 0-300-03218-8 (alk. paper)

The paper in this book meets the guidelines for permanence and durability
of the Committee on Production Guidelines for Book Longevity of the
Council on Library Resources.

---

10   9   8   7   6   5   4   3   2

Truth is not a stagnant property. . . .
Truth is *made*, just as health, wealth and
strength are made, in the course of experience.
WILLIAM JAMES

for Charlie
generous prompter of others' books
less prompt with his own

Contents

Preface

"Afro-American life and history," Larry Neal has written, are "full of creative possibilities." This serene conviction has not always held sway. To the contrary, the eminent Thomas Jefferson once thought that, despite the paradoxically favorable environment of suffering, the Afro-American had no aptitude for poetry or, by extension, for creativity. We know better, have long known that Neal emphatically gets the nod in this debate.

Though Negro spirituals have been shown to levy on the European hymnic tradition, it is manifest that they, like the blues in the secular sphere, were bearing the substance and flair of Afro-American creativity, beyond a Jefferson's ken. Yet spirituals and the blues were not performed in public. They were sub rosa forms. The one form of Afro-American expression that most white people would have commonly encountered is known as "signifying." And one of the home traits of signifying was that it did not confess itself, but kept an innocuous air; it was a way of using words that mean one acceptable thing to resonate with or *signify* another of a dangerous or insubordinate or forbidden character. Moments of signifying are noticed by writer after writer, from Hurston to Ellison and Wideman, but as a phenomenon in Afro-American art-as-language-and-survival it proves as transient as a moment. Thus it was not until quite recently that signifying came in for separate, systematic scrutiny.

It is possible now to recognize how naturally and effectively signifying and the blues, though in themselves single, discontinuous expressions, represented an early stage in the reality of Afro-American creativity. Stressing the verbal art of the blues, I treat that form and signifying here as synecdoches for a whole that was not even known to exist, let alone established in its lineaments.

This study, then, sets out to identify and illuminate the essential structure of Afro-American literature in our century, that is, in the period from its earliest genuine flourishing to its present prominence and power. Neither minimizing nor reverencing social circumstances and political forces, the book centers on the *intrinsic development* of this literature out of the secret matrix of signifying and the blues into successive conditions of (1) *self-veiling*, (2) *solitude*, (3) *kinship*, and (4) *intimacy*. Each of these conditions manifests an advance, a lessening of limitation in relation to its antecedent, with intimacy achieving an exemplary orientation of lucidity, courage, and aptitude in the Afro-American vision. The first three terms I adopt—self-veiling, solitude, and kinship—ask for no special gloss at this point; the reader will feel at home with them. The fourth term may call for a definition in this context. Intimacy is used to signalize a condition in which the Afro-American protagonist (male or female, pugilist or philosopher, activist or ascetic) is depicted as realistically enjoying a sound and clear orientation toward the self and the world. It denotes a state of mind where one is, in Wordsworth's paradoxical phrase, "free to settle," or, in other words, comely and resolute in one's own being as well as sensitive and effective in dealing with social entities and forces. More than this, it suggests at once a thorough involvement with the world and along with that a degree of immunity from and superiority to sociopolitical shibboleths, as a result of what Alice Walker has called "a wider recognition of the universe." Here, then, is no easy "intimacy" of gesture, but a full and unforced communication with the given, the available, and the conceivable in human experience in a particular time and setting.

In a sense this is a study of the gathering to greatness of Afro-American literature. Even in a crude Darwinian sense the sheer fact of survival in an unfostering environment must tell of strong positive capacities; recent evolutionary theory even goes so far as to say that positive advances occur in pockets of adversity and afterwards disperse, as indeed black people have done, throughout a wider terrain. But we need to be aware that Afro-Americans have not absorbed adversity alone. As Ellison says in *Shadow and Act*, Afro-Americans have been affected totally,

by the climate, the weather, the political circumstances—from which not even slaves were exempt—the social structures, the national manners, the modes of production and the tides of the market, the national ideals, the conflicts of values, the rising and falling of national morale, [and] the complex give and take of acculturalization which was undergone by all others . . . within the American democracy. (p. 250)

Albert Murray brings home this point with peculiar force when he observes that even during slavery people of African extraction were "living in the presence of more human freedom and individual opportunity than they or anybody else had ever seen before," and that they were inevitably affected by such an enriched "conception of being a free man in America" (*The Omni-Americans*, p. 18). A formidable variety of figures evince independent vision and force in the annals of Afro-American experience, during enslavement and again in the strenuous and deeply problematical decades leading into the Second World War: Nat Turner as a revolutionary actor; David Walker (best known for *Walker's Appeal*) as a revolutionary writer/thinker; Frederick Douglass as an orator of emancipation; Sojourner Truth and Harriet Tubman as fountains of strength and beacons of hope in the struggle for freedom; the team of Williams and Walker as creative minstrels and poignantly misguided dreamers of change; Alexander Crummell, valiant and thwarted as the first black Episcopalian minister in America; Booker T. Washington as a fiercely calculating conciliator; W. E. B. Du Bois as an intellectual champion and far-sighted activist; and Marcus Garvey as a gorgeous visionary and would-be practical savior. In short, if racial griefs and grievances made an effective hub for the experience of the Afro-American, collectively taken, the individual Afro-American one after another created a powerful and distinctive radiance off that hub.

It is startling, and troubling, to find Stephen Butterfield, in his important scrutiny of *Black Autobiography in America*, denying distinctive selfhood-in-context to the Afro-American, and categorizing him instead as a uniform "soldier in a long historic march toward Canaan" (p. 3). Even LeRoi Jones declares that the Afro-American "never moved into the position where he could propose his own symbols, erect his own personal myths" (*Home*, p. 112). But already in 1965, when Jones took this stand, Wright and Ellison and Hayden and Baldwin, not to mention Hurston and Hughes and Toomer and Du Bois and of course Jones himself, had established a place on the map of American literary culture.

One recalls Hazlitt's definition of genius as "some strong quality in the mind, answering to and bringing out some new and striking quality in nature," and one wishes to say that the Afro-American genius had come to the fore. But *genius* might imply some peculiar and invariable or fated quality. That is not intended, and will not do. Instead, we might take up the synonym Hazlitt himself resorted to: "genius or *originality*." For a kind of centering originality does manifest itself in Afro-American literature: an ability to find a fresh center where old resources have dried up or been crushed. The continual prominence of grandmothers and, of latter days, grandfathers in this body of work is a testament to (a) stamina, in that the oppressed survive into advanced years, and (b) an increase in savvy and grace, in that they also thrive and become models and champions of their people. It also embodies a value of stability and continuity without eliminating surprise, that is, the coming of the newborn child. In some respects the spectrum from grandparent to newborn could stand as an emblem for Afro-American literature, in which the ability to bring forth the new without rude disruption is less a matter of genius than of generosity. John Coltrane, one of the great originators in the Afro-American artistic tradition, neatly sums up the case:

There is never any end. There are always new sounds to imagine, new feelings to get at. And always, there is the need to keep purifying these feelings and sounds so that we can really see what we've discovered in its pure state. [Quoted by Nat Hentoff in the liner notes to the album *Meditations*]

This study represents one effort to get at the true feelings and sounds of Afro-American literature, hewing to the line of its inner development with full knowledge, all the time, that there is never any end.

1

INTRODUCTION *Building on "Signifying"*
and the Blues

> Instead of inciting the Slaves to rebellion with
> eloquent oratory, I soothed their hurt and elo-
> quently sang the Blues.
>
> Eldridge Cleaver

EVER since James Joyce and *Ulysses*,
experimentation has been the order of the day in Western literature.
Inspired by Joyce, T. S. Eliot brought a dazzling formal complexity
into the mainstream of poetry; his work was reinforced by the
rediscovery of the metaphysical poets and by the emergence of the
crabbed art of Gerard Manley Hopkins, a Victorian Jesuit whose
poetry first came to public notice at the end of World War I. Eliot
embodied what he preached against, a "dissociation of sensibility";
the tortured form of *The Waste Land* reflected what the poem
expressed: the fragmentation of personality, the dilapidation of the
edifices of culture and value, the loss of cohesion and force in human
undertakings. The *Shantih* of the poem's conclusion, the peace that
passeth understanding, is an allusion to a system not only distant and
strange, but incommensurate with the poem's staccato form and its
trick of making contentious juxtapositions of otherwise harmless
elements. The ironic, allusive style of Eliot, or Joyce or Pound,

1

amounts to a mischievous spray of the ocean in which they are immersed.

The idea of alienation that Marx had introduced in a strictly politico-economic context (the worker shall not be alienated from his labor) began to be used as a basic cultural metaphor. It became fashionable to be alienated, not from anything in particular, but in the nature of things, and there would develop the anomalous and amusing situation where sizable groups of people, say at cocktail parties, would be talking about their alienation, which obviously had become the source of *community*, or at least of what Thomas Pynchon ambiguously designated "a crossing of solipsisms." It was as though Leibniz's monads found themselves connected in a preestablished cacophony of complaint. Furthermore, with the increasing vogue of the philosophy of existentialism, with its stress on individual exposure and the absence of inherent principles or structures of meaning, alienation found a tongue, and a dignity that proved close to overbearing. For the first time in centuries a common mood coincided with a major formal philosophy in Western society.

The social conventions and practical assumptions that entered into Victorian literature even where it was, as so often in Dickens, scathingly satirical, lost their force. The kind of incertitude that Cézanne had introduced into art by virtue of a sense of parallax, a sense of the difference the observer's perspective and even the moment of observation must make in the judgment formed, became widespread. What Darwin in the mid-nineteenth century had done to shake the concept of institutional sacredness Freud did to the concept of individual organization. Both nature and the mind seemed to subject the human scheme to random pressures and immedicable influences. Not only in its early stage of object-fracturing geometry and shallowness of plane, but also in its later phase of trompe-l'oeil collage, cubism further induced a sense of human devaluation. And the conviction of incertitude took on cosmic status when an eclipse corroborated Einstein's enunciation of the theory of relativity.

With exquisite care literary artists, encouraged by critical theorists, cultivated not gardens but something akin to thickets. Narrative form in literature sought virtually to embody the cube of cubism; the treatment of time was thrown into disarray; and even character lost solidity, not to say centrality, in major twentieth-century writing. Form or, rather, complex and ingenious deformity took over the limelight and became the standard of value for purposes of literature. The French alone in the space of a few decades generated surrealism and the "antinovel" novel, with personality, value, style, psychology, and form thrown head over heels. Literary works took on the look of something fashioned by a troika of Ptolemy, Rube Goldberg, and F. A. O. Schwarz. A penetrating study by William Barrett, *The Illusion of Technique*, demonstrated that the phenomenon of gratuitous intricacy was all but pandemic in intellectual culture. Artists themselves plainly declared the dominance of technique; as Thomas Pynchon puts it, "Our beauty lies . . . in [the] extended capacity for convolution."[1]

It is startling how little the passion for formal invention has reflected itself in Afro-American literature. Some other force, some other *goal* takes precedence.[2] Perhaps it was symbolic that *Fire*, one

1. Thomas Pynchon, *The Crying of Lot 49* (New York: Bantam Books,1982), p. 20.

2. With valuable emphases differing from mine, the following critics have enunciated a vision of the Afro-American literary enterprise in the American scheme: Robert Bone, *The Negro Novel in America*, rev. ed. (New Haven: Yale University Press, 1965); Blyden Jackson, *The Waiting Years: Essays on Negro American Literature* (Baton Rouge: Louisiana State University Press, 1976); George E. Kent, *Blackness and the Adventure of Western Culture* (Chicago: Third World Press, 1972); J. Saunders Redding, *To Make a Poet Black* (Chapel Hill: University of North Carolina Press, 1939); Addison Gayle, Jr., *The Way of the New World: The Black Novel in America* (Garden City, N.J.: Anchor Press, 1975) and *The Black Situation* (New York: Horizon Press, 1970); Robert B. Stepto, *From Behind the Veil: A Study of Afro-American Narrative* (Urbana: University of Illinois Press, 1979); Houston A. Baker, Jr., *The Journey Back: Issues in Black Literature and Criticism* (Chicago: University of Chicago Press, 1980); Sherley Anne Williams, *Give Birth to Brightness: A Thematic Study of Neo-Black Literature* (New York: Dial Press, 1972). In the introduction to his study *Black Fiction* (Cambridge: Harvard University Press, 1974), Roger Rosenblatt also makes telling and wide-ranging comments on the critical, political, social, and

early attempt to produce a quasi-surrealistic organ that would "burn up a lot of the old, dead, conventional Negro ideas of the past,"was short-lived. The first issue went up in fire. The venture never rose from its ashes. Thus, the kind of experiment with sexual candor that James Branch Cabell undertook (*Jurgen*, 1919) and the clinical sentiments and style of the Lost Generation do not find a counterpart in black writing. Black humor proved a white phenomenon, and the fabulator's sense of life as unreal and mad, though this might seem highly germane to black experience, has not really taken hold in black writing. Ishmael Reed may seem to come close to the likes of Barthelme, Kosinski, and Vonnegut, but he is of another stripe. He has a social vision, even a social mission to convey. Reed is not blatant about this; in *Yellow Back Radio Broke-Down* he skewers the "neo-social realist gang" and the principle that "all art must be for the end of liberating the masses." But when he counters, through the Loop Garoo Kid, that art "can be anything it wants to be, a vaudeville show, the six-o'clock news, the mumblings of wild men saddled by demons" (p. 40), he is making his own thinly veiled political statement. We may recognize it as a politics based on revolution, though not in the spasmodic militant sense espoused by his adversary Bo Shmo. Indeed, Bo Shmo's position resembles a case of misguided practicality, and could at worst boil down to little more than another fantasy of wish fulfillment, as Sherley Williams's judicious summary, "The Limited Solution of Revolution," makes clear.[3] By contrast, Reed espouses the incessant pursuit of freedom in art *and thus* in society, and, in the same terms, the superiority of abundance and variety to monotony.

---

philosophical issues that were paramount in the thinking about Afro-American literature in the intensely engaged period of the 1960s and 1970s. The reader should also consult Amiri Baraka and Larry Neal, eds., *Black Fire: An Anthology of Afro-American Writing* (New York: Morrow, 1968); Addison Gayle, Jr., ed., *The Black Aesthetic* (New York: Doubleday, 1971); Stephen Henderson, *Understanding the New Black Poetry: Black Speech and Black Music as Poetic References* (New York: William Morrow, 1973); and Stephen Butterfield, *Black Autobiography in America* (Amherst: University of Massachusetts Press, 1974).

  3. *Give Birth to Brightness*, pp. 118–31.

While modernism in white literature took the form of hothouse virtuosity and detachment (if not revulsion) from the human, in Afro-American literature it took the form of a centering upon the possibilities of the human and an emergent sense of intimacy predicated on the human. The crumbling of traditional structures of support in the society at large may have called up wild echoes and startling manifestations in the aesthetic vanguard, but it entailed no more than a mild dislocation for those who had passed generations in a milieu of dispossession. The Afro-American situation that had obliged its people to count on themselves or nothing now became the foundation for building a new structure of experience in the common ground that stood devoid of any cultural great house. In effect, even as the literature of the ascendant society continued to preoccupy itself with traditional structures in *the mode of absence or perversion,* Afro-American literature was undertaking to reincarnate and reinvest with value the culture's lost sense of being and belonging.

We may with advantage look at one very influential, indeed "classic" modern text, Kafka's *Metamorphosis,* in relation to the use of metamorphosis as a motif in Afro-American literature. Kafka does not transmit metamorphosis into Western literature as concrete incident (at best direct imitation would seem wan), but rather as a principle. Gregor Samsa's story catches the sense of radical instability in spirit and form that has invaded our self-conception in this era, and it catches also the corollary impulse of intolerance toward the presence of others in their casual solidity and toward other viewpoints with their determined plausibility. Gregor Samsa as cockroach embodies a guilty hypersensitivity in the self, a condition that first leads to inadequacy in action and in relationship, and beyond that leads to a stubborn, defiant pride in such inadequacy. His metamorphosis is a way of boasting ineptitude and courting victimization. It is also a way of imposing on others, as Jean Genet does, by insisting on the low order to which we fear being assigned, rather than submitting to a common standard and extending ourselves to surpass it. In sum, the metamorphosis restricts the sphere and forms of operation pertinent to the self, and further controls others by forcing them to treat as given and weirdly physical what is really an optative and final degeneration.

Recent studies have shown that Kafka had no experience, either biographical or cultural, to provoke such a vision. Far from making Melville's Bartleby seem a model of acumen and efficiency, Kafka attained considerable success and recognition as a functionary in the Austrian government (he was born in Czechoslovakia). Not even his notoriously tragic love life seems to have escaped his powers of management; he fostered its unsuccess, and elected the enchantment of distance over the enhancement of presence in love. In some sense, then, Kafka can be said to have done something gratuitous, grotesque, in *The Metamorphosis*.

Perhaps the chasm between experience and literary artifact could be construed as a testimony to the span of the Kafkaesque imagination. No one supposes that a mere correspondence must exist between the artistic work and the phenomenal data of our experience. Such a view would be almost perverse in the century of abstraction. On the other hand, there is some justice in scrutinizing the fact that the imagination in question has an intensely introspective bias. In *The Metamorphosis* we are in the chasms of Kafka's spirit. As John Aldridge has noted, this is the modern position, where the conditions of actuality outside the jealously treasured parameters of the self are thought unpalatable, unnecessary, even improbable.[4] The point is that modern writers did not need to fear that the other selves necessary to their existence, that is, readers, would turn away in equal solipsism. Rather, in ironic collaboration, the readers saw themselves graphically articulated in the writers' work. Even ostensibly realistic writers like Bellow and Updike end up with characters like Henderson and Rabbit drawing circles of self-indulgence and isolation around themselves.

It counts to Kafka's credit that an era should have gone so wholeheartedly into that space, and have emerged with a sense that

4. John W. Aldridge, *The American Novel and the Way We Live Now* (New York: Oxford University Press, 1983), pp. 10, 17–18, 118ff., 128ff.

one man's neurosis was every man's norm. Still, without invidious-
ness, the point may be made that those who take Kafka's vision as a
mirror of Western culture tend to be the ones whose mirrors have
g(u)ilt frames. One has more time to imagine oneself a cockroach if
one's rooms are not overrun with such insects, or if one is not
commonly treated as such.

In Afro-American experience, metamorphosis is more than a
matter of singular imaginative projection. Zora Neale Hurston in
Their Eyes Were Watching God records the view that black women
are the "mules" of the world, being the ones who must carry the
burdens that all others, even black men, can foist off. In *Narrative of
the Life of Frederick Douglass, An American Slave,* Douglass continually reports how circumstances put him in the status of an animal.
For Hurston and Douglass the metaphor of metamorphosis cuts
close to the bone. It expresses the loss of social and practical freedom, as well as the baffled confinement and depression of felt
powers that Kafka exploits.

Apart from Hurston and Douglass, the tradition of "conjure"
takes metamorphosis in Afro-American experience into the domain
of an unremitting psychosocial threat. "Conjure" (or "goopher," as it
is colloquially termed) is cognate with voodoo and obeah, but
differs from them in one important way: it does not reflect a homo-
geneous or self-sustaining community, but operates in a world of
basic insecurity and compromise. Conjure reflects a world where
knowledge is as dangerous as it is privileged, and where ignorance is
one with daily dread. In this dispensation, power is arbitrary and
unsystematic. Though the exercise of conjure might confer a momentary benefit on a black person, its very existence tells of unpredictability, vulnerability, and disintegration.

Even so, the outstanding effect of metamorphosis in black
experience is not negative. A resistance, a resiliency, even perhaps a
human teleology keeps metamorphosis from triumphing, if not from
getting into play. Avoiding alike the portentousness of Thomas
Pynchon's *Gravity's Rainbow* and the giddy, antic posture of John
Irving's *World According to Garp,* black literature makes metamorphosis a datum, not a determinant or a definition. In addition,

metamorphosis as datum slowly loses its psychosocial grip from the early instance of Charles Chesnutt's *Conjure Woman* to the latter-day *Autobiography* of Malcolm X. Malcolm himself, though occupying a "fast-changing world," comes through a series of personal metamorphoses—identifiable in turn as Malcolm Little, Homeboy, Detroit Red, Satan, Malcolm X, El Hajj Malik El-Shabazz—to ever-increasing stability and lucidity. He goes through the social quandaries and existential contretemps we are fond of calling modern, and yet wins his way to himself. Ultimately, his metamorphosis is of the mind, at once given and made, inevitable and creative. Surviving the long stages where metamorphosis possesses him, Malcolm finds himself joyously "transformed," for he is transformed into "a complete human being" (*Autobiography*, p. 365).

It is arguable that the sense of intimacy—that is, freedom from compulsion and a lucid, prompt communication with his spirit and world—lies at the root of Malcolm's power as a writer, if not as a man. His ability to repudiate error enables him to grow, but what makes him grow great is the capacity to embrace the person who made the errors, the person he has been, as an integral stage of his life. That is what makes him "complete." His life contracts from the killing off of his father and of his hopes for a professional career, narrows down to the depths of evil in prison, then expands, in a virtually Dantesque way, to the breadth of vision that is his on the pilgrimage to Mecca. Prior to his assassination, which he prophesies, he is palpably grappling with, growing into, a new catholicity of spiritual and political outlook. (By contrast, *The Metamorphosis* merely dwindles and rigidifies.) Malcolm X's capacity for blind devotion and extremism in behavior evolves into a balanced and lucid fullness of being in the world. From impossibly wanting all of anything, and at once, he comes to wait for the most of the best of everything. He achieves the kind of intimacy with his mind and with his world that is the antithesis of Kafkaesque obsession. In a sense, Malcolm X may have been driven, by the very denial of conventional and evanescent success, into his singular excellence. What Hegel says of the bondsman holds good: he has and is close to powers that the privileged lord cannot touch. The power of any intimacy that goes beyond mechanical gestures and slogans is uncommon in our society. Perhaps—because privilege shelters us not only from harm but also from unknown good—that power of intimacy proves possible in a degree corresponding to the conventional powerlessness of Afro-American people in the society.

For Afro-American literature the sense of intimacy takes the form of reaching, or being invited, out of the self and into an unguarded and uncircumscribed engagement with the world. As Malcolm X declared: "I'm for truth, no matter who tells it. I'm for justice, no matter who it is for or against. I'm a human being first and foremost" (*Autobiography*, p. 366). Such a declaration is a prelude to intimacy, resting on (1) a faith in coping, (2) a precise apprehension of the complex play of experience in the society no less than in the individual, and (3) a creative conviction that bearing means fruit as well as pain. In this sense intimacy is to be distinguished from privacy, in that privacy thrives on exclusion whereas intimacy comes with an unforeseen recognition of the self in the world and with an unbounded interaction of the self with the world.

This is not to make intimacy sound like ecstasy or a joyride to self-realization. It is a process, an experiment in human modality, and it is laden with risk. Implicitly it takes away the protections, learned and instinctive, with which the personality routinely operates, and in return it holds out as much a prospect of exhaustion and rebuff and ridicule as it does an enhancement of the spirit and the terms of life. There need be no surprise, then, that intimacy should be risked most by those with the least to lose, that is to say, the Afro-American writers who derived the least gain from the canonical forms and goals of the society.

By the same token it will come as no surprise that the achievement of intimacy did not come about overnight. We can see adumbrations of intimacy and antecedent developments as early as James Weldon Johnson and Jean Toomer and Claude McKay; but not before the inspired production of Robert Hayden does the genuine and authoritative phenomenon of intimacy appear. It will be timely here to illustrate the work of intimacy in an as-yet-uncelebrated poem of Hayden's, before proceeding to set forth something of the progressive pathway that brought Afro-American literature to that extraordinary modern consummation.

On its surface "The Crystal Cave Elegy" (*Angle of Ascent*, p. 5), the culminating poem in a five-part series entitled "Beginnings," simply captures a meteoric piece of local journalism. But swiftly a complex triangle of identification develops in the relations among the young boy speaking, the grandfather who is the primary subject of the poem, and Floyd Collins, whose plight in the Crystal Cave sets the old man remembering his own experience of the "Kentucky coal- / mine dark." The indistinction between coal and crystal has three analogs in the poem: between black and white, between old and young, between former times and the present. The title incident can be said to be focal, but the issue of "The Crystal Cave Elegy" is the permanent precariousness and pain of human experience. Within that scheme, the traumatic isolation that seems to be the occasion of the poem proves the basis for a deep unison among the poem's elements. The obvious sympathy we would expect between the boy speaker and the boy victim gets no play. Sympathy goes from the old black man to the young white boy, in a mode at once unexpected and irresistible.

The creation of a blended sense of surprise and naturalness is intrinsic to the poem's intimacy. Not superficial association but deep involvement and identification apply. The "Elegy" raises a sensational and pathetic episode to a higher dimension. It does so on the fulcrum of the old man's interjection, "I taste the / darkness yet." What is happening to the boy, the "poor game loner" in the cave, comes home to us with a wrenching clarity. He is undergoing the kind of experience that in its Bergsonian intensity redefines the process of time. The old black man is not just remembering but ceaselessly living in secret the fate of the trapped white boy. His spontaneous prayer for the boy is then a tacit prayer for himself, as one who has faced the ultimate loss of the "greenhorn dream of / life."

Following the paradoxical reflection, "Alive down there / in his grave," the prayer is simple and brief:

Open
for him, blue door.

The "blue door" may be construed as the sky, implying a restoration to the liberal upper air. Or it may refer to death, as a quick release from the agony of encagement and slow dying (the poetry of Negritude abounds in this powerful use of the color blue). Or the blue door may convey both death and redemptive escape, fused in a redemptive heaven.

The essential weight of the poem falls on the transformation of the sensational Floyd Collins story into an emblem of grief and compassion and courage, by virtue of the old man's intimacy with its substance, as opposed to its surface details. The synesthesia of tasting darkness shows how far the incident has been taken inward. The tasting may be associated with a child's orality, the instinctive attempt to identify and relate to a novelty. It also has about it a seasoned frankness and integrity, in that the old man does not deny or suppress his cruel memory. Rather he faces the symbolic power of darkness, with all it suggests of emotional, social, and spiritual deprivation, and he is able to sustain the morbid social identification of that deep psychic dread with the incidental shading of his epidermis. More than this, he seems to sense that the white boy trapped in darkness cannot cope with it, and he extends a spontaneous sympathy to his new fellow-sufferer.

The human closeness established among the characters arises in proportion to the inhuman closeness of darkness to the human actor/sufferer. By this I mean that darkness, symbolically conjuring up regressive, disordered, destruction-bearing forces, seems to inspire antipathy and dismay in the human breast. But darkness *in fact* is more variable and ambiguous than darkness *as symbol*. Apart from the fact that a perverse taste for it can be developed, darkness can be put to positive, isometric use in the spirit. The mystics demonstrate this in their experience of the dark night of the soul, and on a lesser, more practical plane the old man also makes good use of darkness in "The Crystal Cave Elegy." The very inhuman closeness of darkness paradoxically brings out a special power, of endurance and generosity, in the human sphere. The old man evinces it in himself, and seems to will it telepathically to the trapped boy. Clearly intimacy with darkness is not chosen, but given; it is converted into a positive agent by the capacity for intimacy itself.

A certain freedom from *fixed* canons of conduct or thought comes with intimacy. "Pa Hayden" thinks like a black man, enough so that the "darkness" he tastes may be his own, but he does not think dogmatically like a black man. He does not say that an accident, rather than a systematic cultural conspiracy, put Floyd Collins in a hole, and that accordingly the boy falls in a different sphere from himself and need be accorded no recognition. The old man spontaneously displays a sort of self-recognition in otherness, and it is this that, as we will see later, the ill-fated boxer in "Free Fantasia: Tiger Flowers" elicits from "the sporting people" and the "Creole babies" of St. Antoine. It may appear at first blush that disaster is the preferred setting for intimacy. But in fact intimacy means going beyond disaster, and sharing in something like what Wordsworth calls the "grandeur in the beating" of the human heart.

Now it need hardly be said that elegy is predicated on sympathy between speaker and subject, or that the form has had a wide appeal for the twentieth-century artist. Hayden's work may then have something of a conventional air. But it is in substance quietly independent and even revolutionary. To begin with, this elegy pertains to a freak accident, no very probable occasion for the form. It gets its justification from the singular power that the grandfather brings to bear so as to find an ageless humanity in a chance occurrence. He makes the poem not a specific memorial for a death, but an elegy for our basic mortality, for the bonded human condition itself.

A further departure from convention comes in the use of the boy as speaker and mediator in the poem, though it is the old man who bears the elegiac consciousness. In effect the boy is learning to recognize human need and pain and solidarity. The old man is not only embodying human intimacy in relation to Floyd Collins, but communicating it to his grandson, thereby making a tradition of intimacy. That sense of tradition makes the poem's intimacy more than just a triumph of personality, while the dynamic continuity from personality to humanity carries elegy into new amplitudes.

The force of the poem is so easy and so profound that we may at first overlook one important fact: the old man has not been in the habit of expressing himself in this vein. Depths of his being and of his understanding are called up by the young stranger's predicament. In other words, it is not only the human capacity for intimacy that emerges in the poem, but also the reserved old man's qualities of magnanimity and eloquence. Both the intimacy and the magnanimity, which are inseparable, must be seen in light of two prevailing factors that stunt human possibility: happenstance and cruelty. Here happenstance refers directly to Floyd Collins in the cave, but it also harks back to the abrupt fall of Africans into the hands of slave-traffickers; the hold of the slaveship would correspond to the trap of the cave, thus linking the old man and the trapped boy even on the physical level. Cruelty consists of course in enslavement. And again there is an implicit connection between the old man who has known slavery and the young white boy whose life seems so remote from it. The boy has lost his freedom, not to other people, but to the play of circumstances. And the old man's prayer for the boy's freedom becomes a perpetual prayer for his own freedom from the undying memory of his enslavement.

The richness of structure and substance in a poem like "The Crystal Cave Elegy" springs from a condition of human alertness and involvement. No exceptional effort is made to brandish the poem's value in terms of a striking form. Rather than taking a strange and rigid new posture, the poem serenely draws on the immemorial plasticity of content in unaggressive molds to do its work.

If we consider the fact that as literature has become more and more experimental, more and more obsessed with form, it has lost more and more of its common appeal, then we might say that black literature has spared itself a certain penalty. But it may be more to the point to say that black literature could not afford the luxury of formal involutions because embroidery is not the first interest of people who are still busy with the basic fabric of experience. Even Ralph Ellison, William Demby, Ishmael Reed, and Alice Walker, keenly modern, sophisticated writers who continually pose themselves difficult formal problems, do not seem primarily *experimental*. Their primary concern continues palpably to be the centripetal human engagement. In the teeth of social pressure and cultural fashion, an inveterate bent toward the human factor and human valences in all events manifests itself in black literature.

What is extraordinary about a Ralph Ellison and an Alice Walker is the fact that they should have attained international stature, putting themselves among the greatest of their generations, within the scant decades that Afro-American literature can plausibly be said to have existed. For though we fondly point to Phillis Wheatley and William Wells Brown and, of late, to *Our Nig* as a beginning, an occasional work in a discontinuous idiom does not make for a literature. This is not to take anything away from the honorable habit of writing and of reading that sustained the black periodical press in the nineteenth century, or from the moving urgency of expression that materialized in the slave narratives. The question I am raising has to do with the character or impress of the writing, and here a distinction must be drawn between Afro-American work that is dependent on the ambient culture and work that is at least reacting against that culture and thus tending toward an idiom and shape of its own, that is, original and intrinsic self-expression. We must note that reaction retains traces of influence; though it may advance into originality, it may as readily fall back into dependence. It follows thus that dependence belongs to another *order* of experience than originality, whereas reaction is more truly of another *degree*. As regards the Afro-American tradition, the early stage of dependence is marked by *black literary productions*; essentially *black American literature* takes its rise from the end of the nineteenth century, when not only reaction but also a gravitation toward originality became manifest.

But it did not, like Venus from the boiling sea, spring full-blown into being. There had in fact been a long and strong, if oblique, tradition of black expression in the United States. Two forms, one now widely recognized and the other only lately coming into public notice, formed the effective matrix of black American literature. These were (a) the blues, and (b) "signifying," the disingenuously conciliatory habit, perfected by blacks on these shores, of maintaining the critique oblique.[5] In general, signifying is a form of metacommunication, where the surface expression and the intrinsic position diverge—a phenomenon well known to psychiatrists and marriage counselors. In one dimension signifying might take the form of modes of speech and gesture that, while pleasing to the white power structure, carry an undertow of freedom and critical distance. In another dimension signifying might function as a nimble mental maneuver for fending off *any* overweening claim or *any* attempt to constrain and overdetermine the play of life. It is a negotiation along two axes of power, the social and the mental, the public and the covert. The accompanying diagram will illustrate.

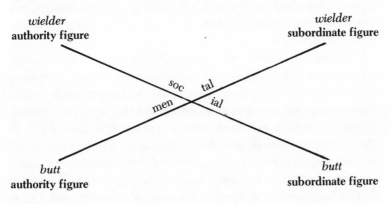

5. Houston A. Baker, Jr., in *Long Black Song: Essays in Black American Literature and Culture* (Charlottesville: University Press of Virginia, 1972), emphasizes the importance of black folklore to the black literary tradition. I agree with Baker, as with many others, on the crucial and *current* standing of folklore, which I go on to treat as the basis of a complex and urgent evolution into various forms and values in the great manifestation of Afro-American literature.

It is not without significance that in music the blues and in language the art of signifying should have sustained the black cultural tradition when its very existence was mischievously denied. This mischief, grave enough in itself, was made worse by one of those paradoxes of social repression: Mary Frances Berry and John Blassingame demonstrate, in *Long Memory: The Black Experience in America*, that the very people who denied the existence of any black cultural substance and style busied themselves in trying to root out its ever-springing signs. Frederick Douglass, penning the narrative of the life he had led as slave and antislavery spokesman in the middle of the nineteenth century, declares himself "utterly astonished" at the way white people take the slaves' song as a proof of contentment, and even happiness (p. 32). Earlier still, in his *Notes on the State of Virginia*, Thomas Jefferson recognizes that "among the blacks is misery enough," and yet manages to convert the implicit summons to sympathy into a source of disparagement. Jefferson links misery with "the most affecting touches of poetry," and blames black people for having "misery . . . , God knows, but not poetry." He goes on to call love "the peculiar oestrum of the poet," but finds that the Negro's love is "ardent" in a way that "kindles the senses only, not the imagination."[6]

On the face of it this seems a grave indictment of white indifference or cruelty in regard to the reality of black people's victimization. But let us frankly face the fact that the signs of black culture were sometimes not easily read, or meant to be read, by nonblack people. (It would take more than a century after Jefferson for Du Bois to come forward and show the lack of imagination and of accuracy in his view.) We must be mindful that an adaptive skill in misleading was an important basis of survival for blacks. Ellison calls it "our long habit of deception and evasion" (*Shadow and Act*, p. xxi), and Du Bois speaks of a message "naturally veiled and half articulate" (*The Souls of Black Folk*, p. 186). Ostensible simplicity and candor arose from consummate personal and social veiling. This

6. Thomas Jefferson, *Notes on the State of Virginia*, edited with an introduction and notes by William Peden (Chapel Hill: University of North Carolina Press, 1955), p. 140.

using of a veil (as opposed to the Du Boisian state of being relegated to a position behind one) ensured the continuance, as in a private greenhouse, of a vital black culture in the hemisphere. But the perfection was also the peril of the veil—an effect well known to actors who play a role too long. Either fatigue or forgetting would set in, and the double vision of the inner reality and the public veil would collapse, producing a harmful effect on what Carter G. Woodson, founder of the *Journal of Negro History* and in his time only slightly less well known than Alain Locke, aptly called "the development of the public [Negro] mind."[7] The pose turned into the personality, the exploiter of a role into its helpless incarnation.

A kind of wry explanation and vindication of white mistaking comes from the mouths of black people themselves. First we have the blues lyric that runs:

> Got one mind for white folks to see,
> 'nother for what I know is me;
> he don't know, he don't know my mind.[8]

The art of concealment that gives rise to this avowal may well have been tacitly enforced by the circumstances of slavery; slaves suffered for expressing an interest in freedom or even in improved conditions of existence. But the art of concealment was pervasive; Langston Hughes depicts it in "Dream Boogie" (*Selected Poems*, p. 221), and Countee Cullen confesses it in "Heritage (for Harold Jackman)," a poem partially meant to proclaim pride in the black tradition:

> *All day long and all night through*
> *One thing only must I do:*
> *Quench my pride and cool my blood*
> *Lest I perish in the flood.*   (*On These I Stand*, p. 28)

7. Carter G. Woodson, introduction to *The Mind of the Negro as Reflected in Letters Written during the Crisis, 1800–1860* (New York: Russell and Russell, 1969), p. v.

8. Not surprisingly, there are many variants of this general position in the recorded canon of the blues. The reader may with advantage consult Giles Oakley, *The Devil's Music: A History of the Blues* (Harcourt Brace Jovanovich, 1978), pp. 15ff.

Clearly this mastery of self-concealment or self-enclosure advanced, if it did not cause, the myth of the happy slave and, after Emancipation and the collapse of Reconstruction, that of the darky happy in nature and deprivation. Still, a slow movement toward self-enunciation, rebellious in the early case of David Walker's *Appeal*, more tempered in the case of Frederick Douglass, could not be headed off.

At the beginning of the twentieth century W. E. B. Du Bois picks up Douglass's brief lament and spells it out. In *The Souls of Black Folk* Du Bois uncovers not only the fact of sorrow in the slave songs, but also the rich intrinsic life of the slaves: its endurance and fortitude in the face of burdens more than physical, its compassion, sensitivity, vision, and grace, its plangent creativity, in short its human soul and worth. As Robert Stepto observes, Du Bois sought "nothing less than a new narrative mode and form in which empirical evidence, scientifically gathered in a literal and figurative field (i.e., the Black Belt) performs the authenticating chores previously completed by white opinion."[9] At the same time, of course, Du Bois did engage himself to reorient and recreate white opinion, as a necessary part of uncovering the intrinsic life and reality of black experience. Veils deprive people on both sides.

Du Bois's uncovering, or let us say his discovery, of the souls of black folk might have been done from outside. It is singularly important that it was done *from within*: "I who speak here am bone of the bone and flesh of the flesh of them that live within the Veil" (p. v). It is important to recognize that Du Bois is not just identifying himself racially but also claiming important new psychic territory. A half-century earlier no less a figure than Frederick Douglass had tacitly taken this double position to be unattainable: "I was myself within the circle; so that I neither saw nor heard as those without might see and hear" (*Narrative of the Life*, p. 31). Clearly Du Bois commands the worlds within *and* outside the circle or, as he construes it, the veil. He is identifying knowledge as well as power,

9. Robert Stepto, *From Behind the Veil*, p. 63.

for while the possession of a power, a gift, a quality is a positive thing off the bat, knowledge of that possession is better yet. To illustrate, the argument of Franz Boas that black speech is rich and complex and has the same integrity qua language as standard white speech matters less, from the black point of view, than the work of black linguists in the same vein. And if the work of black linguists such as J. L. Dillard, Geneva Smitherman, and Claudia Mitchell-Kernan had preceded that of Boas, the value from the black perspective would have been much enhanced. For as knowledge is more than mere possession, so is prior knowledge, leading knowledge, reforming and revelatory knowledge more than mere knowledge. It may even be said that to know and deploy one's own powers, gifts, and qualities in relation to others constitutes the only full-fledged possession. As Alain Locke wrote in the influential title essay of his "interpretive anthology," *The New Negro*, in 1925: "Lacking self-understanding, we have been almost as much of a problem to ourselves as we are to others" (p. 4).[10] A full quarter-century earlier Pauline Hopkins had urged that self-understanding must come from within: "No one will do this for us; we must ourselves develop the men and women who will faithfully portray the inmost thoughts and feelings of the Negro with all the fire and romance which lie dormant in our history."[11]

In this light, when Du Bois as a young man takes the negative that had been the state of black folk and develops it into a positive and cogent idea of the souls of black folk, a major event takes place in the black American scheme. For Du Bois, though perhaps falling short of full-fledged possession, has it in mind and in sight. He announces possession as a legitimate claim and a likely state for black people. And it is possession not just of a gift but of one's very definition as a being. Before, there had been only knowledge of being possessed by others, on top of an inner sense of possession that

10. Robert Hayden uses the phrase "interpretive anthology" in his preface to *The New Negro*.

11. Quoted in the introduction to *The Black Aesthetic*, ed. Addison Gayle, Jr., p. xvii.

had no articulation, no clear and secure public form. To say this is not
to underestimate the fact that the Fisk University Choir had in a
measure paved the way for Du Bois when, beginning in the late
nineteenth century, it instituted its tours throughout the United
States and abroad, singing Negro spirituals. But the same distinction
must be drawn between the Fisk University Choir and Du Bois as
between a pathway and a vehicle. The former established the presence of the spirituals in the public mind. The latter brought home
their meaning and values. As Du Bois himself noted in *The Negro*
(1915), American Negroes made vital progress when they found
"their own voices, their own ideals" rather than being "led and
defended by others" (p. 231).

The Souls of Black Folk (1903) offers itself forthrightly as a text
of "dawning," not only for black people but for the entire new
century: "The problem of the Twentieth Century is the problem of
the color line" (p. 23). It may indeed be seen as a work of resurrection, showing forth the life of what is "buried"; and it may finally be
seen as a work of apocalypse, in that it involves the removal, however briefly and tentatively, of the veil. Clearly Du Bois has thrown
off the attitude and idioms of dependence. He sees American history
afresh, and its social mores and personal involvements. And he
wishes the black American to be seen afresh. If he is still operating in
the orbit of reaction, that is, shy of setting a standard of his own, his
style of reaction is pliant and broad-gauged, and it brings a defiant
gaze almost to the level of independent vision.

In justice to Du Bois it must be recognized that he is no mere
hectoring polemicist or one-note champion of the black cause. *The
Souls of Black Folk* is a most pliant (but not compliant) instrument,
ranging through history, fiction, autobiography, sociology, quasi-
mythology, cultural analysis and meditation, psychoeconomics, and
more. Not only the breadth of its vision but the measure of its voice
serve to bring the soul of *The Souls of Black Folk* home with
propriety and conviction: Du Bois was purveying an embodiment of
soul along with its apologia.

The victim of bias transcends it: "How curious a land is this,—
how full of untold story, of tragedy and laughter, and the rich legacy

of human life; shadowed with a tragic past, and big with future promise!" (p. 95). Even the motif of the "Sorrow Songs" and the culminating discourse upon them fail to unbalance Du Bois's temper: "Through all the sorrow of the Sorrow Songs," he writes, "there breathes a hope—a faith in the ultimate justice of things" (p. 189).

The extent and the source of that hope would seem to rest with black people themselves, if we can trust the apparent use that Du Bois made of Tennyson in formulating his metaphor for the Afro-American state. In section 56 of *In Memoriam*, where he laments the ways of nature "red in tooth and claw," Tennyson breaks into the following outcry:

> O life as futile, then, as frail.
> O for thy voice to soothe and bless.
> What hope of answer, or redress?
> Behind the veil, behind the veil.[12]

In this context the life of blacks in society partakes of the character of something red in tooth and claw, but the hope for redress, rather than residing behind the veil of death (as with Tennyson), occurs within the very framework of oppression, behind the redefined veil.

But Du Bois's "After-Thought," including as it does the poignant wish that "these crooked marks on a fragile leaf be not indeed THE END" (p. 192), leaves the whole question of the new day up in the air. Perhaps, after all, full-fledged possession in the metaphysical sphere cannot settle in the realm of the practical unless recognition is forthcoming? Is a gold mine a gold mine before it is discovered?

Perhaps this problematical factor of recognition helps to explain why black American culture before this century couched itself in the blues and in signifying, because by their obliquity those forms

12. Du Bois also produces a telling and clearly intentional echo of Shelley's "Hymn to Intellectual Beauty" at the very beginning of *Souls*, when he says the "Shadow" of being a problem "swept across" him in the midst of childhood pursuits. But here there is no shadow of a transcendent good, only of immanent disaster. In the final chapter, "Of the Sorrow Songs," Du Bois rectifies this grim fact by pointing to the way his "ten master songs" grope toward "some unseen power," the very words Shelley applies to Intellectual Beauty: "The awful shadow of some unseen power." Orientation and even activity (groping) toward the true ideal yet informs Negro life.

enabled the culture to exist without demanding, indeed without provoking recognition (since recognition was likely to prove hostile). It is a commonplace that the blues originated in songs of lament in the days of slavery. LeRoi Jones also takes a simple, positive view of the blues tradition, writing that "Negro music," because "its strengths and beauties" arise out of "the depth of the black man's soul and because . . . its traditions could be carried on by the lowest classes of Negroes, has been able to survive the constant and willful dilutions of the black middle class" (*Home,* p. 106).[13] But Jones tends to gloss over the extent to which "willful dilutions" were practiced *within* the tradition. Its inwardness is well caught by Ralph Ellison when he derives the blues from "an impulse to keep the painful details and episodes of a brutal experience alive in one's aching consciousness, to finger its jagged grain, and to transcend it . . . by squeezing from it a near-tragic, near-comic lyricism" (*Shadow and Act,* p. 78).

On the printed page the blues have a patiently incremental, not to say a heavily repetitious form. The verbal power of the blues has not readily yielded itself to most commentators; Sherley Williams and Giles Oakley are notable exceptions. The dynamism of performance is another matter, and has led to some grandiose reactions. Richard Wright declares that in the blues the "burden of woe and melancholy is dialectically redeemed through sheer force of sensuality into an almost exultant affirmation of life, of love, of sex, of movement, of hope."[14] The picture here seems too vividly, too positively painted. Wright, given the influence that communism had on him, may have had dialectic and redemption too much on his mind. For this is not the blues singer Langston Hughes saw and put into poetry (see below, chapter 2), nor the one Sterling Brown depicts in "When the Saints Go Marching Home."

13. Elsewhere Jones tellingly writes of "the beginning of the blues as one beginning of American Negroes. . . . The reaction and subsequent relation of the Negro's experience in this country in *his* English is one beginning of the Negro's conscious appearance on the American scene" (*Blues People,* p. xii).

14. Richard Wright, foreword to *Blues Fell This Morning: The Meaning of the Blues* by Paul Oliver (New York: Horizon Press, 1960), p. ix.

The fact is that even in performance, wherever the audience was problematical—that is, in taste, or race, or mood—the blues could underplay itself and be innocuous. Thus Hayes MacMullen thought the renowned Charles Patton "played everything . . . in the same tune," in the same superficial and undistinguished way. And Eddie "Son" House, himself an accomplished Mississippi Delta blues man, thought Patton essentially a showman in his habit of tossing his guitar or playing it behind him or between his legs, and was "genuinely startled by [the] excellence" of Patton's recordings.[15] Both MacMullen and House were looking at Patton's work as an entertainer in clubs or at social affairs, where it is clear he camouflaged his capacities as an artist. The obligation not to upset or offend people's expectations was inseparable from the blues. Doubtless this has some bearing on the "Mumbles," the tradition of indistinct, even unintelligible rendition of the blues, as well as on the more general "fooling massa" tradition.

The blues as we find them may be said to have arisen as late as 1890, but basically, as Booker (or Bukka) White has proclaimed, the blues "came from behind the mule. . . . Now, you can have the blues sitting at the table eating. But the foundation of the blues is walking behind a mule way back in slavery time."[16] And that foundation shows in the reticence and the discreetness if not in the established form of the songs we do know. In *The Devil's Music*, Giles Oakley reports a scene from slavery where the men and women toiling in the fields would "'sing them songs so pitiful, so long' till they would be crying; but 'when they see the boss coming they would make like a gnat got in their eye. 'Cos you know, the boss didn't want them to feel that-a-way, you know, they had to be cool, play it cool, you know'"(p. 15). Even so, there remained the necessity of coping with what the versatile Ray Charles, speaking of the blues, has called "bad dreams and rotten memories." The pent-up spirit would out.

The power of expression, or rather, of intimation concerning the deepest issues of black experience is pregnant in the blues. Let us

15. See Robert Palmer, *Deep Blues: A Musical and Cultural History of the Mississippi Delta* (New York: Penguin Books, 1982), pp. 66, 67.

16. See Giles Oakley, *The Devil's Music*, p. 7.

look at just one example, Henry Thomas's "Shanty Blues," remembering that in performance the song would be much extended by repetitions and virtuoso musical interludes, and might contain a wealth of unique and transitory features.

> Trouble in your time, I tired in your mind,
> Show me that woman you can trust.
> I done lying, lying down, my head to the wall,
> Show me that woman you can trust.
> Well the law's on your side, I'll never get a dime.
>
> I'll make it to my shanty if I can,
> If I can, if I can,
> I'll make it to my shanty if I can.
> Dog's on my track, man's on his horse,
> Make it to my shanty if I can.[17]

The first impression here is of a love affair gone sour, and certainly sexuality has a prominent place in the blues. But even in the first section the reference to the law creates a wider amplitude, while the phrase "my head to the wall" quietly draws on the fact that turning to the wall is an age-old sign of the moment of death.

This association of death and the law becomes central in the second section. The dog on the track and the man on the horse combine to suggest a manhunt, with all power in the hands of the pursuer. Perhaps the fear of getting caught extends to a fear of being lynched. It is clear that reaching the shanty will not mean safety but only avoidance of a stark death in some random place. The shanty means home, and the dignity of dying from one's own ground rather than in the woods like an animal. In effect, then, this love blues carries undertones of a cry against injustice (law's on your side), against deprivation (I'll never get a dime), and even against the extreme inhumanity of abuse and power involved in manhunts and lynching. And we know that when Ma Rainey sang about the "Bo' Weavil" she meant us to hear about more than an agricultural pest that consumed more than its share; that famous blues song contained

17. Quoted in Oakley, *The Devil's Music*, p. 69.

veiled references to the inequity of distribution and inequality of races in her history and life.

"Signifying" has been the counterpart of the blues, in terms of (a) its centrality within black culture and (b) its relative obliquity in expressing that culture to the society at large. In a sense signifying has done better than the blues at guarding its secret freight of purpose and value, but in another sense the higher the degree of success the higher, paradoxically, becomes the prospect of failure: self-possession is held in abeyance.

Only in recent decades has signifying come in for adequate explication and evaluation. Roger Abrahams calls signifying a "technique of *indirect* argument or persuasion," the "ability to talk with great innuendo," a "propensity to talk around a subject, never quite coming to the point," and a style that requires one to operate "by indirect verbal or gestural means."[18] But Abrahams misses the basic thrust of signifying, while dwelling on its occasion and form. Pursuing what he later, in *The Man of Words*, would call a "cultural deprivation argument," he traces signifying to a negative self-image or spirit in black folk. Closer observation reveals that the negative quotient is derived from the public image the folk had to contend against, and from the small favor any dynamic self-affirmation could be expected to win. Critics such as Mitchell-Kernan and H. L. Gates, Jr., have properly objected to Abrahams's explanation of signifying, but no one has basically gone beyond his identification of indirection as its intrinsic mode. Some attention, too, may be paid to the underlying positive thrust of signifying, toward correcting inequity or falsehood.

In fact, two different sets of relationships need to be recognized in the process of signifying: the first, between two equals where the position of one party relative to the rest of the world has taken on distortions of definition or value; and the second, between two people where a long-standing and yet not intrinsically legitimate

18. Roger D. Abrahams, *Deep Down in the Jungle: Negro Narrative Folklore from the Streets of Philadelphia*, 2d ed. (Chicago: Aldine Publishing, 1970), p. 52; italics added.

authority is given to one over the other. In both cases a disturbance in the system of value needs to be corrected. The first class, as Gates shows in a bold, far-flung study of the subject, is increasingly literary and widespread. Gates emphatically documents the anthropo-mythological origins and valences of signifying.[19] My concern here is narrower, more topical and social; I take up signifying, even where it occurs in "literary" texts, as a direct encounter, a folk phenomenon apart from calculated, sophisticated, formal adaptations by modern writers. In the present context what stands out is the second of the two classes of signifying mentioned above, in which the imbalance between a marked authority and its designated inferior is subtly rectified. This is the stage of preservation and protection of the black tradition, as in the status of an encarped seed. For at the outset "signifying" took place typically between an underdog and an authority figure; this type of signifying occurs even now, as between the grandchild as underdog and grandmother as authority figure in "The Watermelon Story" in John Edgar Wideman's *Damballah*, or in the extraordinary scene of reading the will in David Bradley's *Chaneysville Incident*, where John Washington signifies upon his erstwhile "superior," Randall Scott. (A more involved case of signifying occurs in William Melvin Kelley's *Different Drummer*, where Rev. E. T. Bradshaw, even as he calls himself "Uncle Tom," gets out of his chauffeured limousine and offers the white Southerner Harry Leland ten then twenty dollars to "buy" Leland's son "for an hour.") Zora Neale Hurston offers a simple but cogent case of signifying at its very inception: "The women took the faded shirt and muddy overalls and laid them away for remembrance. It was a *weapon against her strength* and if it turned out *of no significance*, still it was a hope that she might fall to their level some day" (*Their Eyes Were Watching God*, p. 11; italics added).

Signifying always involves questions of power on two levels, the social and the mental, and the signifier is the one who as best he can makes up for a lack of social power with an exercise of intellectual or critical power. As Abrahams astutely observes, one person is

19. H. L. Gates, Jr., "The 'Blackness of Blackness': A Critique of the Sign and Signifying Monkey," *Critical Inquiry* 9:685–723.

"almost always trying to manipulate, coerce, or use" another (*Deep Down in the Jungle*, p. 19). But such an exercise carries obvious social risks. The trickster figure that is the signifying monkey sees more than it is prudent to say, and more than it is wholesome to deny. Instead of making scenes, he creates scenarios that amply indicate his sense of the Lion's credulity, insecurity, pride, and proneness to painful error. He submits only to subvert.

The primary stage of signifying is embodied in the classic figure of the tradition: the Signifying Monkey. In this trickster figure we find perfectly fused the arts of conceding and contesting racial stereotypes. As a *self*-assigned sobriquet "monkey" tends to shrug off or treat with humorous affection the term of degradation often visited upon black people by whites. A black person calling another "nigger" can work in the same way. But "monkey" may have less the character of an antidote than of a homeopathic dosage. The sister term *nigger* will help to clarify the case. As James Baldwin puts it, in "My Dungeon Shook: Letter to My Nephew on the One Hundredth Anniversary of the Emancipation," "You can only be destroyed by believing that you really are what the white world calls a *nigger*" (*The Fire Next Time*, p. 14). Internalized, name-calling carries a threat to the health, and the disease is self-humiliation. The caustic comedian Richard Pryor has trenchantly observed that "nigger is a word we give to our wretchedness."[20]

That is where the idea of signifying takes on singular force. The term fuses with "monkey" to create a bold oxymoron. In a sense the title of the archetypal trickster *translates* oxymoron, or wise fool, into the black idiom and context: signifying monkey. Thus on the one hand the monkey may not simply be dismissed, while on the other its signifying may not easily be absorbed, as it is unexpected, unconventional, and unexplicated.

Let us observe, to begin with, that signifying has two elements. The monkey signifies by its mere existence in a different mode from that of the lion, its theriomorphic counterpart:

20. Quoted in *Newsweek*, 3 May 1982, p. 54. Wallace Thurman had earlier called the use of the word *nigger* in the presence of whites "a symptom of some deep set disease" (*Infants of the Spring*, pp. 59–60).

"What I was going to tell you," said Monkey,
"Is you square so-and-so,
If you fool with me I'll get
Elephant to whip your head some more."
"Monkey," said the Lion,
Beat to his unbooted knees,
"You and all your signifying children
Better stay up in them trees."
Which is why today
Monkey does his signifying
A-*way-up* out of the way.

                                    (Hughes and Bontemps, *The Book
                                    of Negro Folklore*, pp. 365–66)

The monkey further signifies by persevering under adversity and
persisting in that mode. Rather than capitulating to force, the lion's
mode, he uses the mode of guile to recapitulate and subtly to reprove
the mode of force. The slave who conjures the signifying monkey
manipulates his manacles to make an ironic and a consoling music
under adversity. In the tacit declaration "I am the monkey *that can
call itself so*" (as opposed to the case in Kafka's *Report to an
Academy*, where the speaking ape professes *not* to be "an ape"), the
first self-possession of consciousness is brought about; and in the
adoption of signifying as a cultural device the further stage of
self-possession that comes with independent action and purpose
becomes manifest.

But signifying harbors a danger that should not be ignored. Let
us recall the fact that Bert Williams and George Walker, two highly
creative and effective performers in the black theater around the
turn of the century, billed themselves as "Two Real Coons" in order
to get some footing on the treacherous boards of white prejudice.[21]
In their minds, Nathan Irvin Huggins records, they were not portraying "real coons" but only giving "style and comic dignity to a fiction
that white men had created and fostered and with which black men
(on and off stage) conspired, [it] being one of the few public selves

21. See Nathan Irvin Huggins, *Harlem Renaissance* (New York: Oxford University Press, 1971), p. 280. Subsequent citations are given in the text.

that they were permitted" (p. 258). Walker, performing as a min-
strelsy comic in plays about Dahomey or Abyssinia, thought he was
representing "a black royalty, a black power, a black elegance, and a
black beauty," even as black and white audiences laughed at the
ludicrous goings-on (pp. 281–82). It is possible, of course, that the
two W's were catering to a ludicrous white ignorance of, and prejudice toward, black kings. Williams and Walker may have been busy
signifying, but no one could tell. Signifying and sheer wishful thinking tend to coincide here. Signifying becomes an idle secret and, as
Gates has justly remarked, dangerously close to tomming. In this
light it is inaccurate for Ralph Ellison, in *Shadow and Act*, to say that
the "'darky' entertainer is white" (p. 47). The "'darky' entertainer"
was both black and white, in rare collaboration. Both black and
white come out the worse, the white for believing a black king
would be so ludicrous, the black for playing not so much on as down
to that belief.

The same sort of perverse collaboration occurs in real life in the
case of Zora Neale Hurston, a more gifted and more important
figure in the black tradition than either Williams or Walker. As white
friends and supporters flocked to her, Hurston developed the curious mannerism of telling them "darky" stories over the phone and
at the same time giving the wink to her black friends standing by.
Should this be considered an example of successful signifying, when
the people most in need have absolutely no access to the significance? In essence we may know that Zora Neale Hurston had none
of the "darky" about her, but in phases of her existence she enacted
one quite convincingly (and in fact profitably); and such enactment
has its bearing on one's being. Wallace Thurman depicted Zora
Neale Hurston as Sweetie May Carr in *Infants of the Spring*, and
commented on her "darky" sagas: "It seldom occurred to any of her
patrons that she did this with tongue in cheek" (p. 229).[22]

22. Hurston's *Dust Tracks on a Road* indicates a certain difficulty she had getting
in tune with black people as a group, though she poignantly calls out to "My People!
My People!" The reader should also see Hurston's "How It Feels to Be Colored Me," in
World Tomorrow 11 (May 1928), p. 216.

No doubt Hurston meant to signify as well as to survive. But there is one ominous note of reaction from her "Godmother," her principal patroness, who would check her whenever she would say anything of seriousness or substance with the chilling question: "Does a child in the womb speak?" In addition, the Godmother strictly enjoined Hurston (as also Langston Hughes, another protégé) not to divulge her name (see Huggins, *Harlem Renaissance*, pp. 129–36). On the one side, Zora Neale Hurston is very discreetly signifying, while on the other Mrs. R. Osgood Mason, the worthy lady in question, is forcing her to be *silent*, especially about herself. It will be necessary to come back to the question of the black figure finding a voice, but for now we should recognize that signifying, like the blues, provided a compromise between enforced silence and a free voice. Let us only bring to mind the way Brother Jack tells the eloquent invisible man: "You were not hired to think" (Ellison, p. 458).

The foregoing caveat concerning signifying obviously leaves a fair amount of room for successful performance. Langston Hughes ceaselessly signifies in the *Simple* stories and in poems like "Advertisement for the Waldorf-Astoria" and "Seascape." But the classic case comes from the minstrel theater, when the Jim Dandy figure dressed to the nines in "white ruffled collar and cuffs, bright blue velvet pants, and red velvet jacket," for then Jim Dandy was reincarnating those models of elegance, Count D'Orsay and Beau Brummell, and further reflecting what Huggins in his *Harlem Renaissance* sums up as the "full evening dress . . . adopted by the 'Four Hundred'" (see pp. 270ff.). Even as Jim Dandy made himself laughable, he signified: I'm a fool, *like you at your best*. This was indeed to bring the signifying monkey to life, wearing a significant "monkey suit." A transaction of power has tacitly taken place, and from it a correction of imbalance and distortion can be inferred. (On the other hand, the splendid regalia of Marcus Garvey as Provisional President of the African Republic constitutes not signifying, but emulation.)

This form of signifying has an explicit biographical analog in the early youth of no less a figure than Ralph Ellison, who confesses in

Shadow and Act to the "absurd activity" of "projecting archetypes, . . . legendary heroes . . . most of which violated all ideas of social hierarchy and order and all accepted conceptions . . . handed down by . . . tradition" (p. xvi). Ellison initially defends this activity on the grounds that it was psychologically needed, but he quickly turns to signifying on any possible white criticism, and on comparable white activities: "It was no more incongruous . . . for young Negro Oklahomans to project themselves as Renaissance Men than for white Mississippians to see themselves as ancient Greeks or noblemen out of Sir Walter Scott" (p. xvii).

And yet, at best, the signifying monkey fell short of expressing the substance and value of black being. It was a delicate and demanding role that implied unsleeping resistance and unflagging aspiration, without upsetting the public image of acquiescence. Thus, even at best, by its very mode of being, and by intentional, subtly calibrated signs of that being, the signifying monkey announced with ironic humor what the blues announce with sorrowful yearning, the presence of powers and qualities as undeniable as unrecognized. Brother Tarp's chain in *Invisible Man* has "a heap of signifying *wrapped up in it*" (p. 379, italics added). The wrapping protects but also obscures the signifying.

Much of black American literature in the twentieth century has been shaped in the vise of this paradox: the possession of powers that are dangerous to contain and dangerous to express, powers existing under clouds of self-reluctance and clouds of public denial and abuse. One of the chief purposes of the Harlem Renaissance of the 1920s, with its proclamation of the New Negro, was to break the black American vise. But this led to another paradox: the assertion of the black artist and the black individual carried with it a tendency to minimize the importance of blackness.[23] Thus Langston Hughes, Countee Cullen, and Jean Toomer are solid in refusing the necessity

23. Robert Hayden makes a comparable point in his introduction to *The New Negro*, ed. Alain Locke (see p. xi); and James A. Emanuel sees the period as "free of individual restrictions and racial recriminations" ("Blackness Can: A Quest for Aesthetics," in *The Black Aesthetic*, p. 208).

of fighting for recognition of blackness and in refusing the complementary burden of representing blackness.

   Writing in *The Crisis*, an organ of the NAACP with the militant
Du Bois (but not enough so for *The Messenger*, "The Only Radical
Negro Magazine in America") in the editorial seat, Cullen declared
on behalf of the entire group that black writers have the right to "do,
write, create what we will, our only concern being that we do it well
and with all the power in us."[24] Hughes, in "The Negro Artist and the
Racial Mountain," was even more explicit about the indifference of
blackness:

We younger Negro artists who create now intend to express our individual
dark-skinned selves without fear or shame. If white people are pleased we
are glad. If they are not, it doesn't matter. We know we are beautiful. And
ugly too. The tom-tom cries and the tom-tom laughs. If colored people are
pleased, we are glad. If they are not, their displeasure doesn't matter either.
We build our temples for tomorrow, strong as we know how, and we stand
on top of the mountain free within ourselves. (p. 694)

Hughes always drew on a special sympathy with "low-down folks,"
but his refusal to be an artificial black champion or to curry favor
with whites was a genuine and abiding position. It may be recalled
here that even Alain Locke, the driving and guiding force behind the
epochal collection of essays *The New Negro*, advocated "self-
expression" and "spiritual development" (pp. xv, 15) at the same
time that he pressed for a heightened sense of communal identity.
The Harlem Renaissance is touted as a collective political movement
with a literary vanguard, but its literature had in view personal, even
metaphysical development for its artists.

   In the case of Jean Toomer, the desire to be a comprehensive
writer and elude the pen of blackness takes on complex ramifica-
tions because Toomer, though he deliberately and exultantly went

24. "Countee Cullen on Miscegenation," *Crisis* 36 (1929): 373. In the poem "To
Certain Critics" Cullen pointedly asked: "How shall the shepherd heart then thrill / To
only the darker lamb?" This impulse to inclusiveness, or nonsegregation, is part of the
philosophy of countering blackness *as a constricting social concept* while pursuing the
potential of being black. On this point, see Houston R. Baker, Jr., *A Many-Colored
Coat of Dreams: The Poetry of Countee Cullen* (Detroit: Broadside Press, pp. 26ff.).

back into the black South of his birth for substance and inspiration in writing *Cane*, also on occasion chose to pass for white. This counts as—so to speak—a black mark against him. But if we look at Hughes's and Cullen's literary philosophy beside Toomer's, the difference is hard to detect. And yet the imputation of at least a literary "passing" never—again so to speak—darkens the door of Hughes or Cullen. The important point remains that the same force acted on Toomer as on Cullen and Hughes, and they all three acted on the same principle. (Toomer's basic impulse was not to pass for white, but to brush aside the factitious criterion of race: "My poems are not Negro poems, nor are they Anglo-Saxon or white or English poems." That may have been his gravest offense, to all parties.) To focus on the individual practice of "passing" is to be blind to a deeper collective dynamism involving the issue of self-possession; for passing is only the most superficial and unstable and idiosyncratic form of breaking the bonds of blackness. It also serves as the most concealed manner of proving the quality of black folk, in that pigment must be a figment of judgment if nothing else gives the black person away in supposed unworthiness. Finally, passing is the most paradoxical resolution of the social problem of blackness; it is self-assertion as self-denial, self-annihilation as self-fulfillment.

In the nature of the case it would be impossible to prove that passing has declined in step with the practice of lynching in the last few decades, but certainly "profession" has tended to take the spotlight from "passing." This has not been an unmixed good. Part of the act of profession hardened into slogans (black is beautiful), part of it vulgarized into Godfrey Cambridge and his watermelon humor, part of it congealed into the Cleaver-Carmichael reaction of defiance and debunking, and part has sunk into toying with the word *nigger*, the name we give to our wretchedness. We do well to recall Ray Charles's pungent summary of the reaction to nomenclature a few short decades ago: "A man could get cut for calling another dude 'black.' That expression wasn't exactly the rage in the forties. . . . You'd be very careful about how you'd shade your description of a brother. If not, someone soon be describing you as red—bloodred" (*Brother Ray*, pp. 101–02).

It is really easier to find progress than satisfaction in contemplating various phenomena at different stages of black experience in America. To attain a new position only raises the problem of maintaining it; to maintain an old position must raise the specter of stasis, for in the conditions of life so much may drift or shift into altered terms of being. Thus, in 1939 the U.S. military forces were harshly segregated, and the Daughters of the American Revolution refused to allow Marian Anderson to sing in a Washington auditorium they controlled; in 1979 the peacetime U.S. Army had a black general (B. O. Davis, Sr., was promoted to general during World War II), and black people's privilege of entering American institutional life had so far advanced with affirmative action that a counterforce was being created, behind the initiative of a man fetchingly surnamed *Bakke*. Bryan Gumble wakes up America for one of the major TV networks, but as the bottom falls out of the job market in late 1982 "last hired, first fired," a phrase that might have originated in playing the dozzens, sums up the black situation nationally. The George Wallace who vowed "segregation forever" in 1963 reenters the Alabama State House in 1983 on the confession that his attitude was wrong, but though *Brown* v. *Board of Education of Topeka* opened up so much in 1954 and even a George Wallace has come around, in 1982 a spokesman for the American Council on Education sees grounds for "some real fear about the future for blacks in higher education." In 1983 the winner of the Miss America contest was a black woman; so was the first runner-up. And the *New York Times* reported the news as an "extraordinary anomaly." And so the seesaw goes.

Still, it seems possible to discern a shape in black self-expression in our century. A development has decidedly taken place. Alice Walker remains compatible with Zora Neale Hurston as a woman writer working in a realistic vein, blending domestic and political interests, and equally sensitive to tragedy and to ecstasy. But Walker operates on a different pitch and scale. Hurston is compatible but not commensurate with her. The same may be said of Ishmael Reed in relation to Charles Chesnutt or Langston Hughes, for Reed has taken the underground mischief that marks the entertainer's humor of Chesnutt and Hughes and made it almost volcanic.

With the caveat that, outside of nomenclature, nothing works as simply as black and white, we may discern four major modes and stages in black American literature. These modes affect both the responses of individual figures in the texts and the pattern that the texts themselves display.

SELF-VEILING

The first stage we find is self-veiling, or an unassertive, undemanding adaptation to the environment. In relation to Du Bois's formulation, this results in a *double* veil: the one the society interposes between the black person and full participation in its resources and opportunities, and the other assumed by the black person in any particular encounter with that society. The effect of the double veil is to render the action of the black person into an *act*, a performance pro tem; this is one important sense of Ellison's title *Shadow and Act*. Charles Chesnutt's *Conjure Woman* gives us a telling example of self-veiling, not so much in the individual stories as in their cumulative structure, and J. W. Johnson's *Autobiography of an Ex-Colored Man* may be looked on as the classic case. Johnson's work was of course a precursor to the Harlem Renaissance; our image of that movement as bearing a stamp of self-expression and self-enhancement will be shown to be counteracted by a stubborn impulse to self-veiling. Jean Toomer's *Cane* in one dimension is a study of the endless causes and guises of self-veiling.

In effect self-veiling functions as the artificial antithesis of intimacy. Its motive—to survive—is positive, but its vision limited. The survivor's existence is bound within the maneuvers that sustain it. Self-veiling embodies the old adage of "playing fool to catch wise," but it carries a danger with it: the player is caught by the game. Uncle Julius in *The Conjure Woman* means to be craftily agreeable, but ends up being agreeably crafty, a kind of Uncle Tom under a thick patina of humor. And yet that humor has singular merit in the period following the Civil War that the historian Rayford Logan calls the nadir of black experience. We will find that there are varieties and degrees of self-veiling, but as bad as things may get, self-veiling seems to have an absolute limit in black literature; it approaches but does not fall into self-cancellation, even in the case of the ex-colored man. The fact that suicide is an extremely rare occurrence in Afro-American literature deserves emphasis. A blues line suggests a degree of inborn clear-sightedness and resolution that does not accord with suicide: "Black nigger baby gonna take care of myself." LeRoi Jones's *Preface to a Twenty-Volume Suicide Note* provides a valuable insight into black attitudes, for the prospective suicide will remain forever prospective; suicide is a subject of contemplation, not an act. Or if it is to become an act, the necessary prelude or preparation, that is, the suicide note, will last long enough to preclude performance. The same phenomenon occurs in "Prisoner's Talking Blues," by Robert Pete Williams, in which grief and frustration drive the prisoner to, but only to, the contemplation of suicide:

> Sometimes I feel like, baby, committin' suicide.
> I got the nerve if I had anythin' to do it with.[25]

The aural proximity of "nerve" and "knife" helps to suggest that the missing instrument "to do it with" is will or consent; he could if he would.

In this context the actual suicide of Rufus Scott in Baldwin's *Another Country* has a startling singularity (though it is consistent with the scathing, obsessive, incontinent relationship he has with Leona, the white Southern woman, and it is of course analogous to her going insane—that is, she dies to normal life). We may note too that a minor character in *Go Tell It on the Mountain*, Elizabeth Grimes's former common-law husband, resorts to suicide after being humiliated by a policeman. But it seems more typical of black literature for the negative-minded character to put himself in the way of being destroyed by someone else, as Tod Clifton does in *Invisible Man*, or Clay in Jones's *Dutchman*.

25. Quoted in Harry Oster, *Living Country Blues* (Detroit: Folklore Associates, 1969), p. 4.

A radical clinging to life, even when unbearable and insoluble, proves a basic feature of black literary response. We need to recognize that self-veiling, besides being a form of social accommodation, is a product of self-consciously impotent hatred, the turning toward the self of feelings and purposes that are not admitted, let alone pursued, in relation to others. An important feature of this response is its impersonality. It is not concerned with individual enemies, but with the hostile system itself. The futility of individual response is apparent when the invisible man takes out his wrath on the white man under the streetlight; the victim neither adds to nor lessens the burden of prejudice the invisible man feels, so that the latter's reaction only accentuates his ugly mood and powerlessness. Perhaps he could be said to be doing something, as contrasted with the ex-colored man, but his dream of his own castration shows that he is still thinking of himself as a person to whom something is done.

The ex-colored man reacts uniformly at the level where the problem exists, at the level of the system. As a result we see in him a depersonalization of response to the perpetrators *and* to the victim of the lynching. The corollary of this is a depersonalized response to *himself*. In Ernest Gaines's "Bloodline," Captain Christian Laurent appears to be caught between a response to personality and an assault on the system. He himself, though seeing the systematic nature of his oppression, has no systematic counter and withdraws into a suspended state of thought. Whatever we may think of John Williams's military solution in *Captain Blackman*, it does have the virtue of being *systematic*. (Further examples of a systematic military perspective are found in W. E. B. Du Bois's *Quest of the Silver Fleece* and James Baldwin's *Tell Me How Long the Train's Been Gone*.)

But self-veiling is obliged to be a curiously alert and thoughtful state, with more virtues at its root than appear on the surface. It carries its own recoil toward self-assertion. The ex-colored man does not quite break the surface, but he contemplates it with the savage glee of someone of superior gifts confronting a humdrum order that has forced him down.

SOLITUDE

The recoil toward self-assertion becomes manifest, following upon the Harlem Renaissance, in a condition of *solitude*, in which the black character stands out from the veil and survives, but survives without sustaining or amplifying connections. This is the second phase of development in the Afro-American literary scheme. Richard Wright's *Native Son* and Ralph Ellison's *Invisible Man* are the classic embodiments of this condition.[26] Another special case emerges in Zora Neale Hurston's *Their Eyes Were Watching God*, where solitude takes over to resolve an almost Manichaean conflict between veiling and a singular romantic-naturalistic fulfillment.

We may note in passing that the experience of separation and solitude has marked an earlier text, Claude McKay's *Home to Harlem*. But McKay presents a blank or dead solitude, a sort of obverse of the reckless enthusiasm to share and belong in blackness that the protagonist adopts. In fact, the theme of belonging is haunted throughout the novel by the threat of disaster, as Jake is first AWOL from the Army and then makes himself anathema to the wrong element in Harlem. When he finally flees with Felice, the text shifts from the realistic to the idyllic mode, inevitably with some loss of substance or plausibility. They are like Keats's lovers running away at the end of *The Eve of St. Agnes*. One action is over and the pair has escaped its worst consequences, but there is no new action to frame or sustain them.

26. It may at once be objected that these two novels, despite their closeness in chronology, have acquired almost antithetical standing. *Native Son* is treated as a mainstay of the protest movement, *Invisible Man* as often as not in the vein of a sell-out to the dominant white tradition. In addition, Ellison expressly takes a position athwart *Native Son* in his discussion of *Invisible Man* (*Shadow and Act*, pp. 14ff., 114ff.). But these objections do not go to the heart of the issue. Protest is no more than an element in *Native Son*, and is transcended as mere Achillean derring-do is transcended in the *Iliad*. Indeed, protest would have the ironic effect of placing *Native Son* in the dominant tradition, in association with Sinclair and Farrell and Steinbeck. LeRoi Jones, whom no doubt many would see as belonging in that tradition, bluntly repudiates it on this ground: "The Negro protest novelist postures, and invents a protest quite [compatible] with the tradition of bourgeois life" (*Home*, p. 112). As for Ellison's verdict on Wright and his version of his own production, it seems fair to say that an unforced reading comes out elsewhere. And as D. H. Lawrence declared, we must heed the novel, not the novelist.

The state of solitude represents presence without stable or viable connections. The invisible man cannot turn back to Mary, who comes closest to constituting a human connection for him, and by the same token Bigger Thomas cannot draw on either the humane Jan Erlone or the ideologist Boris Max from his cell; in one case time and in the other social rigidity prevent that. We may note here that both Chester Himes's *The Primitive* and Ann Petry's *The Street* leave their protagonists in grim solitude, despite powerful struggles to break into a living social pattern. Like *Native Son*, these novels involve murder, which almost comes to emblematize the ultimate ignorance of how to integrate oneself socially, even while one is experiencing ultimate physical closeness and exposure in society. In solitude, situations and gestures of intimacy occur, but without essential force. Or again, the invisible man may wistfully look out on a prospect of intimacy, but without essential hope.

But solitude remains a movement toward the light. The hole the invisible man inhabits is filled with light not only for him to see but, poignantly and helplessly, for him to be seen. All that light (which seems not to put the utility company in any danger of bankruptcy) should attract attention! The hole is a complex base of operations for him in a way that the ex-colored man's memorial box is not. In fact, the hole is the stage beyond the briefcase in which the invisible man had so foolishly cherished his keepsakes and guides. Those keepsakes had afforded him a false light; the hole by contrast sheds ample light on nothing. The hole becomes preliminary, prefatory. He sallies out into daylight, though to no good effect, and sends his missive-autobiography to speak to, and for, the world. That also is to no good effect, but it envisions an effect beyond the vindictiveness the ex-colored man had harbored in his heart. Veiling has had no notion of a cure. Solitude knows its cure, but cannot accomplish it.

KINSHIP

The third stage of Afro-American literature manifests itself in the form of kinship. Here relationship comes into play, as the conditions of life become ampler and more varied for the black protagonist.

But this amounts to an enrichment without relief. If literally the hold of the ghetto is relaxed, and if contingently the ghetto of the mind opens out to a new sense of encounter and connection, there remains something deliberate, rather than fluent, and defensive, rather than spontaneous. Perhaps any avowal of kinship carries with it an undertone of defense; if so, it is heightened in black writing, where one is kin to grief and injury and inequity, as well as the luminous paradoxical consolation of blues or the sidelong consolation of signifying. The work of Michael Harper virtually assigns itself to this category, with odd anticipation in Wright's *Uncle Tom's Children* and equally odd corroboration in Eldridge Cleaver's *Soul on Ice*.

Again we may see kinship as a natural, though not a necessary, development from solitude. Kinship is what Bigger Thomas rejects, early in *Native Son*, because he thinks of it as amassed pain rather than amassed alliance. He is thinking in terms of himself as subject and others as dependents, burdens, on his feeble and hypersensitive resources. He is in a willful and woeful solitude, shut off even from himself. But where such narcissism does not hold sway, solitude is the platform from which one looks out to the sea (and not the darkling pool) of humanity. As long ago as the eighteenth century the associationist philosophers formalized the concept that self-interest naturally, though not necessarily, leads to sympathy; this progression may be taken as the analog of the movement from solitude to kinship.

In the particular case of black literature, though, kinship is more complex than mere sympathy. It means seeing deprivation and pain, as Bigger Thomas does, but it also means recognizing endurance and dignity, as Bigger does not, and it presupposes feeling compassion and indignation. It means a sense of confirmation and strength for the self, and an experience of enlargement based on unison with the kindred person(s). It means a vision and movement of growth, as in Harper's "High Modes: Vision as Ritual: Confirmation," where personal and communal powers surge together to one goal. But its meaning subsists in the atmosphere of antagonism between endurance and growth, vision and adverse social reality. It is in the nature of kinship to rule out as well as to embrace, and what it embraces it embraces according to fixed criteria. For this reason kinship, though skirting the domain of intimacy, falls short of it.

INTIMACY

The next development in Afro-American literature has the quality of *intimacy*, marked especially by an openness toward the turns of inner life as well as the force of things without, and by a conviction of being at home in any dimension of human experience. The effect is not to dissolve the black connection in some illusion of universality, but rather to reaffirm it in its distinctiveness while observing its play as a datum and *as an instrument*, and not just as a subject matter. A sense of perspective and proportion comes to bear upon the obsession of blackness. The world and the self, held in rigid restriction in the stage of veiling and elided even in the stage of kinship, emerge into the open. And world and self enter into moments of reciprocal exploration.

The poetry of Robert Hayden quintessentially conveys the quality of intimacy, but the work of Alice Walker also provides an important case, especially in that Walker recapitulates the stages of self-veiling, solitude, and kinship within the matrix of intimacy. She helps us to see that self-veiling, which looks like a form of masochism rooted in the despair of color, extends indifferently out into the culture at large; in this regard, the achievement of intimacy entails not just a racial but also a national breakthrough.

While the development from self-veiling to solitude and from solitude to kinship falls within the ordinary curve of human experience, the development from kinship to intimacy veers off into mystery. When it happens we recognize it readily enough, but we can go round the circle often without encountering it. In the present dispensation in American literature where the scope of human personality is baffled in the image of formal intricacy, and where irony and alienation and self-absorption and paranoia run rampant, the adventure of intimacy is breakthrough enough. That it should occur in black literature may seem a surprising breakthrough, unless we remember two facts: (1) originality often is spurred on where privilege and conventional grounding are denied (The Catholic hunchback, Pope, and the lame rebel, Byron, come at once to mind; but we could as easily think of Flaubert or Rimbaud, Pushkin or Dostoevski); and (2) as Wordsworth observes, "power" has the characteristic of "growing under weight."

The development of black literature evinces an internal structure and a psychological dynamism of some elegance, and may in retrospect take on an air of inevitability. But one finds throughout resistance and inconsistencies in the way black writers have limned black experience in our century in America. Ralph Ellison's *Invisible Man* and John Williams's *Captain Blackman* may both conceive of a new America, but Ellison's vision is meditative and depends on revised structures of cooperation and orientation in society, whereas Williams's is activist and cynical about any such revision. Captain Blackman takes correction of injustice into his own hands. In other words, while both Ellison and Williams see change as inevitable, inevitability has not meant uniformity.

The very absence of uniformity is the hallmark of authenticity and of vitality in black literature. All in step, and facing one way, would suggest a crushed and stereotyped culture. And we may ask how that sort of uniformity could arise in the twentieth century, in a time of relative unrestraint, when slavery itself could not confine and crush the black ethos or the black imagination.

2

SELF-VEILING *James Weldon Johnson,*
Charles Chesnutt, and
Nella Larsen

> I could write a hand very similar to that of
> Master Thomas.
>
> Frederick Douglass

JAMES WELDON JOHNSON'S *Autobiography*
of an Ex-Colored Man is a *bildungsroman* with a difference, in that a
personal and social maturation of the central character proves hollow. Born to a pale-skinned, in-service black mother and the up-and-
coming son of a "great" Southern family (he discreetly ships his
embarrassing mistress and scion off to Connecticut), the ex-colored
man is both pampered and deprived as a child. He is pampered with
things like piano lessons and gold coins, yet deprived of stability,
clear principles, and genuine feelings. He makes friends, as with Red
Head, to suit the moment's convenience, and after his mother's
death—which, despite his profession of "sacred sorrow" (p. 419), he
mourns less than her having doted on him might warrant—he drifts
into a vagabond life as a would-be student, factory-hand, musician,
millionaire's private entertainer and traveling companion, aspiring
musicologist, and businessman. He also drifts in and out of function-
ing socially as a black person. His features and complexion *and*
habits cause the millionaire to pronounce him white, and to urge him

43

to settle in the white world of Europe. But his gift, even his passion for cultivating black folk music leads him to an almost heroic choice of coming home and going South, in search of his deepest self—and fame and fortune. In a small town in the South, his true race not having been divulged, he witnesses the lynching-by-fire of a pathetic black man and takes flight in shame and terror. He passes for white, prospers, marries, has children, and suffers the loss of his wife and, to his late, chagrined realization, of his self-respect and soul. His story is a muffled act of penitence, but also a muffled accusation against a society that condones the automatic oppression and casual lynching of some of its members.

On the face of it the ex-colored man's decision to pass for white stems from a single trauma: the sight of a lynch mob, near high noon, putting a black man to death by burning. In a paradoxical way he identifies with the victim, but there is a time lag before that is known, and he takes advantage of the time lag ("I felt sure my identity as a coloured man had not yet become known" p. 496) to make good his escape not only from the town but from the Negro race. The point is of course that his identification with the victim has been merely physical; indeed the victim is depicted as purely physical, showing "not a single ray of thought," deprived of "reasoning power" by his terror, and thus presenting the appearance of an animal "stunned and stupefied" prior to slaughter (p. 497).

But if the identification is purely physical, so must be the escape. Anything more than physical, for example compassion or indignation, would have led to a more complex result in the ex-colored man. He might have felt an altruistic desire to protect the sufferer of evil, or a desire to counteract the doer. He might have had just the selfish desire to get on with his ambitious work, though with sly care and concealment. Either approach would begin with the physical state, but go beyond it, preserving human connection and the power of action. The ex-colored man confines himself to the physical, and puts himself in a socio-psychological box. For he refuses to face and understand, to come to grips with the physical. The burly, good-natured, manipulable black youth Red Head, will do that for him in his school years,[1] and the millionaire will make it unnecessary in his adult life. In other words the trauma of the lynching is not cause but consummation of a denial of physicality on the ex-colored man's part.

When he speaks of being driven by "unbearable shame," we need to hear Kierkegaard discoursing in the background on the nature of shame as a reaction to what one does in the eyes of other men, as opposed to dread, which entails what one is in the eyes of eternity. The ex-colored man has indeed lived a life of self-concealment, self-effacement, and shame. The lynching is not an isolated trauma, it is only a systematic version of the trauma he underwent when the bediamonded black suitor happened to gun down the cultivated white "widow," his keeper, in the "Club" (pp. 460–61). Because it is habitual and predictable violence, the lynching focuses the randomness and subjection that have marked the ex-colored man's life all along. For example, he simply and abruptly gives up all thought of college when his school savings are pilfered; he happens to hear ragtime played as classical music and thinks he has hit upon his life's career; though "anxious to . . . settle down to work, and give expression to the ideas which were teeming" in his head, he "strayed into another deviation from [his] path of life" (p. 494), that brings him to the site of the lynching.

Accident marks the life of the ex-colored man. His reaction to accident takes the self-protective form of seeking instant finalities. That reaction gives us the mark of his mind. He overreads and overdetermines the character of accidents, seeking a pragmatic or material security that will make him immune to change and, thus, invulnerable. Actually his decision to "go back into the very heart of the South, to live among the people, and drink in my inspiration firsthand" (p. 471) is more pragmatic than heroic:

1. It is interesting to note that Johnson's odd mating of school friends had been anticipated in Thomas Hughes's *Tom Brown's Schooldays*, where the frail intellectual Arthur depends materially on the athletic title character.

I argued that music offered me a better future than anything else I had knowledge of, and . . . that I should have greater chances of attracting attention as a coloured composer than as a white one. (p. 474)

It comes as an appealing *afterthought* that he might give voice to "all the joys and sorrows, the hopes and ambitions, of the American Negro, in classical musical form" (p. 474).

Even before he witnesses the lynching, the ex-colored man's pursuit of his hopes and ambitions is tainted. He is quickly distracted by new friends and new experiences, devotes two or three weeks (rather than days) to Washington, D.C. (pp. 477–78), and observes that "it was *with some reluctance* that I continued my journey south" (p. 479; italics added). His desire to make permanent whatever is comfortable for the moment is the obverse of his wish to guarantee the elimination of trials; it is also a prophecy of his recoil from the harsh physical finality of the lynching.

He attributes his prevailing self-indulgence to his benefactor: "through my experience with my millionaire a certain amount of comfort and luxury had become a necessity to me" (p. 480). (The curious power of the possessive pronoun to denote the user's being owned is stark in the phrase "my millionaire.") But the millionaire only corroborates an unlearned and uninspected bent in the ex-colored man's makeup. Let us recall that when his incognito father gives him a ten-dollar gold piece drilled through for wearing around his neck, he spends the greater part of his life wishing "that some other way had been found of attaching it to me besides putting a hole through it" (pp. 394–95). Similarly, when given a piano, he feels "disappointment that [it] was not a grand" (p. 413). His feeling for purely material value is what sets him up as the millionaire's protégé, but it is also what sets him up as the mark of the railroad porter on the way to Atlanta University. The boardinghouse keeper with the "round face beaming with motherly kindness," she on whose "capacious bosom" the ex-colored man wants "to lay [his] head . . . and go to sleep" (p. 424) is a sensual promise of perpetual comfort for which he pays the price of losing his school fees and his chance at a college education (pp. 424–27).

The ex-colored man gullibly throws himself into the insidious clutches of the boardinghouse keeper, in contrast to the "invisible man" whom circumstances prevent from making it back to the healing ambience of Mary's boardinghouse. The ex-colored man never grows up, but keeps seeking a womb-like, motherly situation. The boardinghouse keeper provides the clearest instance, perhaps, but we may also think of the "benefactor" as *motherly*, in that he is (like the ex-colored man's own mother) interested in music and he stays home and gets, as he gives, material sustenance from some unpublished source. This condition of womb-like retreat will also manifest itself in the ex-colored man's marriage.

We may recognize a common danger, even deadliness in the ex-colored man's obsession with the motherly and the comfortable. In actuality the "motherly" woman with the captivating food is an accomplice in his undoing. Again, the "benefactor" millionaire proves the equivalent of "some grim, mute but relentless tyrant, possessing over me a supernatural power which he used to drive me on mercilessly to exhaustion" (p. 459). The millionaire shifts in fact from mother to father, at this early stage. As the relationship matures, and becomes something social in its own right (as opposed to a psychic substitute), it takes on a subliminal homosexual character. It is not a denial of tonal changes in his relationship with the ex-colored man to say that the millionaire is most satisfying in the guise of "mother." And finally the ex-colored man's marriage to an indulgent and protective woman forecasts his condition of being comfortably ensconced in a deathlike box. It will be necessary to look further at the comfort-loving materialism that characterizes the ex-colored man, but here we should note its association with suppression of the true self: "he paid me so liberally I could forget much" (pp. 459–60).

Given his materialistic impulses, it is not surprising that the ex-colored man's two best "friends" should be Red Head and the millionaire, physical and social havens in their turn. He and the Red Head, he and the millionaire are necessary to each other, and make natural complements. The text spells out the former relationship: "wit and quickness" on the one hand, "strength and dogged faithful-

48   SELF-VEILING

ness" on the other (p. 399). But the second relationship is much the
profounder and more vital. It goes well beyond the surface data of
the ex-colored man's ability to entertain on the piano and the millionaire's to pay for that. Basically the millionaire lives in dread of
time—the text plainly says so (p. 472)—and the ex-colored man fills
time for him; on the other side (and the text, the speaker never
recognizes this) the ex-colored man lives in dread of circumstances,
from which the millionaire shields him.

The ex-colored man's materialism, evident in relation to gold
coins and pianos and his avowal that a fine meal realizes one of his
dreams of Southern life, takes its rise less from sensuality than from
sensibility, from fear of pain and a feeling for aesthetic refinement.
Prima facie there is nothing ignoble or even discreditable about that.
But the ex-colored man gravitates toward snobbery ("I was a perfect
little aristocrat" p. 395) and the kind of petulant and vindictive
narcissism that seems a home quality of black youths whose mothers
care too devotedly for them (Basil, in Gloria Naylor's story "Mattie
Michael" in *The Women of Brewster Place*, is a perfect example).
Thus, when the "brown-eyed violinist" marries another, he can
consider himself "partially avenged . . . by the fact that, though she
was growing more beautiful, she was losing her ability" to play her
instrument (pp. 419–20).

The dread of circumstances governing his life keeps him from
becoming anything decisive, just as surely as his mother's dread of
society keeps him from knowing anything concrete and effectual
about himself. The ex-colored man becomes essentially an escapist,
at once acutely self-conscious and fundamentally self-ignorant
(note, again, the embryonic homosexual relationship with both Red
Head and the millionaire, as well as the narcisso-homosexual overtones of his description of "the ivory whiteness of my skin, the
beauty of my mouth, the size and liquid darkness of my eyes, and
how the long, black lashes that fringed and shaded them . . . [were]
strangely fascinating even to me" [p. 401]). In effect he escapes
himself, and when he tries to reverse that escape he can do so only
cryptically. There is no positive energy, no positive purpose for him

to work off. Unwilling to remain a black man, and unable to become a white one, he is in the Arnoldian situation of being both dead on one side and on the other powerless to be born.

The inability to bear his blackness modulates in the ex-colored man into inability to bear mortality, that is, uncertainty, incapacity, pain, loss. He strives to be exempt from his mortality, indeed he strives not even to recognize it. This leads him to harbor with the millionaire, the consummately exempt figure; but it can readily be observed that the millionaire is also the detached figure, the drifting figure, the unwitting Wandering Jew. He is exempt from his own humanity at last.

If we ask what the attributes of the millionaire are, we are hard put to say more than possession of money and insomnia. He does not need more to be human, but he does need more to be mentor, the tacit role he plays in relation to the ex-colored man. His state of exemption is of course important to that role; it puts him in the tradition, alike classical and Christian and Oriental, that says superiority to material pressure and detachment from material desire are essential to spiritual development and teaching. Within that tradition, Thoreau is drawn to Mencius and, more imperceptively, Dorothea Brooke to Casaubon in George Eliot's *Middlemarch*. Perhaps surprisingly, with all the talk of alienation and the decay of heroism, the exempt figure as mentor has had a steady place in twentieth-century writing. If the hero is dead, the hero's hero is not. We may call to witness Dahfu, in Saul Bellow's *Henderson the Rain King*; Pops in Ernest Hemingway's *Green Hills of Africa*; the title characters in Toni Morrison's *Sula* and Alice Walker's *Meridian*; Old Jack in *The Chaneysville Incident*, by David Bradley; Sam Fathers, in William Faulkner's *The Bear*;[2] Magnus Eisengrim, in Robertson Davies's *Deptford Trilogy*; Sarid, in Francis Ebejer's *Leap of Malta Dolphins*; and a variety of figures, most notably Zorba the Greek, in the works of Nikos Kazantzakis.

2. It is arguable that in *The Sound and the Fury* Benjy is an exempt figure and his idiocy a mark of election. But the reader sees this more than the characters in the text, so that his position becomes an ironic reflection of their confusion and distress.

But we must note that the millionaire leads the ex-colored man into materialism, not toward freedom or spirituality. Even more than his getting married, the ex-colored man's breaking away from the millionaire holds out the prospect of his becoming human, vulnerably and powerfully so. When he turns away from the commitment to enter into black culture and retrieve its value for itself and for the world, he gains the final exemption—passing—at the expense of his humanity. His allusion to the Old Testament story of Esau (Gen. 25:29–34), who sold his birthright for a "mess of pottage" (p. 511), is most appropriate, reminding us of (a) his materialism and fear of suffering, and (b) his failure to sustain his identity as a result of his falling victim, like Esau, to the force of the moment.

His failure to develop his inner self, his soul, means that he is an ex-man more truly than an ex-colored man, and his book is the dead remnant of his being, coming like the voice of a ghost, or like a ventriloquist's self-dummy from the box in which is kept the tenuous evidence of what might have been.

His wife remains the sole and very attenuated link to his being as a member of the category "human," as opposed to his mere existence as an isolated creature. Her death effectively throws him back upon himself, and it is significant that he chooses the risk of writing to the safety—and emptiness—of silence. His situation is rife with paradox: his safety is a form of death, the cancellation of his soul, while his possible "undoing," the act of writing, in actuality restores him to his kind, by way of both defiance and atonement.

The ex-colored man goes through a series of self-veilings. His various jobs are forms of veiling, and none more emphatically than that with the millionaire. In this position he cannot let himself express something as raw and involuntary as fatigue; his music continues to present itself as formal experiment and local entertainment when deep down it involves his definition of himself and his distinctive humanity; and even when he "comes out" and breaks from the millionaire, he continues to play it safe and keeps his true identity hidden rather than accept the full (positive musical *and* negative societal) impact of his blackness. In effect, each of the ex-colored man's self-veilings carries him a step further than the previous one, so that his ultimate decision to pass looks somewhat less than enormous beside his constant reluctance to go all-out black, just as on the other side the risk he finally takes for his music looks smaller than it should, owing to his continual efforts to come forward in his own person. In short, the pendulum of his commitment slowly increases in amplitude until it has carried him to the extreme stage when the lynching confronts him. And he falls plumb into passing.

He reaches thus an extreme of self-veiling that, even to him, closely resembles self-cancellation. His story is an effort to bring himself back from the dead. He has given up far, far more than Uncle Julius McAdoo, in Chesnutt's *Conjure Woman, for the same benefits* of material comfort. His sacrifice is so stark that he cannot gloss it over, as we must infer Uncle Julius does his. And the ex-colored man's recoil from his self-cancelling sacrifice cannot quite save him, because by its anonymity it only restores him to a further form of self-veiling.

The ex-colored man, understandably but unwisely looking to immunize himself against circumstances, immures himself out of existence. From a child he is all calculation, and the final sum of his calculations with circumstance is near zero. Everything has cancelled out for him; he has been no more than "a privileged spectator" of Negro life, or "a deserter," a nonentity suffering from a placeless and baseless nostalgia—"a strange longing for my mother's people" (p. 510). By his own testimony he has neither "history" nor "race" (p. 511), because to have that he would have to forge it, and he has fled appalled (white with loss of blood, but also white with loss of soul) from that. As a result he is left without an identity, without realized or articulate human relationship. His whole life has depended on enclosures, but ambivalently so: he loves the nightclub but hates the risk it entails, loves the millionaire's apartment but resents its obligations. Finally he has enclosures he can count on, in his narrow protected home and then, with the loss of his wife, in his even narrower, secret, autobiographical box. But he is ultimately deceived, betrayed. That box is his cryptic casket, the proof that he is surviving in a living death. Basically there are, as Ralph Ellison bluntly observes in *Shadow and Act*, "no exemptions."[3]

What makes the ex-colored man noteworthy is not his passing or its concomitant loss of conviction and character and identity. That would happen to any sensitive and conscientious person. But one is struck with the gap between his superior knowledge and analytical power (the text is larded with essayistic interpretation and explanation) and his sense of impotence. Du Bois's redeeming and empowering knowledge does not apply. The ex-colored man evinces helpless knowledge or useless knowledge, though there is a hint it might be otherwise in the interest and respect "Shiny," the cultivated black man, inspires. Acknowledging helpless knowledge, the ex-colored man chooses a mere pragmatic, materialistic course, in which he makes money rather than "history and a race," a phrasing that provides a startling anticipation of Joyce's great promise in *A Portrait of the Artist as a Young Man*. In so choosing, he substantially effaces himself. His gifts and powers and promise are all *as a black man* and we need to see his defection, his self-veiling in light of those gifts. He is not a representative black man, passing, but a singular one, with vision and ambition and prowess, denying the burden of that singularity for himself and, by association, to his race.

The self-veiling of the ex-colored man, let us hasten to note, is socially intelligent, and only disastrous at the metaphysical (or private) level. In most cases the state of self-veiling in black literature comes about in less explicit and less calculated ways. Tod Clifton has none of the ex-colored man's analytical bent or cultural depth; he is a street kid.[4] He is confrontational where the ex-colored man is evasive, but he has the same meaning to convey, and the same reaction to that meaning: living as a black man is insufferable, and he will call

3. But the yearning for exemption persists, as evidenced in the heroine of Margaret Atwood's *Bodily Harm* (New York: Simon & Schuster, 1982).

4. Tod Clifton is used here to show both the persistence and permutations of self-cancellation, not to characterize *Invisible Man*, which will be more amply analyzed below.

it off. His first effort to break from behind self-veiling is in the politics of the Brotherhood, but all he finds is that one authoritarianism has supplanted another; he is not expected to become his own man, but the organization's tool. Tod rebels and takes to the street. In this he must seem to be definitively throwing off his personal veil. It is hardly so in fact. For Tod Clifton is not an obscene and mercenary opportunist, peddling nasty dolls to bored and unprincipled people. That is his veil. The reality of his spirit includes baffled disillusionment, and a near-tragic assumption that life leaves him no other role but that of the outlaw sidewalk vendor.

Like the ex-colored man Tod goes through materialism and finds it wanting. But all he can conjure up in response is the obscene sidewalk doll that reflects both his attitude toward society and his image of himself. He is using it aggressively to pronounce life obscene, and using it passively to bring disaster down on himself, to cease to live at all if he cannot live as a man (represented in the primordial, or, in literary terms, Hemingwayesque symbol of fistic prowess). Tod Clifton cancels himself at the hands of the N.Y.P.D.

Lacking both the philosophy and the organizational power of a Ras, while being confined to Ras's militant mode, Tod brings out the radical impoverishment of materialism. With the millionaire, the ex-colored man is able for a time to mask that impoverishment, but the millionaire himself confesses it in his deep and grievous boredom. Things distract him, no more. Nothing attracts him, or answers to his ceaseless need to escape from blankness.

Now materialism always amounts to a Satanic credulity toward signs and a tacit faith that objects will generate or at least reflect an inner correspondence. Seeing the Garden of Eden, Satan desires to have a place like that, in the belief that such an outward sign can overcome his inward disgrace, or in other words, that materialism can prevail against the spirit. But such materialism has shown itself early and late in black literature and experience.[5] *The Autobiog-*

5. Special attention should be called to Nella Larsen's *Quicksand*, originally published in 1928.

raphy of an Ex-Colored Man stands out in portraying the self-confessed victim of this illusory materialism. In Tod Clifton *Invisible Man* presents its instinctive victim. Charles W. Chesnutt's *Conjure Woman* contrives a veritable fusion of the two, the victim who knows and wryly, obliquely resists his fate, only to embrace it and veil himself at last in a rush of instinctive sentimentality.

If it would be plausible to call *The Autobiography of an Ex-Colored Man* a novel in the quasi-picaresque form, *Conjure Woman* should be thought of as a parade novel, that is, a novel where the copious action passes by a static character for review and evaluation. Uncle Julius McAdoo is essentially a pragmatist-with-a-purpose, the kind of man who uses the story of "The Goophered Grapevine" to try to preserve his carefree advantages in the abandoned scuppernong vineyard, but who smoothly settles for a position as a coachman. While his stories carry intimations of what may be called metaphysical value (the peripatetic slave Sandy complains of living in a state in which he "ain' got no home, ner no marster, ner no mistiss, ner no nuffin" p. 44), their basic concern is with coping, with keeping up a position or function in an immediately comfortable or profitable arrangement. It is striking then that in "Po' Sandy" the striving for comfort leads to a metamorphosis into a pine tree and the prospect of a second metamorphosis into a wolf. Classical antecedents or no, this is a blatant case of *cancellation*. It is minimal and unnatural survival that defeats its own purpose. Wordsworth invites us to see the antique penchant for metamorphosis as rooted "in pity or in wrath." Somehow the former, pity, is wanting in Uncle Julius's stories, though the latter, wrath, is never explicit.

We may observe here that the ostensible purpose of escape and comfort is not long served; Sandy, the beneficiary (or victim) of the conjured metamorphosis, is selected for lumber when his master "tuk a notion fer ter buil' a noo kitchen" (p. 52). The cleverly contrived cancellation, like that of the ex-colored man, leads to death, in this case literally so. We must ask why Uncle Julius sees fit to use his characters so, and why so little exploration of Sandy's anomalous experience takes place. There is about the story a stubborn humor that entraps the reader in a grisly, obscure conspiracy. Something important is left unsaid here, something important is veiled from our eyes. The overt end of the story, namely, Uncle Julius's managing not to lose the opportunity of making an abandoned schoolhouse (the last stage of poor dendroid Sandy) into the meeting-place for his seceding section of the Sandy (!)[6] Run Colored Baptist Church, only serves as a stimulus to Uncle Julius's hidden imagination. We are taken in by his success in the end, when we need to inquire into the means, the content of the story itself.

It is easy to overpraise the shrewdness and inventiveness of "ole Julius McAdoo." He is dealing with a master who has "always been too easily imposed upon" (p. 67), a mistress on principle given to sentimentality, and ultimately a malleable collection of figures from "memory—or imagination." These figures, let us note, he is not above killing off in dehumanizing ways: Henry, in "The Goophered Grapevine," dies because he has been "goophered" into imaging the state of the scuppernong vines, which are fatally damaged by a hyperefficient Northerner; and Sandy, converted into a tree, dies to make lumber. At bottom, both die to serve Uncle Julius's present convenience. In "The Conjurer's Revenge" Uncle Julius does not exact death, only metamorphosis into a mule. And if his Ovidian propensity extends also to white folk—in "Mars Jeems's Nightmare" a harsh slaveowner is "goophered" into a black man and suffers accordingly—it does not thereby take on a more complex cast. Uncle Julius's vision is highly *somatic*. If it is politically tendentious, its politics would end in well-fed, often-dancing, happy, hardworking people, slaves or not. Issues like freedom or justice do not substantially emerge. As Chidi Ikonné notes, Uncle Julius's practical objectives weaken the protest feature of *Conjure Woman*.[7]

6. It is worth noting that the name of the slave who introduces Frederick Douglass to conjure is Sandy Jenkins (*Narrative of the Life*, p. 80).

7. Chidi Ikonné, *From Du Bois to Van Vechten: The Early New Negro Literature, 1903 to 1926* (Westport, Conn.: Greenwood Press, 1981), p. 48.

John Blassingame, reaffirming Du Bois's position in *The Negro*, observes that "often the most powerful and significant individual on the plantation was the conjurer," in that he helped the slaves construct "a psychological defense against total dependence on and submission to their masters."[8] In a sense Uncle Julius is living up to this norm, using conjure to avoid dependence and submission. But it is a manipulative and materialistic defense, not a committed and authentic "psychological" one.

The relation between Uncle Julius and his employer puts a premium on manipulation and ingenuity, as Julius uses his stories to protect his access to grapes or honey, or a new suit, or a job for his grandson. The relation between Uncle Julius and his *"employees,"* the figures in his tales, is *also* based on manipulation, but there is the crucial difference that they are being helplessly used, while the employer is only being tested, and tentatively at that. The tales become parables less of human experience and universal meaning than of Uncle Julius's wary efforts to feather his nest. At best, then, we might praise his waging a lone old man's guerrilla war against circumstances, against the imposed passivity of blackness. But even that is brought into question. As he visits cancellation on his "employees," so ultimately does he bring a semblance of it upon himself. A measure of self-veiling, of pulling down a mask over his desire for independence and an unencumbered place, emerges strongly from the body of *The Conjure Woman*.

In fact the storyteller Julius and the narrator John are curiously complementary figures; one is too much given to materialism, the other too much given to rationalism. Each unwittingly serves to raise the other's self-esteem, as John thinks Julius gullible in matters of reason, and Julius proves John gullible in matters of practicality. They even appear alike in their concern with metamorphosis: Julius's tale pivots around conjure, and John's intellectual interests, if we

8. John W. Blassingame, *The Slave Community: Plantation Life in the Ante-Bellum South*, rev. ed. (New York: Oxford University Press, 1979), p. 109. On the meaning of "goopher," Zora Neale Hurston notes "how frequently graveyard dust" or "goofer dust" occurs in voodoo rites (*Mules and Men*, p. 234).

can judge from the massively inapt treatise he reads to his wife to relieve her illness, deal with evolution or long-term "transformations" in nature ("The Gray Wolf's Ha'nt," p. 163). John's reading proves less efficacious than Julius's tales; he is bested there. But this does not make Julius's use of conjure more authentic, wise, or admirable than John's use of transformations. John's transformations remain both natural and abstract, occurring across eons and without individual machination; Julius's conjure occurs in an instant, against nature, and has very much the smack of self-seeking manipulation. In short, each uses the concept of change to manifest the basis of his personality. For the materialist Julius change is topical and pragmatic, for the rationalist John it is general and conceptual. If we compare them, it is only to bring out their opposite but corresponding failures.

The *content* of Julius's tales permits us to see an indictment of slavery, but the *intent* goes athwart that purpose. Julius is too pragmatic for that and, it need hardly be said, John is too taken up with rationality to get into social issues and causes. Even the sensitive and good-hearted Annie, John's wife, does not go beyond immediate sympathy for the suffering detailed by Julius, toward any principle of indignation or resolution to seek betterment for the heirs of deprivation and misery. For giving an air of apparent neutrality to stories of intense political import, Zora Neale Hurston would later also come under fire (intro. to *Mules and Men*, pp. xxiv–xxvi).

And yet there is one level at which an indictment of slavery does crystallize in the unreflective narrative flow of *Conjure Woman*. Paradoxically, Julius is crucial to that crystallization. His very lack of sympathy with or overt concern for the victims of his tales becomes a testimony to the harm that slavery does; he is dull, numb to the suffering of others, and all taken up with his own immediate material needs, because slavery has not made room for him to grow and refine himself as a human being. Treated as matter, he has become materialistic. Thus he is a tainted medium of information about the full range of black response to slavery. Frederick Douglass alerts us to this phenomenon in two ways. He himself suppresses his own reactions, pragmatically, and when he finally comes out of himself, for himself and others, he is pained to note that many slaves take life simply on the surface, from day to day, without reflection or resentment, let alone a will to change. Their passivity, their pragmatism, provides a gloss on Julius's. We must look through his "indifference" to his "employees" and see a deeper indictment of slavery.

There is evidence, in fact, that Julius, when not forced to forage for survival, has magnanimity as well as shrewdness in him.

The final story of *The Conjure Woman* is "Hot-Foot Hannibal," and there Uncle Julius gives over his shrewd materialism and even imaginably risks his job to be a sentimental servant, or what might once have been called a "good" Negro, one who is virtually like a member of the family. By somehow causing the mare to balk so that it becomes necessary to take the long road, he becomes the instrument of a last-minute meeting and hence a reconciliation between the estranged young lovers. This is the sort of thing an "Uncle" does, but that is not the role in which Uncle Julius has been cast (we are reminded that his grandson's name is Tom—"Mars Jeems's Nightmare"). He even goes on to sacrifice an "opportunity to enter [the] service" of the grateful newlyweds (p. 229), though this would have been most profitable. Clearly, his act was without ulterior motive; he was being a good and faithful servant to his employer, the bride's uncle. Emphatically placed as this "goodness" is at the end of the series, it seriously qualifies the shrewdness and challenging of the social odds that have seemed to mark "ole Julius." He may thereby conquer his employer's slow-dawning skepticism about his motives, but he also cancels any faith we may have in him as a character. We may infer rather than document growth and change. Uncle Julius's sentimentality cancels his pragmatism, all we really have of him as an individual. The stories he uses to sustain himself thus at last are turned to the end of cancelling his prior energies and impulses and erecting a personal veil.

From exhaustion? Conviction? Prudence? Or from the devastating logic of his own materialism? The quaint old storyteller discovers what the sophisticated ex-colored man declares, the radical emptiness of material gain. And he has one other thing in common with the ex-colored man, namely, the absence of anyone to carry on in his footsteps. The ex-colored man has two essentially blank off-spring, and Uncle Julius's grandson, as the narrator observes, is an unprepossessing sort. Neither has lived for anything that *lives*.

This fact becomes crucial to our understanding of Uncle Julius's shift from opportunist to sentimentalist. At bottom he is really con-verting from a kind of detached gamesmanship and self-seeking manipulation of the external scene to a recognition of the inner necessity of living in a state of relationship. He has a certain mischie-vous appeal in the former role, but he attains a greater potential human depth and complexity in the latter. We should not blame him for opening up his humanity to his white Northern employer and *his* kin, while failing to come forward as a black champion. Simply put, Uncle Julius is not cut out for the rigors of intimacy, or even the test of kinship (though he does try to do something for his grandson). In effect his final limited attachment to his employer is parallel to the ex-colored man's attachment to his wife: a way to enjoy human connection without a paralyzing exposure to the dark burdens of history and the blunt risks of life that being black entails. Each finds a refuge rather than a solution; neither in refuge has the resources to erase deep mental reservations against true kinship or intimacy.

One further comment will prove useful here. Chesnutt was writing in the heart of the "Booker T." era, when the progressive pragmatism espoused by the black Washington was the order of the day. Chesnutt adds humor to Washington's relentless solemnity. Also, he dramatizes the historical context that made pragmatism obligatory. Chestnutt avoids the academic environment that Wash-ington thrived in and that Ralph Ellison would come to sear with satire (the Tuskegee Institute ironically embraces both these out-standing figures).[9] Still, Chesnutt is exploring the possibilities of Northern goodwill. The development of sentiment in Uncle Julius's

9. For a valuable account of Tuskegee's history between Washington's death and *Invisible Man*, see Robert G. O'Meally, *The Craft of Ralph Ellison* (Cambridge: Harvard University Press, 1980), pp. 12ff.

attachment to his Northern boss-cum-mentor returns the human touch to the operations of the "Tuskegee Machine." The effect is limited, and indeed clouded by the unsettled social matrix in which the action takes place. Uncle Julius McAdoo goes beyond the submission, piety, and material want of Uncle Tom, but he cannot break out of the materialism that in a sense Uncle Tom had transcended *without taking on an air of regression to Uncle Tom.*

But even as the Tuskegee Machine proceeded like a juggernaut down the years (Booker T. Washington died in 1915), signs of malfunction were becoming evident. Washington himself suffered an assault at the hands of a white man in New York, and his towering stature was not enough to spare him the indignity of a racist dismissal of the charge. This practical proof of the Washington fallacy had been theoretically foreseen by W. E. B. Du Bois in *The Souls of Black Folk*. Du Bois was to spearhead the Niagara movement and he became a founder of the NAACP (1910). A system was in place with equality rather than accommodation as its objective. The Du Boisian alternative to Booker T. Washington, despite the plangent comparison and tender pride of "On the Sorrow Songs," overcame Washington's "humility" only by opting for elitism, favoring devotion to individual excellence and organizational power through the so-called "talented tenth." It is as though Du Bois, for all his attunement to the folk in *Souls*, could not hold that allegiance, but turned to formality and abstraction.

It is often stressed that Ralph Ellison cuts down Booker T. Washington in the academic episodes of *Invisible Man*. Perhaps even the onomatopoetic revolution of Ras's cavalry charge in the riot scene has a sly satirical intent; "bookaty" sounds suspiciously like Booker T., with the implication that one is as rational and effective as the other, and with the further implication, perhaps, that Washington's submissiveness has led to his being ridden helplessly in what he least desired, all-out conflict. It needs also to be recognized that Ellison also satirizes W. E. B. Du Bois in the other scene of mass conflict at the novel's outset, the battle royal. There are nine contestants besides the "invisible man," and they represent the talented and privileged ones, with the select "ten" standing for "tenth."[10] The implication is that even the Du Boisian position ends up as a performance, a piece of controlled entertainment.

That sort of assessment may seem harsh. It is certainly exaggerated by hindsight and distorted by waves of progress that petered out and hopes that failed of fruition. It is not wholly without merit, however. The movement of the Afro-American imagination past the compromised materialism and sentimentality of Chesnutt's work would not come easy. Johnson signals a plausible way out, in *The Autobiography of the Ex-Colored Man*, but the upshot is to show that the dissatisfactions of Washingtonian pragmatism are exceeded by the debacle of racial idealism.

An even better measure of the inertia holding back change may be found in the negative reaction to Du Bois's brilliant essay "Reconstruction and Its Benefits," read before the American Historical Association in 1909. In brief, Du Bois was charged with special pleading, and it would be decades before white historians would confirm his analysis of what Reconstruction added to American life: refined democratic constitutions and state governments; new forward-looking social legislation; and establishment of a free public school system. Du Bois further pointed out that far from being helpless or shiftless after Emancipation, black people in "10,000 local bodies touching the majority of the freed population," had set about building churches, schools, and colleges, and instituting self-help projects. His summary position was that "the main body of Reconstruction legislation stood," and that "practically the whole new growth of the South" after Emancipation came about "under laws which black men helped to frame."

10. In espousing the talented tenth Du Bois may have been influenced by Lincoln's suggestion in 1864 that "some of the colored people may be let in, as, for instance, the very intelligent, and especially those who have fought gallantly in our ranks." Du Bois approvingly quotes this "cautious" recommendation in "Reconstruction and Its Benefits."

It remains essential to see that the dead end of materialism and self-veiling variously projected by Chesnutt and Johnson is not given in the nature of blackness, and neither does it spring from the nature of black-white interaction. It stands as a stage in the enunciation of black temperament. Materialism, which for all its inherent deadliness originates as a mode of survival, had to attract black writers in the early stage of finding an acceptable voice. Or, to put it another way, where the environment threatened annihilation at every turn, to veil the inner self and invest in material facades was at least to be responsible for decision and action. We have seen that self-veiling usually was a recoil from actual essayings of a positive self. Furthermore, to have the veiling in one's own hands tended to assure that it would not—again note the absence of suicide—become too thorough. In this regard, more attention should be paid to the way Frederick Douglass holds back, or backs off, after a certain point of self-assertion, in *Narrative of the Life*. The limits beyond which Douglass would not go reveal themselves in the fact that, when Henry Highland Garnet advocated a slave strike in a speech (based on his reissue of David Walker's *Appeal*) before a national convention of Negroes in Buffalo, New York, Douglass came out against the motion, which went down to a narrow defeat. But it is Douglass himself who purposely establishes the limits, he who frames the principles on which limits shall be established. There is a freedom, even a fulfillment in that.

The paradoxes of self-veiling are sharply etched in the title piece of Langston Hughes's first volume of poems, *The Weary Blues*. The blues singer in the poem transcends "his rickety stool," which seems to represent his life condition and not just the appurtenances of the joint: "He played that sad raggy tune like a musical fool" (p. 23). We can reasonably infer that nothing in his life conveys the concentration and depth of his music. He collapses after he plays, and it almost seems that he must alternate between comatoseness and music. His life, then, deeply veils what his music expresses.

But how much certainty do we have concerning what his music expresses? The manner of playing ("like a musical fool") and the matter involved do not chime together. Where his play is vivid, sure, superior, what he sings is all depression and defeat:

> I got the Weary Blues
> And I can't be satisfied.
>
> . . . .
>
> I ain't happy no mo'
> And I wish that I had died.   (p. 23)

His stamina as a singer ("far into the night he crooned that tune") does little to offset the intensification of woe in the song, and woe finally seems to have undone him when he "stopped playing and went to bed," for "he slept like a rock or a man that's dead" (p. 24). He has played himself *out*, and it is impossible to tell whether his woe or his playing has contributed more to his undoing. The blues may give us more than the life, but it gives us meanings veiled in paradox.

But the poem contains a complex reversal. The blues singer's apparent self-exhaustion (for his state is a product of his will, his soul) is counterbalanced by the fact that he has played himself into the heart and mind of the speaker in "The Weary Blues." This effect is less obvious here than in Wordsworth's "The Solitary Reaper," a strangely analogous poem, but the speaker's attachment comes out in two ways. First, more than the coming of daylight is indicated in the line "The stars went out and so did the moon"; we may understand also that the speaker is possessed by the singer's woe, and his art, and so loses a sense of the world beyond. And second, the speaker is telling as much about himself as about the singer when he says:

> The singer stopped playing and went to bed
> While The Weary Blues echoed through his head.
> He slept like a rock or a man that's dead.   (p. 24)

Has the speaker followed the singer home in fascination, in obsession? And in whose head does the echo of the weary blues play? The singer's, yes, but not his alone. The speaker is also bearing "that music," as Wordsworth says, in his heart. Not even the speaker's empathy with the blues singer, though, can enable us to penetrate the latter's veil of sleep, a veil as opaque as rock and as deep as death.

It is an accident that offsets the singer's repetitious self-veilings. Clearly he goes through his routine, his ritual, every night, and as clearly a Langston Hughes does not often happen by. In the case of the women in "Strange Hurt" (*Selected Poems*, p. 84), the offsetting feature is more oblique, or diffused; it is the reader's recognition and sympathy that must come into play. "Queer pain" has turned the woman's world upside down. She seeks "burning sunlight/Rather than the shade," and

> In months of snowy winter
> When cozy houses hold,
> She'd break down doors
> To wander naked
> In the cold.

Such behavior is both self-injuring and, cryptically, self-assertive. The narrative line of the poem is very stringent, but we are clearly dealing with habit here again, and may thus infer that the woman is neither abused nor mocked, nor comforted by her neighbors. Only the reader is left to feel curiosity and indignation about what may have turned her so, and sympathy for her sort in his experience. At best a tacit correction is urged. No doubt that tacit desire for correction may help to cause stories of self-cancellation to be cast before the public, which is stimulated to respond with sympathy or responsibility for the victim. The ex-colored man may be our most articulate "victim," and his story with its final cry of self-condemnation may be obliquely meant to manipulate its readers into pity and redress for his race if not for his anonymous self.

But Hughes also depicts a state of self-cancellation in which no real correction is possible. The short poem "Border Line" (*Selected Poems*, p. 81) has a far deeper weariness than "The Weary Blues," and a level of pain that goes beyond upending into ultimate paralysis of the personality:

I used to wonder
About living and dying—
I think the difference lies
Between tears and crying.

I used to wonder
About here and there—
I think the distance
Is nowhere.

Of course the sadness of self-cancellation is ready-made for a lyrical voice like Hughes's, but as a writer coming into his own with the Harlem Renaissance he intended something more dynamic, more upbeat.

A positive intent with a privative outcome appears again in Nella Larsen's *Passing* (1929). We should make special note of the fact that Larsen's work appeared well after Chesnutt's and Johnson's, at the latter end of the Harlem Awakening. The Great Migration stemming from the First World War had wrought as powerful a transformation of American society as the great westward trek of eight decades earlier, with the result that the black population had shifted from a postslavery, Southern agricultural regimen to an unpredicted urban scheme. In the interval between the suspension of old routines and the emplacement of new rigidities, Harlem became ad lib the focus of a major experiment in American mores. From dancing to couture, from literature to social thought, the great northward river of black people bore and bred new forms.

It is striking, then, that Chesnutt and Larsen should have both shown the force of self-veiling, despite the surface difference between the world of a field-hand-turned-house-favorite in the 1890s and the vibrant, open order that seemed to prevail in the 1920s. *Passing* is more frank in its aspirations than *The Conjure Woman*, and more complex in its resources. But it ultimately shows little more than the way the Great Migration had turned the old post-Reconstruction cabin into the Depression ghetto.

Passing concerns two young black women who share two things: friendship from childhood, and skin pale enough to allow them to live at will in the white world. One, Clare Bellew (née Kendry) chooses to do so, out of a taste for adventure as well as material advantage; the other, Irene Redfield (née Westover), stays at home in Harlem, reflecting both a sterling solidity and a kind of stolidity of character. Their Christian names, Clare and Irene (rainbow), suggest the color bias of the novel's title, with the further suggestion of peace in Irene's case. But in fact Irene's is a precarious, even volcanic peace. She is prone to feelings of anger that she does not know how to express or correct, and these feelings increase in frequency and force as the novel goes on, becoming paranoid and little short of murderous: she continually desires the demise of whatever does not chime with "her own way" (p. 107). Clare, who has been known to have frank bouts of rage (the word "catlike" is used of her, in an obviously feral sense), exudes an air of mystery ("some creature utterly strange and apart" p. 77), and possesses the power to "transform" others (p. 78). If Clare is passing for white, both are passing for content, sophisticated beings. They meet as it were in passing in a fashionable Chicago hotel, after more than a decade apart. And in that chance meeting they trigger depths in each other that the years had lidded over all but completely.

Tension and trouble develop rapidly when Clare takes to visiting Harlem on the sly, drawn by its familiarity and, paradoxically, also by its new aura of danger—her husband is not just white, but grossly bigoted: "no niggers in my family. Never have been and never will be" (p. 76). She and Irene's husband, whose desire to leave the United States for Brazil to escape racial strain and restriction causes consternation in Irene, are drawn to each other by complex feelings of novelty, sympathy, and opportunity for the green freedom of what folk wisdom calls "the other side of the mountain." But Clare's husband has grown suspicious of her frequent absences and trails her, courtesy of a private detective, to a private, penthouse party in Harlem, where in a melee Clare falls out of a window to her death.

The implications of the story are as harsh as its resolution is melodramatic: one goes out to a stifling emptiness if one "passes,"

but one returns to death if one returns. Thomas Wolfe was luridly
upstaged by Nella Larsen with his idea that "you can't go home
again." But even staying at home, as Irene does, proves unfulfilling
and, in an oblique way, deadly, for the narrative leaves open the
possibility that Irene helped speed Clare out the window. Irene has
become not just conservative but inert, clogged with the egotistic
anger that effectively defines her;[11] and the threat of losing her
husband to Clare has made her will to give Clare's secret away and
also, we may believe, to take Clare's life ("If Clare should die!" p.
169). Be that as it may, her own way of life is not preserved; her
husband can only be less happy than before at being stuck with
Harlem and with her. The very structure of things, in Harlem or out,
seems to suggest that no vision of life is tenable, that self-veiling must
be the unconscious impulse of the characters. For Clare, passing
cancels Harlem, sneaking into Harlem cancels passing, and she is
invested in both. For Irene, staying does not protect her from the
radical threat of the outside, and her inability to make of staying the
life she desires cancels its value for her. But the salient feature of
Passing, at last, is its insistence on clinical inquiry, in a pointless
detective spirit ("Let's go up and have another look at that window"
p. 189). The novel is insistently nonelegiac: "Gone! The soft white
face, the bright hair, the disturbing scarlet mouth, the dreaming eyes,
the caressing smile, the whole torturing loveliness that had been
Clare Kendry. That beauty that had torn at Irene's placid life. Gone!
The mocking daring, the gallantry of her pose, the ringing bells of
her laughter. *Irene wasn't sorry*" (p. 185, italics added). If Clare
cannot live the deprivation of blackness, Irene cannot live its dynamics. If Clare, though capable of "the heights and depths of feeling"
(p. 114), refuses to feel, Irene "can't feel" (p. 178). The attempt to
break the Du Boisian veil on Clare's part, and to hide behind it, on
Irene's, only brings the personal veil into cruel play. Neither can cope
with the double veil. Perhaps no one could, while Harlem was so

11. "Security" is the key word that identifies her egotism. Her anger comes out in
a host of forms: scorn, contempt, irritation, vexation, sharpness, ferocity, resentment,
bitterness, and so forth.

much in the limelight. We will see that it takes an obscure, unheralded boy out of an unlikely Chicago slum to stumble upon a way to dispel the veil.

In James Weldon Johnson, Langston Hughes, and Nella Larsen we have looked at writers on the eve, in the heyday, and at the tail end of the Harlem Renaissance. We have been looking at them, however, in a dynamic context that moves on purpose beyond the formulation of a fixed period. There is a need, I would hold, to avoid treating the Harlem Renaissance as some sort of cometary apparition, Kohoutek perhaps, in the firmament of Afro-American literature. As the only period with a ringing sobriquet, it has enjoyed a nominal domination that has entailed a detriment to the body of later work. Though not taking up, at this point, what is indisputably the outstanding text of the time, Jean Toomer's *Cane* (see below, chapter 6), I have given a fair, essential view of the cast and the striving, as also the strains and the inhibitions, of the era. Toomer will have his turn, after the full exploration of the phase of intimacy in Afro-American letters. His singularly halting heroism of vision can then be seen in better perspective, and so can the difficulty of the Harlem Renaissance in coming into its own.

Marcus Garvey's "Back-to-Africa" movement, espoused in *Negro World* and embodied in the Universal Negro Improvement Association, had foundered in the financial morass of the Black Star Line, and roughly a decade of devotion and animation and hope, from 1914 until 1925 (when the U.S. government put Garvey in prison, prior to deporting him to his native Jamaica) came to a wallowing end. By the end of the 1920s another tributary of black self-enhancement, in the Harlem Renaissance, had also been virtually blocked up and rendered stagnant by massive financial problems; only this time the problems were impersonal, taking the form of the Great Depression. The patrons, both major individuals and a popular throng, who had given star status to black work in literature, art, music, theater, and dance, fell aside. The artists themselves lost some of their munificence and panache. Perhaps the novelistic career of Claude McKay provides an emblem of the case. In 1927

McKay came out with his first novel, *Home to Harlem*, a fond and tangy celebration of a creative, keen, frank, daring, challenging, and dear hub of life. By 1929 McKay was producing *Banjo*, set mainly in France, portraying an uncentered and unoriented way of life. Four years later came his third and final novel, *Banana Bottom*, concerning the abandonment of America by Bita Williams and her election of a rural life in Jamaica. It is almost as though Jamaica had taken on the status of a symbolic *finale*, the mark that the great urban collective dream and drive had come apart, involuntarily for the self-made hero Marcus Garvey, voluntarily for McKay's heroine.[12]

Much as the primitive brain persists under the sophisticated cortex, so does self-veiling persist in black literature in the presence of more highly articulate and complex structures. Tod Clifton gives evidence of that, and *at the early stages of his career* so does "Jack-the-Bear," the protagonist of *Invisible Man*. He cancels himself in two ways in the battle royal scene, first sexually and then intellectually, fearing equally to be seen as a man with power and as one with thought. As late as the eviction scene he is still cancelling his own ideas, trying to speak correctly rather than truly, and as late as the encounter with Sybil he cancels his own intention. But these latter episodes show a powerful advance in his constitution. After initial, one might almost say atavistic reluctance, "Jack-the-Bear" does say what he thinks of the eviction, and of the social system and the social character out of which such evictions characteristically come; and his reneging on the scene of primal lust with Sybil is a mark of his preoccupation with larger interests and concerns, a refusal to be used sexually as he was abused by the very denial of the battle royal. It remains true that the novel is framed by scenes of failed sexuality (which is pretty much the only sexuality it affords), but that is a question better taken up when we come to the phase of intimacy in black literature.

12. Bita Williams should also be compared with Janie in Hurston's *Their Eyes Were Watching God*, as a female figure finding self-realization against all conventional conceptions. On the other hand, Helga Crane's attempt to do so in *Quicksand*, by Nella Larsen, leads to dismal and crippling failure.

What we are seeing in *Invisible Man* is of course proof that the materialistic dead end has been broken through. Ellison has advanced far enough to put the materialistic seeker—and his counterparts, the Norton millionaires and Bledsoe/Jack managers of the world—under ironic scrutiny. Long gone is the self-elegy of the ex-colored man, long gone his cryptoinfantile passivity and love of "comfort and luxury." The "invisible man" knows aggressive rage, and finds that he must struggle unremittingly to have much less than comfort. Eventually he realizes that he is struggling for much more, for something other than comfort. He learns that comfort, whether as position or possession, is a trap. He does not come thus far by abrupt, miraculous transportation. There have been crucial, evolutionary figures intervening between him and the ex-colored man.

Zora Neale Hurston's Janie, in *Their Eyes Were Watching God*, is such a figure, and Bigger Thomas, the protagonist of Richard Wright's *Native Son*, another. Both figures, let us recall, end up killing to preserve their "selves," the very antithesis of self-cancellation. This is the grim but ineluctable passage toward taking a place *as someone definite and distinctive* in a scheme of some significance. Notably, both Janie and Bigger Thomas give unflinching utterance to their lives, whereas the ex-colored man and even the storyteller Uncle Julius are respectively stifled and mediated voices. Janie uses dialect not like Uncle Julius to beguile, but *to become*, and it is striking that that becoming involves counteracting a metamorphosis so thorough and pervasive as to pass for ordinary life, that is, the way "de nigger woman is [made] de mule uh de world." As self-cancellation weakens, the trick of metamorphosis that helped to element it also modulates into a fresh idiom and domain.

3

SOLITUDE *The Beginnings of Self-Realization in Zora Neale Hurston, Richard Wright, and Ralph Ellison*

> If man's life goes
> Beyond the bone
> Man must go lonely
> And alone,
> Unhelped, unhindered,
> On his own
>
> Sterling Brown
>
> And find sweet grace alone.
>
> LeRoi Jones

ZORA NEALE HURSTON has been regarded as a daughter or heir of the Harlem Renaissance. It is truer to think of her as a fully grounded and amply evolved post-Depression figure, and to think of the Harlem Renaissance as an explosive but foiled striving in the fissure between the First World War and the Depression. In the main, characters of the 1920s—whether McKay's or Larsen's or Toomer's (or for that matter the proto-Renaissance J. W. Johnson's)—have about them a sort of self-exhausting mobility, a rootlessness in time or space. Langston Hughes's *Not Without Laughter* may be said to resist this tendency, but at the ironic cost of merely breeding up a black bourgeois. They are as it were unwittingly *in transition*. Hurston's Janie is as subject to circumstances, as much in motion as they, but bears with her a brooding power of inevitable development. The more she is threatened, the more resourceful she becomes. The more she is deprived, the more self-sufficient she becomes. That inner stability and outer indomitability mark her off from anything that has gone before; these traits will not appear again before Alice Walker's *Meridian* in the 1970s. The confinement of this phenomenon to women's hands is perhaps telling itself, showing the capacity to bear not just children, or the continuance of life, but to bear life itself. It is a rare phenomenon, even among women.

The story of Janie Crawford in *Their Eyes Were Watching God* (1937) is the record of black development from materialism and passivity (her grandmother's belief that money and/or white patronage are the essence of a good life) to self-respect, self-reliance, and (qualified) self-realization. Janie is said to be "full of that oldest human longing—self-revelation" (p. 18). The difficulty of getting a bead on that self is severe enough. Hurston renders the stock scene of racial discovery with rare delicacy, complexity, and resonance. Not social prejudice or personal meanness but *affection* leads to Janie's discovery that she is black. Without distinction, along with the white children of the family her grandmother works for, she has lived and played and been naughty and gotten "a good lickin'" (p. 21); and in that spirit she is included in a photograph of the group. She looks for herself in the picture and where she is supposed to be sees only "a real dark little girl with long hair," whom she does not recognize. "Where is me?" Ah don't see me," she complains. She has taken the image, perhaps the imprint, of her white companions.

It is a poignant rather than a wrenching or crushing scene; "everybody laughed" at her failure to tell herself. Her reaction to instruction ("Aw, aw! Ah'm colored") evokes further laughter (p. 21). In this unusual rendition there is little of the trauma of repudiation, and a good dash of humor and consolation. But Hurston reinforces the "discovery" scene with what we may term the *nemo* syndrome: the little girl who doesn't know her own face also doesn't know her own name. "Dey all useter call me Alphabet," Janie recalls, "'cause so many people had done named me different names" (p. 21). As a nickname Alphabet implies something both extravagant and defective, the elements of any name or all names without the shape or strength of one. Janie's grandmother sets forth her ambition for the child: "Ah wanted you to look upon yo'self. Ah don't want yo' feathers always crumpled by folks throwin' up things in yo' face" (p. 37). But Janie, as the photograph proves, can't look upon herself with recognition or confidence. In the burgeoning tradition of Afro-American literature, her grandmother's desire to see her "safe in life" (p. 30) resounds ominously. The desire to be "safe" has undermined every value and underscored every disaster for Irene Redfield, in Nella Larsen's *Passing*.

The source of confidence and safety her grandmother contrives harks back to the materialism we have identified in black literature, here in the form of marriage to the old farmer Logan Killicks. The deadliness of that age-old materialism, though, is intuitively grasped by Janie, who sees Killicks as "some ole skullhead in de grave yard" (p. 28). It is not clear whether Killicks, destroying Janie's sense of sunup and blossoming pear trees, is destroying Janie's spirit or her sexuality. The two perhaps intertwine for her. Some naturalistic romance of beginning summons her; and Killicks, who "don't take nothin' to count but sow-belly and corn-bread," can only detain and thwart her with his sixty acres of "seed p'taters" and "manure." Johnson's millionaire has shown us abstract materialism, his money detached from work or any particular source; Logan Killicks brings materialism down to earth, and shows it is not only deadly but dreary and foul.

At first blush Janie's resistance to Logan Killicks's needs and ways must seem like the old May-January pattern, and more so as she quits her kitchen to run off (bigamously) with dapper Joe Starks. But much more is afoot. Not only does Janie Crawford-Killicks not cancel herself in the interest of materialism, but she puts materialism on the defensive. Logan Killicks is made to feel that he has no leg to stand on, and soon to feel ugly and impotent. He reacts by redou-

bling rather than revising his materialism, trying to make Janie into a
surrogate mule on the grounds that the farm requires more and more
work. When she refuses, he makes a gesture that embodies the
philosophical weakness and functional despotism of the materialistic
way: Logan Killicks threatens to take an ax to Janie and kill her.

With Joe Starks, Janie enters the terra incognita beyond materialism. Two pieces of data furnish preliminary clues to this world.
First, Joe Starks appeals to Janie's yearning for the "far horizon,"
without touching her feeling for "sun-up and pollen and blooming
trees," which is to say that he probably won't be able to satisfy her
deepest, primary needs. And second, Joe Starks takes overnight,
where Logan Killicks took at least a few weeks, to stop "making
speeches with rhymes" to Janie, which is to say he probably won't be
out to satisfy those needs. As things develop, Joe publicly prevents
Janie from speaking in public ("her place is in de home"), and has so
much to do as "Mayor–postmaster–landlord–storekeeper" of the
"colored town" of Eatonville (incidentally the name of Hurston's
birthplace in Florida) that he has neither time nor thought for her.
"You oughta be glad," he intones, "'cause dat makes uh big woman
outa you." In short, Janie finds herself in a world of paradox, where
to be neglected and belittled is to become "big."

Materialism, which in its own terms means access to possessions
and comfort and luxury, has yielded to political power as a goal.
(This is a notable turning point; as late as 1933, Jessie Fauset's *There
Is Confusion* and *Comedy, American Style* had shown materialism's
tenacity.) Joe Starks's profits prove secondary to his control over
other people. He will not let Janie, or anyone else, near that power,
but what he is offering to Janie alone is the opportunity to be the
beneficiary rather than a victim of materialism (as the other people
of Eatonville are victims, disliking and even mistrusting Joe Starks
but putting up with him and admiring him in return for creature
comforts like street lights and a provisioned store).

Though in terms of social history what Joe Starks is doing may
look necessary and desirable, the way he does it changes from bold
to coercive and cold before our eyes. (William Melvin Kelley in *A*

Different Drummer brings Tucker Caliban, like a Moses, to the stage where one would expect the founding of a black township, but does not delineate any way in which Eatonville's pitfalls might be avoided.) An ominous quality clings to Joe Starks's work both publicly and domestically, and Janie has neither instinct nor argument—as with Logan Killicks—to protect herself against him. Nothing brings out more sharply the harmful development of Starks's town than the images of metamorphosis that grow up around him.

The first metamorphosis is cumulative and has to do with Joe Starks's appurtenances. The townspeople see him turning into a white man, or a cento of white men, with a "promenading white" house like that of "Bishop Whipple, W. B. Jackson and the Vanderpool's," a desk "like Mr. Hill or Mr. Galloway over in Maitland," and a "gold-looking" spittoon like "his used-to-be bossman used to have in his bank . . . in Atlanta" (pp. 75–76). We recall in fact that when Joe Starks first appears "he acts like [white] Mr. Washburn . . . to Janie" (p. 47). She intuits at once what the townsfolk will only slowly and obliquely recognize. But she is not bred to act on her intuitions. The second metamorphosis goes beyond trappings into the basic makeup of the character: "It was like seeing your sister turn into a 'gator" (p. 76). Strictly, this is analogy rather than metamorphosis, but the townspeople are representing a moral and social passage in Joe Starks from one state of being to another, and representing equally—such is the consciousness of analogy—a change in their own attitude.

What they do defensively and passively to Joe Starks, to keep some perspective and self-esteem, he eventually does to Janie in a forthright and hostile way. He metamorphoses her into a barnyard animal, again not literally, but as a way of expressing a social judgment: "Somebody got to think for women and chillun and chickens and cows" (p. 110). In point of fact, Janie has been reduced to a projection of Joe Starks's ambition, without substance or activity of her own. It is striking how little of the Eatonville section of the novel deals with her, as her existence falls into a pattern of seeing others as real, and seeming rather than being an individual.

If Janie has escaped materialism,[1] or being "run off down a back road after *things*" (p. 138), she has not advanced very far. She has attached herself to a believer in images, and it seems truer to say that she has herself become, than that she has developed, an image. Her lack of self-image in the photograph scene entailed at least a poignant humor. Her capitulation to the Killicks order of images has a grim, stifling air. Thus it is important that when Joe Starks slaps her around for presenting him a "tasteless mess" of a meal, "her image of [him] tumbled down and shattered" (p. 112). This clears the way for a further stage of development. She has seen mere substance in Killicks, illusory substance in Starks. Now Hurston alerts us to another level of experience in Janie by reinvoking, and exorcising, Janie's naturalistic romance:

She had no more blossomy openings dusting pollen over her man, neither any glistening young fruit where the petals used to be. She found that she had a host of thoughts she had never expressed to him, and numerous emotions she had never let Jody know about. (p. 112)

The change that occurs in Janie is at first internal, secret; she bears her new realization a long time before she is driven, by Joe's carping insults, to retort it against him: "You big-bellies round here and put out a lot of brag, but 'tain't nothin' to it but yo' big voice. . . . Talkin' about *me* lookin' old! When you pull down yo' britches, you look lak de change uh life." As she says this in the presence of townsfolk, the whole world of illusion evaporates. In that moment, the text draws a distinction between power and possessions on the one hand and personhood on the other. Joe Starks feels that Janie has "cast down his empty armor before men. . . . They'd look with envy at *the things* and pity *the man*" (p. 123, italics added). We may note the blunt assault on Joe Starks here, as opposed to the metaphorical distancing in the townsfolk's judgment. They refer to their "sister" as a "'gator" and only thus convey their shock and distress at Joe Starks's transformation. Attention is called to the transformation more strictly

1. Melvin Tolson memorably defines "the materialism of the West" as "a steatopygous Jezebel / with falsies on her buttocks" (*Harlem Gallery*, p. 118).

than to Joe himself, and they retain at least a baffled sympathy: "You keep seeing your sister in the 'gator and the 'gator in your sister, and you'd rather not" (p. 76). But Janie holds Joe directly before us, not so much transformed as *exposed*, and exposed as an unmanned being in a state of decay; the "change of life" pertains to a woman whose fertility is past. She not only unmans but feminizes Joe Starks.[2]

If the townsfolk were addressing Joe, they might be said to be signifying. Janie has all but lost the patience or style to signify. She puts her husband down, and out, sexually and socially. Indeed, she does not even address Joe Starks, she *categorizes* him in the merciless synecdoche of the verb "big-bellies." The townspeople might have set the example in unmanning Joe Starks, but they use the term "big-belly" *of* rather than *to* him (p. 78), and at least retain enough of a sense of human relationship to adopt the indirection of signifying and think of him as a metamorphosed sister. They say Janie is "really playin' de dozens" (p. 123); in fact there is little verbal play on Joe's part, and on Janie's a deadly bluntness that seems to crash through signifying and into denunciation. She is rectifying an imbalance of power, as signifying fundamentally sets itself to do. But she is working head on, whereas signifying leads the mind to an awareness of entities and forces and values not explicit in the actual words used. The signifying gesture instigates a conclusion that it does not itself reach. To illustrate, the word *abraxas* is significant of the supreme power, yet still observes the law that the supreme power must go unnamed. The monkey never goes up into the lion's face, but signifies at a distance, from the trees.

Joe Starks experiences her action as a deliberate attempt to kill, though she only means him to live in another light. It takes him a good second to realize what her retort amounts to, and that is an omen of his unwillingness or inability to change. In imputing to her a desire to kill, he is indicating that he will die to hold on to his position.

2. Janie, in fact, makes her first husband feel impotent, tells her second publicly that he is so, and kills the third. It is an arresting, anthropophobic pattern which the text does not allow us to search to its foundation.

78   SOLITUDE

Change would be tantamount to death. He is wholly accustomed to
putting her down with impunity; she takes him, and herself, by
surprise when she rises up to keep from being psychically *put away*.
For all her long-suffering, for all her willingness to present herself in
his image, Janie will not be cancelled. Her attitude here poignantly
anticipates her confrontation with the maddened, deadly, beloved
Tea Cake.

It gives proof of *her* mind's going beyond images, beyond
credulity, that when Joe Starks calls in a conjure man she can
withstand that worthy's manipulation of the townspeople's minds.
Both materialism and image-bearing are past for Janie. Before she
announces Joe Starks's death to the waiting townspeople (the conjurer can neither harm Janie nor help her husband, unlike the Chesnutt pattern of a scant four decades earlier), Janie looks at herself in
the mirror, and recognizes herself, though changed, and approves of
herself (pp. 134–35). For the first time in her life, from the childhood
photograph through the dreaminess under the pear tree to the coercive facade of life as Joe Starks's mate, image and substance fuse, so
that image as such loses its force. When she lets down her rich hair
(p. 137) that Joe had jealously obliged her to bind up (pp. 86–87), she
is asserting not only the rightness of her beauty and her confidence in
it, but also the rightness of her self. Janie takes a place in the long
tradition, from the Bible to *La Femme du Boulanger*, of expressing
inner freedom by freeing the confined hair. To evaluate this freedom, let us look at what Janie has been through.

Despite the marked differences in manner and purpose among
them, the three principal persons in Janie's life to this point, her
grandmother, her aged-farmer husband and then her entrepreneur-
politician husband, all make the same demand on her: to cancel
herself. She appears to yield to her grandmother's devotion and
emotion, and again to Joe Starks's presence and rhetoric, but at
bottom she holds fast to something as unknown as indomitable.

That "something" is her freedom, or her ability as a forty-year-old
widow who has been largely silenced and set aside to move with

eloquence and direction into the town and beyond it into the future. Let us note that she is not bursting out afresh and full of vigor from a comatose state, like the sleeping beauty. Rather she has been tacitly prepared to cope by her entire experience since puberty, in that her experience with her grandmother and both her husbands has been one of essential *solitude*. She has not joined or shared with anyone. Her life has been an unconscious preparation for being by herself. Only now she is aware of it, and herself links freedom and solitude: "She liked being lonesome for a change. This freedom feeling was fine" (p. 139).

At this stage Janie's solitude is simple, that is, uncomplicated by desire or deficiency, and her freedom is rudimentary—it is freedom from falsehood or obstacles, but without any positive expression or form. Her relationship with Vergible Woods, "Tea Cake," first gives Janie to herself by confirming and eliciting her powers, physical and social and moral. There is a dash of sentimentality or hyperbole in the treatment ("He was a glance from God" p. 161), but Janie and Tea Cake share something with all the propriety of what is genuine and all the unorthodoxy (in relative age, wealth, position) of what is original. The upshot of the relationship is to give form to Janie's freedom while paradoxically also giving depth and force to her solitude.

Janie and Tea Cake occupy a world of applied pastoral, with a dash of the Wife of Bath—that is, their feelings are elevated and lovely, but their setting is a rather realistic environment of gambling and railroad workers and "money and fun and foolishness" (p. 192). In this situation Janie, who has withstood two husbands and considerable social pressure, submits herself wholly to Tea Cake, the way Chaucer's Wife gives "maistrie" to her devoted, young, fifth husband. Like the Wife of Bath, Janie fulfills herself by surrendering herself, in that surrendering to one who surrenders to her causes the fiction of domination to disappear: "Janie . . . felt a soul-crushing love. *So* her soul crawled out from its hiding place" (p. 192, italics added). If on the face of it the phrase "soul-crushing love" does not

quite have the favorable ring the context suggests it is meant to,
perhaps the best response would be to take the soul as nutmeg or
oregano, its flavor and aroma elicited by crushing.

The violence and unpredictability that from the outset dwell on
the edge of the relationship between Janie and Tea Cake slowly
close in, culminating in the hurricane and Tea Cake's being bitten by
a rabid dog from which he is trying to save Janie. They learn too late
that he has been infected. It is a cruel irony that he, who had a pattern
of abrupt disappearances and who has taught Janie a legitimate faith
in him absent, cannot stand to have her out of his sight. The symptom
of his illness is the symptom of his love gone mad. A sense of irony
becomes almost overwhelming when Tea Cake, paranoid in illness,
comes at Janie with a gun and is shot in horrified self-defense by the
woman he has lovingly taught to shoot. And yet the final air of the
novel is neither tragic nor melodramatic.

Beginning in accidental solitude with her grandmother, and
passing to accepted solitude with Logan Killicks and Joe Starks,
Janie ends in what may best be called accomplished solitude. Tea
Cake, part bean-planter and part happy-go-lucky gambler, has
shown her not only the far horizon Joe Starks promised but also
sunup and pear trees in bloom, which her instinctive mind had
desired: "he could be a bee to a . . . pear-tree blossom in the spring"
(p. 161). Life has shown her the rest, including the need to kill even
the beloved for the sake of life. Above all, Tea Cake and life together
have shown her herself, *Janie* (Crawford and Killicks and Starks and
Woods are inadequate surnames, appendages). And Janie is a
woman with (1) the strength to survive and to even forgive the
slanderers (first Tea Cake's friends in "De Muck" and then her own
friends back in Eatonville) who would belie and befoul her time
with Tea Cake; and (2) the command and lucidity before experience
to see that "Love is lak de sea. It's uh movin' thing, but still and all, it
takes its shape from de shore it meets, and it's different with every
shore" (p. 284).

Finally, Janie is a woman with power enough to transcend her
two greatest ambitions: to have a man like Tea Cake and to have the

gift of ready speech. Perhaps she has the first transcendence forced upon her, but that takes little away from the merit of being able to sit, grieving over killing and being nearly killed by Tea Cake, and thanking him "for giving her the chance for loving service" (p. 273). She is, as Arnold enjoins, seeing things steadily and seeing them whole. The second transcendence, of silence, is again bathed in paradox: even as she resorts to words to tell her story, Janie can say of the word-mongers:

Talkin' don't amount tuh uh hill uh beans when yuh can't do nothin' else. And listenin' tuh dat kind uh talk [the slanderers] is jus' lak openin' yo' mouth and lettin' de moon shine down yo' throat. (p. 285)

The problem of finding a voice haunts black literature. Even in 1981 David Bradley harks back to it in *The Chaneysville Incident*: Moses Washington (the name explains itself) carefully marks the passage in Jeremiah that says "I cannot speak; for I am a child," thus giving Biblical authority to the difficulty of finding a voice. The passage contains God's promise that "thou shalt speak," which represents a positive breakthrough. But it is to be noted that the central character, who tells the story, encounters resistance to the black world and people of the story from his wife. And she is white and named Judith (who undid the foreign Holofernes). One hesitates to extrapolate any special intimation on Bradley's part.

Needless to say, difficulty in finding a voice is hardly an exclusive burden of the black writer. Gibbon experienced it, and so did Coleridge. Repeatedly rewriting the first chapter of *The Decline and Fall of the Roman Empire* constituted an attempt on Gibbon's part to sound right before he spoke out; as soon as the voice came right, the work swept on to its grand conclusion. And Gibbon had the same sort of experience when he came to pen his autobiography. For that, he got up to six versions, none of them even close to complete. Coleridge, in turn, not only wrestled with an assortment of poems left fragmentary, but largely gave over the will to express his poetic inspiration. The final section of "Kubla Khan" dramatizes his psychic conviction, in the thick of a drug- and dream-induced access of inspiration, that he could not find an effective voice, could not keep alive the desired "symphony and song." We may note with interest here that in his *Preface to a Twenty-Volume Suicide Note*, Jones makes an analogous protestation: "I am thinking / of a dance One I could / invent, if there / were music" ("The Death of Nick Charles," p. 32).

What gives singularity to the black writer's burden in searching for a voice is the twofold factor of frequency and context. Either directly or in projection through a central character, black writer after black writer, generation upon generation, from Frederick Douglass to Alice Walker, evinces the problem of voice. And it is appropriate to regard the most outspoken black writers of the protest movement as bearers of the burden in another guise. Theirs is not so much a free voice as the forced voice of reaction and resentment.

The matter of context gives a special poignancy to the black writer's problem of voice. Let us recall the obliquity of blues and of signifying, and set that beside comments made by Jonathan Edwards in Puritan America and William Faulkner in modern secular America. In his Nobel Prize speech, which we tend to remember mostly for the comment on surviving and prevailing, Faulkner in fact explains *how* man will prevail. Man alone, he says, "has an *inexhaustible voice*" (italics added). Edwards's comment is personal, whereas Faulkner's is generic, but it assumes the same freedom and the same global import as Faulkner's:

I spent most of my time in thinking of divine things, year after year[,] often walking alone in the woods . . .; and it was always my manner, at such times, to sing forth my contemplations.[3]

Wordsworth, we may recall in passing, composed poetry in a similar way. In other words, the woods in which black people hid and counted on silence were fields of stimulation and expression for others.

Freedom of voice was not only limited in practice but was

3. *Personal Narrative*, in Jonathan Edwards, *Representative Selections*, with introduction, bibliography, and notes by Clarence H. Faust and Thomas H. Johnson, rev. ed. (New York: Hill and Wang, 1962), p. 61.

positively curtailed for black people. Frances Anne Kemble, in her *Journal of a Residence on a Georgia Plantation, 1838-1839*, records that she has "heard that many of the masters and overseers prohibit melancholy tunes or words, and encourage nothing but cheerful music and senseless words."[4] To encourage "senseless words" goes beyond denying an authentic voice; it insures that there will be no voice at all. As we find in Dorothy Porter's important edition of *Early Negro Writing*,[5] another form of the same insurance was recorded by a black man, James Forten, Sr.: slaveowners, Forten wrote, simply could be expected to send off to a proposed colony "those among their bondmen who feel they should be free" and who are thus "dangerous to [their] quiet," while "the tame and submissive will be retained and subjected to increased rigor" (p. 267).

Other sources of the problem of voice also come readily to mind. The separation of family and friends and the denial to black people of the right of assembly were decidedly inhibiting to communication. As even the uncomplaining slave Equiano complained, in *The Interesting Narrative of the Life of Olaudah Equiano, or Gustavus Vassa, the African* (1789), "I had no person to speak to that I could understand" (*The Life*, p. 91).

But one of the most poignant and arresting cases of the problem of voice[6] occurs with Frederick Douglass, who reports that at the deathbed of the aged and debilitated Captain Auld, his former master, he was "speechless." Douglass was by then a noted figure in his own right, and came in a position of strength. What made him "speechless"? Unexpected nostalgic grief, which it would have been unseemly to express? Unexpected living resentment and vindictiveness, which decency obliged him to contain? A spontaneous upsurge

---

4. Frances Anne Kemble, *Journal of a Residence on a Georgia Plantation, 1838-1839*, edited with an introduction by John A. Scott (New York: Alfred A. Knopf, 1961), p. 164.

5. *Early Negro Writing: 1760-1837* (Boston: Beacon Press, 1971).

6. It is important to distinguish between the attainment of *literacy* and the achievement of a *voice*. Richard Wright effectively defines literacy as "at best, no more than vicarious cultural transfusions" (*Black Boy*, p. 282). A voice means, in addition, independent strength and form and clarity.

of feelings of subjection and inferiority? A century later Ralph
Ellison will speak of "the barriers of [the] stifling, provincial world,"
but indicate that he somehow collaborated: "my struggle became a
desperate battle which was usually fought . . . in silence; a guerrilla
action in a larger war in which I found some of the most treacherous
assaults against me committed by those who regarded themselves
either as neutrals, as sympathizers, or as disinterested military advis-
ers" (*Shadow and Act*, p. 122).

Janie Crawford inherits or rather embodies such quandaries in
Their Eyes Were Watching God. To say that Janie has reached a
state of accomplished solitude is to recognize both the progress she
has made in personal development and the denial she encounters in
the social sphere. Her home is a symbol of her condition, free and
proud and yet radically unshared. She is not disposed to come out to
the community, and the townsfolk are in one sense afraid and in
another unfit to come in to her. Phoeby (whose name, as a variant of
Phoebus, may be meant to convey light)[7] comes in, but she does not
carry word, or light, back out. The reverence she comes to feel for
Janie will if anything baffle the community, since her very reverence
will prevent her from profanely broadcasting the story. Phoeby
confirms rather than offsets Janie's solitude. Hers has become an
inner world, where all light concentrates on Janie: "The light in her
hand was like a spark of sun-stuff washing her face in fire" (p. 285).

Janie's transcendence of Joe Starks's image-world is tacitly reaf-
firmed in the closing scenes of *Their Eyes*. She remains wholly
unconcerned about the image the townsfolk have of her. She neither
courts nor defies their opinion. Her life is beyond that. Phoeby will
not be a sunrise for the new Janie, for that Janie, while unable to
express herself at large, cannot be reduced to a superficial image.

But Janie's tacit renunciation of image-making is far from settling the issue in black literature. Though images will cast injurious

7. Is her surname, Watson, a buried pun on light (watts-on)? We may note that
as "phoebe" she would be a small, dull-colored bird. From any standpoint Phoeby's
name suggests light but not in such a way as to make it clearly available.

spells on the protagonists in Wright's *Native Son*, Ellison's *Invisible Man*, and Chester Himes's *The Primitive*, LeRoi Jones will make a defiant, a desperate stand on their behalf. Raising the image to the level of a philosophical standard, Jones writes in "The Revolutionary Theater":

Imagination (Image) is all possibility, because from the image, the initial circumscribed energy, any use (idea) is possible. And so begins that image's use in the world. Possibility is what moves us. (*Home*, p. 213)

Perhaps there is justice or even wisdom in this. But one notes also a certain pathos in the adoption of an instrument that has been so antipathetic to black people and their cause. Images do matter, but reflection on them and judgment must matter more, if we are not to be victimized by chasing a will-o'-the-wisp or taking up residence in a mirage.

Jones is both too shrewd and too committed to a practical goal not to have seen this pitfall. He advocates but is also wary of "the changing of images" (*Home*, p. 247). And yet there is also about him an extremist, apocalyptic streak that leads, in "The Legacy of Malcolm X, and the Coming of the Black Nation," to a certain turbulence of direction: "God is man idealized," he writes, and immediately adds: "The Black Man must idealize himself as Black. And idealize and aspire to that" (*Home*, p. 248). Realization is not congruous with aspiration in these lines, and a realized godhead sorts with neither. Devotion, frustration, and pain: these come through the language more clearly than the purported program.

Though Africa had had a significant impact upon the American and Afro-American scene in the opening decades of this century, it did so more as an idea than as a reality. In aesthetic circles African art and "primitivism" had helped to stimulate a desire for the "freedom" of approaches at once natural and new. Marcus Garvey's "Back-to-Africa" movement had given focus to feelings of tradition and dignity and brotherhood. W. E. B. Du Bois had conceived of a pan-African movement that would realize political, social, and cultural strength for black people. But none of these approaches to

Africa took into account the actualities of that vast and various continent. Africa was being manipulated as an image.

By the late 1940s and early 1950s the situation had changed from cultural manipulation to cultural coincidence and even reciprocity. The nationalism that yielded independence for one African nation after another in the decade and a half from 1951 to 1966, beginning with a single Libya and culminating with tens of erstwhile French and British possessions, both stimulated and reflected the pressure for equality and self-determination among black people in the United States. The epochal Supreme Court decision on school desegregation (*Brown* v. *Board of Education of Topeka*, 1954) and both the serial explosions of protest and the sustained Civil Rights movement of the 1960s wheeled into and spun out of African aspirations. It was at the level of a community of purpose and value (adapted to local circumstances), rather than a community of persons located in one place, that the African tie was finally to take hold. Malcolm X, launching the Organization of Afro-American Unity in 1964, would differ from Garvey and Du Bois, his predecessors in conceiving an international black political structure, precisely in the concreteness of purpose and value that he stressed; the race struggle in the United States was parallel to and part of the struggles for independence throughout Africa. A groundwork had been laid for Malcolm X by no less a figure than Richard Wright, who works from detached observation through complex emotions and interests to a rousing, hortatory political identification with African independence movements. As LeRoi Jones observes, a *"brotherhood of purpose"* was forming (*Home*, p. 239).

Richard Wright's visit to the African Gold Coast, recorded in *Black Power* in the year of the school desegregation decision, clearly brings out the change that has developed in the black American's relationship to Africa. First, Wright's trip comes about almost casually, without the apocalyptic fervor of Garveyism or the millennial aspirations of Du Bois's pan-Africanism. Wright of course brings his novelist's eye—the Las Palmas whorehouse (pp. 22ff.), the purchase of the pan (pp. 83–84), and the story of the stolen purse (pp. 245ff.)

make for brilliant scenes. He also applies the prism of his black experience and his residual Marxism, but he clearly follows through with an unplanned and untendentious sojourn. What he finds, finds him. Some gestures or states he grasps intuitively, others simply elude him, and yet others are almost deliberately left obscure (the behavior of Kwame Nkrumah often falls into the latter category).

Wright's posture is that of an observer, an analyst. His view is panoramic, but its center in the nature of things becomes Nkrumah and the popular drive for "FREE—DOOOOM!" Wright effectively ends up analyzing "the quintessence of passion" on a national scale. Both the intensity and the scale create an obvious object, and at the same time entail, at the level of practical data, "ever-winding avenues of searching" that forbid "any immediate satisfaction." In other words, Wright does not go back to Africa, but goes onward into Africa, as much exploring himself as it. He is all the more justified, accordingly, in making much of the complex surge for freedom that joins his American experience and his African encounter.

But the fusion of analytical finesse and emotional openness that Wright displays in *Black Power* puts him in a vastly different position than he had held a mere fourteen years before in *Native Son* (1940). And the difference goes beyond the effects of genre. The travel report and the novel are alike in detailing the coming into self-realization of a nation and a human being, respectively. But in the travel report a presumption of inner substance and value holds sway, whereas in the novel the threat of worthlessness is radical. The treatment of the movies provides a convenient measure of the distance between the two texts. Bigger Thomas is captivated by the illusion of the movies, which set unreal and unhealthy boundaries for his life. In *Black Power* the influence of the movies on Mary, the girl in the taxi outside the prime minister's office (pp. 161–65), is shown as degrading and silly, *and she herself knows that she is exploiting it.*

Richard Wright's *Native Son* evinces a remarkable number of likenesses to *Their Eyes Were Watching God*, including coming to a conclusion with a formal murder trial and a personal scene of human reconciliation that yet leaves the protagonist in a state of solitude. Bigger Thomas, moreover, begins under a threat of self-cancellation and is seduced by materialism and then by images, in the pattern held up before Janie. But where Janie naively begins in a corner of the white world and contracts from there into the black enclave of Eatonville and further into "De Muck," Bigger expands out from the ghetto into the white world and beyond that into the levels where social philosophy and political power are struggled over. The difference in scale is significant, not least because *Native Son* puts the figure of solitude—saved however traumatically from self-cancellation and materialism and its sequel, image-worship—into a public position, whence the kind of representative encounter is possible that the domestic concentration of *Their Eyes Were Watching God* in itself precludes.

Bigger Thomas's experience represents a series of violent swings between self-cancellation and self-assertion, with the urgency of his moods of self-cancellation gradually diminishing while the lucidity and control of his self-assertion correspondingly grows. The opening scene of the novel cryptically blends self-cancellation and self-assertion. The context is oddly Hamletic. The "light tapping in the thinly plastered wall," the presence of a creature that is shifting and invisible ("I don't see 'im") and the pervasive sense of dread all suggest the visit of the ghost with the message that something is rotten in the state (pp. 8–9). At this juncture the rot seems all domestic, symbolized as much by the rat that invades and haunts the Thomas family's one-room life as by the mother's telling her first son she wonders why she had ever "birthed" him (p. 11). The son, Bigger Thomas, clearly dreads and abominates the rat as much as any of them, but once he kills it his hysterical cursing turns into a mixture of vicious play and macho display—he holds the fearful creature toward his sister, and she faints.[8]

The fear Bigger shows toward the rat is involuntary; his attack

8. It is noteworthy that Wright himself, in *Black Boy: A Record of Childhood and Youth*, evinces crippling fear of the dead kitten his mother insists that he bury (p. 18). Perhaps he displaces the scene into this form, rat for cat and sister for brother, as an act of exorcism. Bigger is clearly guilty of such displacement.

on his sister is quite voluntary and represents an effort to recover and reestablish himself. But in actuality he has been the one the family has turned to and depended on for protective action. Far from being hostile, they are implicitly complimentary (his younger brother looks up to him with feelings next to idolatry, and his mother cries him down in proportion to her obvious high hopes for him). Why then is Bigger so hostile and self-assertive? The episode with the rat seems less a symbol than a catalyst for feelings of helplessness and worthlessness that Bigger has carried unexpressed for some time. It is a sort of uprising against such feelings that causes him to disappoint his mother and distress his sister:

Vera [his sister] went behind the curtain and Bigger heard her trying to comfort his mother. He shut their voices out of his mind. He hated his family because he knew that they were suffering and that he was powerless to help them. He knew that the moment he allowed himself to feel to its fullness how they lived, the shame and misery of their lives, he would be swept out of himself with fear and despair. So he held toward them an attitude of iron reserve. . . . And toward himself he was even more exacting. He knew that the moment he allowed what his life meant to enter fully into his conscious-ness, he would either kill himself or someone else. So he denied himself. (pp. 13–14)

It is striking that Bigger, who here suspends all reactions in order to keep from killing, goes into "a deep physiological resolution not to react to anything" *after he kills and is captured* (p. 255). The appar-ent identification of not feeling and not killing does not stand up under scrutiny. Killing does not release feeling in any basic way, but merely rebounds into not feeling, into not daring to feel. This result has in it less paradox than meets the eye, in that the killings are not undertaken out of an uncontrollable upsurge of feeling, but as a way of stifling feeling. When Bigger identifies himself with the act of killing, then, we need to take close account of two facts: (1) to acknowledge the killing is to go past the mere act and the ensuing "physiological resolution not to react," into a stage of open aware-ness and responsibility; and (2) to accept this stage is to defeat the numbing depression that kept him from himself, his family, and his society, and thus it entails the beginning of his active humanity. It is his ability to *face* the killing, not merely to *perform* it, that counts most in the end. The performance is in itself a reflex of the self-cancellation that marks Bigger at the outset.

Wright sets forth without mercy the state, and the cause, of self-cancellation. He brings home in a radical philosophical way what may have looked like a physical reflex in Janie, or an animal impulse in the cornered rat, namely, the siamese continuity between self-cancellation and a drive to undo others, or murderousness. "Naw; it ain't like something going to happen to me. It's . . . like I was going to do something I can't help" (p. 24). A passive-aggressive seesaw is manifest even in the approach to the holdup; Bigger feels "like a man about to shoot himself" (p. 28). In relation to the job interview he has with Mr. Dalton, Bigger's sister chides him: "you know how you can forget" (p. 15), but it is his very ability to forget that keeps him at the minimum level of stability he exhibits. "Forgetting" essentially means that he suspends "the way he lived; he passed his days trying to defeat or gratify powerful impulses in a world he feared" (p. 44).

The foundation of such a response in the self-protective realities of the human psyche is easy enough to recognize. We may also note that Wright records identical feelings in his own family, in his own life. The situation, with his mother on her deathbed, is admittedly extreme, by contrast with the "normal" signs of weakness and inadequacy in the Thomas household. But the weight of repetition would seem to aggravate the "normal" into the intensity and finality of dying. Here is the pertinent passage from *Black Boy*:

> Once, in the night, my mother called me to her bed and told me that she could not endure the pain, that she wanted to die. I held her hand and begged her to be quiet. That night I ceased to react to my mother; *my feelings were frozen.* (p. 111, italics added)

Clearly Wright in the emotional realm matches his mother's position in the physical: he cannot endure the pain. She dies, according to the dictates of nature. He makes himself as good as dead, according to the demands of his spirit. Seeing the same reaction in Bigger gives us important if paradoxical evidence of his sensitivity and makes plausible his eventual emergence, or rebirth, from the extreme of self-protection that causes him to kill Mary Dalton and Bessie Mears, as he has earlier metaphorically killed himself.

It is clear that Bigger's response to self-cancellation early in the novel portends his homicidal behavior with Mary Dalton and Bessie Mears (we must remember that Bigger dreads Mary from the start—"*Goddamn that woman!* She spoiled everything!" (p. 54)—so that his near-discovery by Mrs. Dalton in Mary's room aggravates an already hostile attitude). But this gives the novel, and Bigger's life, an unduly dark fatalistic cast and favors the view of the attorney Boris Max, which Bigger himself rejects. The novel in fact urges us from the outset to see Bigger as more than a defiant and negative character just spoiling for a chance to do harm. The powerful impulses he wishes to gratify must also be taken into account, for though these do not necessarily exclude killing (himself or others), they go far beyond that.

Bigger's notions of positive gratification are not spontaneous and, as it were, age-old, like the nubile Janie's hankering after sunup and pear-tree blossoms and the kisses of the first youth strolling by. They are in their way sophisticated, secondary notions, stemming from sociocultural observation and from the media ("he tried to decide if he wanted to buy a ten-cent magazine, or go to a movie" p. 16). The advertising plane that banners USE SPEED GASOLINE brings out Bigger's response to what he sees in actuality and what the media inspire him to conceive: "[White boys] get a chance to do everything"; "I *could* fly a plane if I had a chance"; "Send your men over the river at dawn and attack the enemy's left flank" (pp. 19–21). It soon becomes clear, in the first encounter with the Daltons, that Bigger is as much governed by *images*[9] as by desire for material comfort; materialism and image-worship, which occur discretely in *Their Eyes Were Watching God*, overlap here, and complicate Bigger's responses. In the Daltons' neighborhood, for example,

9. On the power of images, the work of the South African playwright Athol Fugard, and especially *Sizwe Bansi Is Dead*, is well worth noting, and so is Ed Bullins's short play *How Do You Do*. The pathological extreme of the power of images unfolds itself in Toni Morrison's *Bluest Eye*.

where he comes in search of a job, he cannot square his inner feelings of "fear and emptiness" and his outward sense of something reduced in power: "he did not feel the pull and mystery of the thing [the wealthy neighborhood] as strongly as he had in the movie" (p. 45). We should recall that *Native Son* was published five years before the passage of the Ives-Quinn Act (1945), the first law forbidding discrimination in employment. Besides the personal conviction of helplessness that he has formed at home, there is a social stamp of hopelessness and uselessness for Bigger to bear. When in actuality he finds that the very neighborhood of the Daltons does not simply overpower him with the compounded weight of magical association and practical exaltation, that is to say, when he finds that he can keep walking, his mind makes a curious compensatory turn. He will be dangerous to "the white man" if the white man is not after all overwhelmingly dangerous to him. Bigger reacts to the loss of movie magic by investing himself with magical propensities: "he wanted to wave his hand and blot out the white man who was making him feel like this [afraid and worthless]. If not that, he wanted to blot himself out" (pp. 49–50).

The fact is that Bigger blindly cultivates solitude at this point, desiring to be away from others or desiring others to be absent from him. This is the solitude of incapacity, which he must outgrow. The contrast with his final poised and poignant solitude in his jail cell is a measure of his growth in the novel. At that point, Bigger will exhibit a great but ineffectual capacity for communication, in the ambiguous condition of solitude that Wright enunciates in *The God that Failed*:

Perhaps, I thought, out of my tortured feelings I could fling a spark into this darkness. I would try, not because I wanted to, but because I felt that I had to if I were to live at all.

I would hurl words into this darkness and wait for an echo; and if an echo sounded, no matter how faintly, I would send other words to tell, to march, to fight, to create a sense of the hunger for life that gnaws in us all, to keep alive in our hearts a sense of the inexpressibly human. (p. 162)[10]

10. As meager and tentative as is the hope Wright expresses here, it represents a distinct advance over Jean Toomer's position in *Cane*. The speaker in the "Harvest

In the early stages of *Native Son* Bigger Thomas needs as much to recover from a philosophical sense of magic as from a social and physical sense of terror and destruction. The further he goes into the latter, the more the former takes hold of his mind. He alternates between two complementary states. First, he feels blithely secure, credulously falling asleep after the first killing, for example, and experiencing a "sense of fulness [that] he had so often but inadequately felt in magazines and movies" (p. 141). Second, he takes to feeling omnipotent, a condition expressed by various modulations of the following paradigm: "he wanted to wave his hand and blot them out" (pp. 95, 109, passim). This magical gesture is addressed to his family, black people, Bessie, the world, his visitors in prison (p. 275), the people at the inquest (p. 307), "the sun's rising and setting" (p. 381). It is in the grip of this magic that he can be aggressively jubilant about having "killed a rich white girl and . . . burned her body . . . and . . . lied to throw the blame on someone else and . . . written a kidnap note demanding ten thousand dollars" (p. 175). We see a more realistic reaction when he is "afraid to touch food on the table, food which undoubtedly was his own" (p. 175). Tacitly, of course, the food-reluctance is related to an older magical belief that one fell into the power of those who gave one food. But in Bigger the fear of eating reveals a personal visceral distress and an unfocused, guilty feeling that others are secretly concocting harm for him.

The desire to sleep that overcomes Bigger when Mary's body is found and again after he takes Bessie's life represents the exhaustion of his sense of magic. His sense of reality will develop slowly, because it must be based on relationship and he is little versed in that. But the very idea of sleep grows complex for Bigger; rather than oblivion, it comes to mean peaceful courage and confidence and a religious sense "that all life was a sorrow that had to be accepted" (p. 237).

Song" is the counterpart to Wright's lonely figure, except that it is the mud from his labors rather than an abstract darkness that keeps him from seeing whoever else might be there. Toomer's harvester not only cannot remove the mud from his eyes, but actually "fear[s] to call" to others.

At this stage, the threat of annihilation no longer leads Bigger to homicidal defiance and magical self-inflation. In the novel's final section, "Fate," it is as though sleep has become metaphysical, and to rise from it a sort of resurrection. The language of resting "eternally" gives way to that of the rotted hull of a seed "forming the soil in which it should grow again" (p. 255). The dream of "a vast configuration of images and symbols whose magic and power could lift him up and make him live so intensely that the dread of being black . . . would be forgotten" gives way to a sense that "maybe the confused promptings, . . . the elation . . . were false lights that led nowhere" (p. 256). He can still resent being made a spectacle and a "sport" for others, especially white people, but he is now open to Jan Erlone in a way inconceivable before; and he is open to himself.

It is probably from Jan, with his comment that Bigger "believed [in himself] enough to kill" (p. 269), that Bigger takes the elements of his metaphysical self-proclamation; we may recall his anxious effort "to remember where he had heard words that would help him" (p. 386).[11] His outcry flabbergasts his attorney, Boris Max: "I didn't want to kill! . . . But what I killed for, *I am*! It must've been pretty deep in me" (pp. 391–92). But this is after all a retrospective posture. More current is his desire for reconciliation, and the fact that "the impulsion to tell" the truth on which reconciliation must be based "was as deep as had been the urge to kill" (p. 286).[12] The same kind of reversal of spirit appears in his desire to console and soothe his family, instead of defying and blotting them out (p. 275).

And yet the last thing we see of Bigger precludes reconciliation;

11. The same phenomenon occurs in Douglass's *Narrative of the Life*, where hearing words of Mr. Auld "stirred up sentiments that lay slumbering" in Douglass, and led to "a new and special revelation, explaining dark and mysterious things, with which [his] youthful understanding had struggled, but . . . in vain" (p. 49).

12. Here again, as in *Their Eyes Were Watching God*, the concept of telling one's story is treated as fundamentally human. The striking point is that, despite such a tenet, black literature so often portrays characters who must struggle grievously to find a voice. There is a fault line between the anthropological imperative of telling one's story and a socio-psychological prohibition against self-realization. In other words, the individual black writer's burden *as an artist* is aggravated by a racial surplus of inhibition.

he is alone in his cell, smiling "a faint, wry, bitter smile," and hearing "the ring of steel against steel as a *far* door clanged shut" (p. 392, italics added). In effect the novel has brought him to personal, say even spiritual readiness for reconciliation, while removing him from the social context that makes reconciliation possible.

This paradox is lightened if we consider the question of Bigger's solitude. It is striking how often, throughout the story, Bigger finds or feels himself alone. Again and again we see him in the middle of a room or surrounded by others, in a state of presence without connection. From the outset, when his "gang" appears so prominent in his life, he is unconnected, and deliberately so, in that he cannot stand connection; it reminds him of his cowardice in the case of Gus and of his powerlessness in the case of his family. Bigger has thoughts of escaping the sense of solitude, but the escape takes the form of magic on the one hand and self-cancellation on the other:

It was when he read the newspapers or magazines, or went to the movies, or walked along the streets with crowds, that he felt what he wanted: to merge himself with others and be a part of this world, to lose himself in it so he could find himself, to be allowed a chance to live like others, even though he was black. (p. 226)

But magical identification (magazines and movies) and social identification with others in the world stand in contrast in no more than superficial ways. Each entails a relapse into self-cancellation. Each is a desire for life as "a beautiful dream," for illusion, for unconsciousness. When the "cold white world" (p. 226) forces in on him, Bigger seeks another form of escape, by substitution: "If only someone had gone before and lived or suffered and died—made it so that it could be understood!" (He rejects Christianity, of course, though his language here conjures up Christ.) Again, he shuns his existential situation to join himself with another, in a passive, cheating unison—he wants it done and made easy for him, he wants to get out of going through it for himself.

It is striking that following his capture Bigger becomes his own Christological figure, coming back to himself after "three days" and "feeling . . . like the rotted hull of a seed forming the soil in which it should grow again" (p. 255). The text is replete with (a) suggestions of original *and individual* creation ("some spirit had breathed and created him . . . in the image of a man with a man's obscure need and urge" p. 255); (b) images of individual growth ("a seed"); and (c) the language of singularity tempered but also confirmed by the force of the category ("he had to go forward and meet his end like any other living thing upon the earth" p. 256). To merge is impossible, but to belong ineluctable. Bigger has striven not to belong, adopting a mélange of materialism (note his retroactive effort to make money off Mary Dalton's killing), magical images, and self-cancelling postures. When he can face the mystery and the misery of being black and, more largely, of being human, he has shut himself off from its benefits by murder. The cry "what I killed for, *I am!*" causes Boris Max to flinch away, but that is not the cause of Bigger's being alone. The cause is in the act, and in the result of the act: "*I am!*" From self-cancellation Bigger has come to self-avowal, but through a passage with a cell at the end.

Bigger Thomas takes a place among the multitude of black protagonists who end up hiding away or running away or held away from some vital consummation. Needless to say, the line does not end with him; given that it is an expression of a cultural evolution, we should not expect it to. Earlier stages persist where new ones arise, and even interpenetrate with them. Captain Christian Laurent, in Ernest Gaines's "Bloodline," voluntarily isolates himself from a context in which *he has both purpose and power*, so that he represents an advanced capacity without an enlarged opportunity for black people. In the same vein, Nell finds herself "alone" at the end of Toni Morrison's *Sula*, alone and *looking back* at a lost opportunity for kinship with Sula and participation in the vision of freedom that Sula sought to embody. Bigger, as a preeminent figure in this line of grievous frustration, stands in the condition C. J. Rawson sees as the role adopted by Jean Genet, "homme et captif . . ., affirming his own solitude."[13] But even in his solitude Bigger has something compelling and resonant for the future of black literature, the quality that frightens the same Boris Max who could take mere murder in stride,

13. C. J. Rawson, "Cannibalism and Fiction, Part 2: Love and Eating in Fielding, Mailer, Genet, and Wittig," *Genre* 11:302.

the ability to say to himself and to the echoing corridors of the society: "*I am!*"

Some difficulty may arise from the fact that Bigger Thomas remains essentially without connections, without amplitude. Ralph Ellison puts it tellingly in *Shadow and Act*:

> I . . . found it disturbing that Bigger Thomas had none of the finer qualities of Richard Wright, none of the imagination, none of the sense of poetry, none of the gaiety. And I preferred Richard Wright to Bigger Thomas. Do you see? [This] . . . directs you back to the difference between what Wright was himself and . . . his conception of the quality of Negro humanity. (p. 16)

In Ellison's view, Wright took an overly "ideological" and deterministic position on the black condition. But it is worthwhile to ask what the essential tenet of Wright's ideology was, and whether at bottom, at least as regards Bigger Thomas, that ideology was sociopolitical or *metaphysical*. For Bigger goes through the naturalistic "fatalism" of the killings and the analytical "fatalism" of Boris Max's courtroom performance (to say nothing of the prosecutor's) into the self-discovery and implicit independence of his basic cry, "I am." In other words, while it would have been attractive to have a more autobiographical figure as protagonist, and a more cultivated personality in the manner of, say, Chester Himes's *The Primitive*, Wright would have paid a price for that. And the price would have had nothing to do with sociopolitical ideology. It would have fallen entirely in the metaphysical sphere, since Wright would have forgone any chance of showing a Bigger Thomas coming out of determinism into determination, out of rigid reaction into mobile being. The victim of "images" that we see in the early chapters emerges as a participant in a life of the spirit: "some spirit had breathed and created him . . . in the image of a man." Here image and identity fuse, so that he is free of illusion, even while the freedom of giving a certain substance to the image comes vainly into his hands.

The mobile and urgent reaffirmation of the phrase "I am" in the opening paragraphs of the prologue to Ellison's *Invisible Man* bears scrutiny. It occurs eight times in sixteen lines (plus once in the preterit "I have been"). It occurs without clamor, without strain. What Bigger

Thomas gets by agony the "invisible man" seems to possess by instinct, or at least by virtue of irony. He plays at once with the fact of his being and with the social conception of his being black. With his unrolling of complements to complete the predication "I am"—"an invisible man," "not a spook," "nor . . . Hollywood-movie ectoplasm," "a man of substance, . . . even . . . [possessing] a mind," "invisible," "not complaining, nor . . . protesting " (p. 3)—he shows that he is marked by urbanity, forbearance, amusement, a wry touch of cultural history and mild debunking, and a gracious eschewing of rightful resentment. All in all, a prepossessing performance, and surely such as to reassure the likes of Boris Max in *Native Son*. The foursquare challenge and demand for recognition posed by Bigger is mollified here, and an easy if not simple mode of intercourse set up; no one need be alarmed about invisibility (caused by the society, suffered by the speaker), or about the social repercussions of invisibility (caused by the speaker, suffered by the society).

But abruptly the narrator shifts from the deft and authoritative "I am" into an impersonal, neutralized "you're" (p. 3), though still talking about himself. A kind of grammatical schizophrenia is taking place. And the evidence builds up that the difference between the unlettered Bigger and the literate, nearly elegant "invisible man" is more apparent than real. Jack-the-Bear also has eruptions of defensive violence, which he transposes on to the audience: "You ache with the need to convince yourself that you do exist in the real world . . . and you strike out . . ., you curse and you swear to make them recognize you" (p. 4). He too experiences self-cancelling dislocations, but into nightmares rather than magical movies and images: "You wonder whether you aren't simply a phantom in other people's minds. Say, a figure in a nightmare which the sleeper tries with all his strength to destroy" (pp. 3–4). There is something of Bishop Berkeley in the idea of an entity existing only as a phantom in the mind, but the basic thrust of the language goes less toward epistemology than toward pathology; and the nightmare (which is the nightmare of reality for the black man) smacks of Goya or Fuseli.

The prologue sets the amplitude of *Invisible Man*, from urbane humor to violence and phantasmagoria. The protagonist goes overnight from being a favored (if also carefully governed) student in a black college in the South to being an unwitting outcast who is "kept running" through a kaleidoscopic world of authoritarian business organizations and authoritarian political groups, on the one hand, and disorganized but rebellious and explosive individuals, on the other. He has the curious attribute of being a misfit everywhere, being too much of an organization man for the rebels and too much of a rebel for the authoritarians. But he is searching for a way to fit in, and keeps credulously thinking that a cryptic deathbed message from his grandfather or a supposed recommendation from his college president or a well-calculated political speech will do the trick. The emphatic repetition of the words "I am" in the prologue is a confession of desperate need rather than a proof of self-knowledge. We will have to come to terms with the fact that, for all his elaborate experience, he ends in a state of confusedly expectant solitude. Ellison himself pointedly comments on the ironic freight of Jack-the-Bear's "infinite possibilities" (*Shadow and Act*, p. 109).

Leaving the prologue for the story proper, one finds the attributes of the "I am" all the more problematical. Jack-the-Bear says he took unusually long to "achieve a realization . . . [that] I am nobody but myself" (p. 15). This seems at first blush a sober and honorable piece of personal metaphysics, but it is shadowed by two pieces of problematical data. First, Jack-the-Bear's grandfather, a cryptic guru of the text, professes to "have been a traitor all my born days" (p. 16), and it is clear that he has been so not only to the white "enemy" but also to his unrealized self. His "yeses" and his "grins" are meant to keep the white man at bay, and perhaps to get the best of him. Presumably they constitute a form of signifying, but both significance and efficacy perish in the perfection of his gestures. Nothing is seen or known save yeses and grins. They are his legacy, but no one is sure how to interpret it, let alone use it. If a yes and a grin do not mean acquiescence, but defiance, this fact is virtually unrecognizable; the old man who advises his heirs to "yes them to death" has brought only himself to death, unfulfilled. His signifying signifies defeat. Ultimately the invisible man, though capable of believing that to ring changes on yes will enable him to "walk around in their guts with hobnailed boots" (p. 498), recognizes this for himself, recognizes that he has been outmanipulated, veritably "out-yessed": "by pretending to agree I *had* indeed agreed, had made myself responsible for that huddled form lighted by flame and gunfire in the street, and all the others whom now the night was making ripe for death" (p. 541).

Tod Clifton would stand as a better case of signifying, which Ellison himself defines as "rhetorical understatement" (*Shadow and Act*, p. 249). Taken on the surface level of his behavior, Tod Clifton, of course, presents little evidence of understatement; even his friend the invisible man looks upon Tod's obscene sidewalk dolls as a shocking sign of degradation. But when Tod stands up for his honor against the policeman, it is clear that he has not simply come apart and sunk into cheap lewdness and greed. The dolls are telling us something besides what they say. In effect they are a prophecy of the revolt he soon makes explicit by defying the policeman; they reveal his opinion of society's taste and his knowledge of society's charac-ter. With Tod Clifton, Ellison condenses the slow social movement from signifying to rebellion. But when Tod in his use of his fists acts forthrightly, instead of signifying, the police take advantage of their position to signify by acting forthrightly: law enforcement is the vehicle for expressing an unstated will to destroy a Tod Clifton. The issue of the form of an act versus what that act signifies is of course a major bone of contention between the invisible man and the leaders of the Brotherhood; they see Tod in terms of what his act says socially, not what it signifies culturally and metaphysically.

Second, as George Kent has observed,[14] Jack-the-Bear's "I am nobody but myself" is echoed exactly by Jim Trueblood, the inces-tuous father who tells of his act with an unsettled blend of shame and humor, and who profits from it with gratification and bafflement: "sings me some blues that night ain't never been sang before, and while I'm singin' them blues I makes up my mind that *I ain't nobody but myself*" (pp. 65–66, italics added). What is entailed in this same-

14. George E. Kent, "Ralph Ellison and Afro-American Folk and Cultural Tradi-tion," *CLA Journal* 13:267–68.

ness, at once linguistic and metaphysical, between the radically unreflective, shallowly sensual, blabbing protodegenerate True-blood and the ambitious, fastidious, analytical, political, cautious, cryptoidealistic Jack-the-Bear? Like the invisible man the highly visible Trueblood has gone through unintended, though not finally unchosen, violations of taboos that *prove revelatory*, and both envision a definitive coming back to society that somehow does not amount to anything more than a suspended state of living off the white power structure. They further share a tendency to materialism, to blink basic human issues for the sake of what the ex-colored man calls "comfort and luxury" (it is not clear whether Jack-the-Bear abandons or is driven away from his materialism). It is notable too that Trueblood's tale shows the same stylistic play of horror and comedy as the invisible man's narration, and that Trueblood, like the invisible man, is a renowned storyteller-speaker. Does Trueblood serve as a shamefully, and shamelessly, visible alter ego for the "invisible" Jack-the-Bear? Does he represent the *action* that identifies and isolates, to Jack-the-Bear's *conception* that identifies and isolates?

The subtlest but also perhaps the strongest link between True-blood and the invisible man is their solitude. The relation between them is not parallel but complementary. Trueblood's is the solitude of an *unthinking* Oedipus. The ax-slash on his face corresponds to the Theban king's lost eyes, and marks him as one to be seen and shunned by the world; his experience has been social and external, and so is his penalty, without the psychomoral complexities of atonement. (Mythology offers us, in Philoctetes and Tiresias for example, the idea of injury as a sign of election. I do not see True-blood as a figure in this scheme of understanding.) Jack-the-Bear knows the solitude of the *enlightened* Oedipus, whose blindness tells of his need not to see, or rather not to have seen a certain world.

In this connection let us recall that *Invisible Man* is framed by oblique violations of sex taboos, with Oedipal overtones. "Had the price of looking," Jack-the-Bear says of the naked blonde at the opening smoker scene, "been blindness, I would have looked," this despite his "irrational guilt and fear" (p. 19). In terms of strength of taboo, we may see here an analogy between incest and sexual activity with a white woman. This analogy is confirmed in Trueblood's dream, in which approaching a white woman is as full of dread as waking to recognize his daughter. The text gives indications that interracial sex may exceed incest in the strictness of its taboo, since Trueblood's transgression is indulged by the surrounding white community and proved dangerously attractive to Norton, whereas the final riot is set off by a black kid making a cop mad "by grabbing a candy named after a white woman" (p. 528). Even so indirect and trivial a "grabbing" as this triggers a possessive and punitive reaction. The taboo is not for the protection of society, but for the persecution and oppression of its black members.

Jack-the-Bear, or "Boogie Bear," is personally involved in this recrudescence of the taboo theme at the novel's end. He deliberately sets out to seduce a white woman, "one of the [Brotherhood's] big shots' wives," in a compound violation of sexual and political taboos. Nothing happens, in fact, but the posture, the *will* of violation is assumed and despite his final reneging the canonical consequence ensues: Jack-the-Bear loses connection with others, and indeed by calculation *chooses* disconnection from others. He has been much manipulated, it is true; when he finally stumbles upon this fact and, almost simultaneously, catches sight of the effectiveness of the protean Rinehart personality, he naturally is inclined to turn the tables and become the manipulator. But it remains true that manipulation equals violation. He inadvertently manipulates himself not only out of the artificial Brotherhood, but also out of the Harlem community, and ultimately out of the human community in his manhole existence.

It will be useful to distinguish between the way the novel associates Jack-the-Bear and Trueblood, on the one hand, and Jack-the-Bear and Rinehart on the other.[15] Jack-the-Bear falls into the role

15. The fact that Jack, the leader of the Brotherhood, is dubbed "The Bear" by the invisible man does not, in my view, generate any deep connection between the two. Perhaps it is Ellison's coy way of associating the Brotherhood with the Communist Party, as the bear is Russia's totem animal.

of Rinehart, much as he falls into the manhole, by accident; and he makes use of the role of Rinehart, much as he does his sojourn in the manhole, to explore both the practical and the philosophical aspects of his experience. But he recognizes that the manhole is a stage, a convenient instrument for him, just as his assumption of the role of Rinehart has been. The invisible man is obliged to leave both this role and his manhole, or at least chooses to do so.

With Trueblood, he has no such choice. The association between them is not social and accidental, but primary and intrinsic. We may note that after each encounter with Trueblood and with Rinehart the invisible man is thrown out of his established world, but in the Rinehart situation the sequence is merely adventitious. In fact, the plunging off the surface of life only extends the sense of instability and incoherence that the Rinehart episode induces. To the contrary, there is a genuine causal connection between the Trueblood episode and the invisible man's expulsion from college. (It is the Golden Day that, in the exposition of the novel, corresponds to the Rinehart episode with its confusion of identities and of values). The identification between Jack-the-Bear and Trueblood, in short, tells us something basic about Jack-the-Bear, whereas the exchange of identity with Rinehart only tells us something about his world.

In the end Jack-the-Bear lives in indefinite solitude, in a world peopled by lights that offer number without substance or variety. It is as abstract as the first day of creation, and as pathetic as the impossibility of the second. The lights represent an obsessive literalization of his symbolic intent to bring light on his own situation and to bring its light to the world. He has a *fiat lux* at his disposal, but it is furtive and defiant. He is as improbable a "God" as Bledsoe, who dares to say to the sophomoric Jack-the-Bear: "your arms are too short to box with me" (p. 142). He is his own final mentor, and no more adept than a Bledsoe or a Jack or the ill-chosen Sybil who, far from making an illuminating and liberating pattern of the fragments of his sociopolitical experience, ties him to the cliché of overpowering sensuality ("you big black bruiser") that his being a black man triggers in her mind.

The fall into the manhole is a happy one, in that it saves his life. It is symbolically important too, not so much because it suggests the plunge "out of history"[16] that he so dreads, but because it consummates the pattern of lurkings, twistings, and accidentality that inform the invisible man's experience. It follows the scene where he is most with others, with Dupre, Scofield, and the rest in the riot, but he joins them as superficially and as meaninglessly as possible, though ironically getting great credit for being there: "Brother . . ., you said you would lead us." It is more as if he were losing himself, "merging" in Bigger Thomas's escapist sense, than as if he were finding an identity. He says as much: "I was one with the mass, . . . my personality blasted" (p. 537).

Nor can he sustain even this limited condition; something impels him to detach himself, to opt for observation where he should take action: "Shouldering my way to the side I stood in a doorway and watched them move" (p. 538). The little he does on his own in tightening the tourniquet on the arm of an injured man only proves that he is essentially a bystander, without any reliable function or position in the scheme of things. He is astonished to be taken for a doctor. As he says, in a symbolic declaration of terrible simplicity: "I couldn't cure a headache" (p. 539). This moment, with its confusion of identity, reminds us of the Rinehart episode, but conveys a sense of beneficial action and healing, whereas Rinehart embodies only protean emptiness and escapism. The sense of possibility is not accepted, let alone sustained, by Jack-the-Bear. In the manhole he pronounces on his "infinite possibilities," but they are infinite mainly by virtue of having neither specificity nor focus.

16. It is well worth noting that "history" is a rather amorphous concept in *Invisible Man* compared with the suggestive concreteness of historical data in Williams's *Captain Blackman* or even Walker's *Meridian*. I would say Faulkner deals with the past, rather than with history, but there too a relentless concreteness prevails. Ellison achieves a singular emotional resonance in an insubstantial sphere. Perhaps this is what Reed is mocking in his poem on "Dualism in Ralph Ellison's Invisible Man" (*Conjure*, p. 50). But in fact Ellison *implies* less a serpentine variety in history than a Hegelian inexorability—either one is going where it is going, or one is cast aside. The dread of being left in the void animates *Invisible Man* (though it is from the void, the hole, that the protagonist sees best). In "Ellison's Zoot Suit" Larry Neal fruitfully addresses this question of history and *Invisible Man* (*Black World* 20 [December 1970]: 45ff.).

Soon, too, pressed by Scofield, he is denying the name of "brother" that he had so proudly and enthusiastically adopted before. (It is ironic that the novel's theory of brotherhood should be confined to the cold political order.) The vocabulary of withdrawal and solitude gathers momentum rapidly: "I ran, going away, leaving Scofield"; "I went on, plunged in a sense of painful isolation"; "I am no longer their brother" (this in the midst of standing solitary against Ras and his henchmen); "If only I could . . . say, 'Look, . . . let's stop running and respect and love one another.' . . . If only . . ."; "as though I sat remote in a padded room"; and finally, in yet another point of identification with Trueblood, "I was caught like Trueblood's jaybird that yellow jackets had paralyzed in every part but his eyes" (pp. 541–56). Trueblood, by analogy, gives us a singular insight into Jack-the-Bear's solitude, in its social and moral or spiritual dimensions. Actually, Jack-the-Bear articulates this:

You stand naked and shivering before the millions of eyes who look through you unseeingly. *That* is the real soul-sickness, the spear in the side, the drag by the neck through the mob-angry town; the Grand Inquisition, the embrace of the Maiden, the rip in the belly with the guts spilling out, the trip to the chamber with the deadly gas that ends in the oven so hygienically clean—only it's worse because you continue stupidly to live. (p. 562)

But the fact that the invisible man articulates his position, and does not only embody it like Trueblood, implies at least a potential possession in the Du Boisian mode, and implies a potential freedom. He communicates from solitude. His knowledge that something is amiss with him becomes the instrument for social scrutiny ("Who know but that, on the lower frequencies, I speak for you?" p. 568) and the basis for a hope, even a program: "I'm shaking off the old skin and I'll leave it here in the hole. . . . And I suppose it's damn well time. . . . There's a possibility that even an invisible man has a socially responsible role to play" (p. 568). Solitude, or hibernation,[17] takes on

17. Both Tony Tanner, in *City of Words: American Fiction, 1950–1970,* and Robert B. Stepto, in *From Behind the Veil,* put special emphasis on hibernation in *Invisible Man.* We need also to note that this image is modified by that of castration/transcendence, and also by Jack-the-Bear's occasional, eruptive ascents to the sidewalk.

an idealistic color or, as Verlaine said of symbolism, *nuance*. Jack-the-Bear's is the voice of solitude, but the voice has a freedom and a mission that the ex-colored man only briefly aspired to, and that Bigger Thomas never even brought to the pitch of aspiration. Cleansed of catchwords like "brother," the invisible man turns out to have more than a paralytic's eyes; he has a voice that speaks from solitude to, and sympathetically for, any man: ". . . I speak for you."

The significance of this projection bears spelling out, for the voice is what the ex-colored man denied himself, what Janie and Bigger Thomas were denied, and what Jack-the-Bear himself had dreaded to use save as a ventriloquist's dummy for a Bledsoe or a Jack. His voice means not only that he has a sense of having found himself, but also that he has found a basis of relationship with others. Someone else is there—the solitude is not perfect—and that someone is likely to be somehow genuinely accessible, akin to him. One goes back to the opening section of the novel with its subtle and complex cadences sustaining the bald avowal: "I am." We may say that the invisible man chooses himself in his hole, whereas the ex-colored man chooses a hole for himself. What Ellison in "Richard Wright's Blues" calls "the American Negro impulse toward self-annihilation and going underground" (*Shadow and Act*, p. 94) is inseparable from the impulse toward self-renovation, self-discovery, and self-assertion or, perhaps better, self-justification. That is to say, the self against all adversity and without glossing over its own weakness and waywardness reaches a point of readiness, a beginning that allows for purpose and tolerance, emphasis and irony, individuality and identification. As Ellison says, "being a Negro American involves a *willed* . . . affirmation of self against all outside pressures" (*Shadow and Act*, p. 132).

This is a hard-won position. It must be remembered that the life condition of the black people the invisible man meets, from rural college days to city life and on to political life and even well into the climactic riot, shames and repels him. That is what he wishes, strives, to get away from. He identifies himself as a black man, rather than with the black man. When he eats the sweet yam on the street—

already a departure from the upswing standards he has set for himself—and pronounces with punning decisiveness, "I yam what I yam," it is a matter of a moment, a mood, rather than a turning point in his philosophy. Tod Clifton's death comes closer to constituting a change, but while it makes the invisible man, down in the subway, speak of "us transitory ones" in relation to the "three boys . . . distorted in the interest of design" (pp. 429–30), it does not cause him to lose his "feverish isolation" or to intervene on behalf of the candy-filching boys near the five and ten (an old woman does that instead).

Only in the ultimate isolation of the manhole ("there is nothing like isolating a man to make him think") does he find a philosophy or a life posture that offers reconciliation with himself, his whole history, and his humanity. He can now "denounce and defend . . ., say no and say yes, say yes and say no." Nor does he speak only for himself. While at the outset of the novel he shifts from "I" to "you," striving for communion, here he shifts from "I" to "we," incorporating himself into humanity and humanity into himself: "Our fate is to become one, and yet many" (p. 564); "sometimes I feel the need to reaffirm all of it, the whole unhappy territory and all the things loved and unlovable in it, for all of it is part of me" (p. 566).

And yet it is clear that the invisible man, like Bigger Thomas and Janie Crawford, has seen things intimately without achieving intimacy through them, just as he has recognized more than he has accepted kinship with other people.

Invisible Man is distinctly Janus-faced, looking back on accomplished events and looking forward to new accomplishment in personal action and being. This latter remains deeply problematical. The novel exhibits a conflict between (1) verification, or the reproduction of experience as having taken place, and (2) validation, or objective possession and articulation of his experience as belonging in a scheme of understanding and value. In fact, the speaker displaces validation unto the reader, unto *us* ("who knows but that . . . I speak for you?"). It might be urged that he has no choice, being uncertain of the reader's position. But that is to presuppose a white reader, indeed a hostile and unjust white reader, whereas the text holds out value and revelation to both black and white, both sympathetic and hostile readers. His tentativeness with us is a projection of inner doubt and irresolution. He says himself that he has accepted "the lesson," but he does not identify it and he is not sure what it amounts to, whether it puts him "in the rear or the *avant-garde*" (p. 559), reminding us of Ishmael Reed's mischievous declaration that "I called it pin the tail on the devil / they called it avant garde "("if my enemy is a clown, a natural born clown," in *Conjure*, p. 53). The invisible man's grandfather describes life as a situation in which one may "start Saul and end up Paul" (p. 372), and here again proves a cryptic if not devious guide. No conversion, no positive new commitment or conviction, actually emerges from the hole any more than the invisible man himself emerges. Indeed, he makes a point of suggesting that if he speaks for us we don't really know what he says: "So there you have all of it that's important. Or at least you *almost* have it" (p. 559). That *almost* does not refer to the few pages that remain to be written but to the reader's essential grasp, or more accurately, the writer's essential intention and conviction. If "all of it" is part of him, but he can't give us "all of it," the reverse becomes critical. We do not doubt him; he has achieved verification. But we cannot follow him, because he is not positively going anywhere; he remains suspended in hibernation, and short of validation.

In effect, Jack-the-Bear seems able to make only set speeches face to face. As he has been a hit-and-run orator in the eviction scene, so he becomes a hit-and-hide orator in the hole; in Addison Gayle's view, he is "faceless, formless, and rootless."[18] If we go back to Trueblood for a moment, we can see that he displaces his will to violate taboo *and* his wish to seem to do so by accident or force of circumstances, unto the dream state, or unto his daughter's supposed sexual knowingness. That trick of displacement gives one sense of the invisible man's message about speaking for *us*. He will not speak

---

18. Addison Gayle, Jr., "The Function of Black Literature at the Present Time," in *The Black Aesthetic*, p. 412.

forthrightly, in his own right; even his falling back on the Constitution is a poignant example of speaking by rote. Though he does invoke the Constitution, his solitude remains not only social and spiritual, but also political. He is cut off from any structure or mode of relationship that would bear on the organization and exercise of power in society. In this connection the invisible man differs from Janie and from Bigger Thomas by virtue of his half-hortatory, half-minatory desire to reach out, whereas Janie has no such desire and Bigger no opportunity.

The three texts of solitude, *Their Eyes Were Watching God* and *Native Son* and *Invisible Man*, represent frustrations of kinship and circumstantial violations of intimacy. If not the central then certainly the culminating action of each text is murder or widespread mayhem; each is marked by human dissociation or abuse. The protagonist in each case gains knowledge of a positive world, but remains unable to act on that knowledge, short of command or possession over anything but his or her own solitude. The failure of fulfillment is both psychic and social for Janie Crawford and Bigger Thomas; the act of homicide keeps one from one's kind.

The invisible man's failure has subtler causes. It is tied on one level to the obscure or displaced taboo violation of his experience, and on another to the fact that he simply does not know how to act on his own. He simply is accustomed to reacting and adjusting, taking his motive force from outside. Left to himself, he comes to a total halt. Still, he is the one who can look to something more than expiation of a specific crime, like Bigger, or devotion to a specific shrine, like Janie. He is the one with a catholic prospect: "all of it is part of me." That prospect is pivotal for the further development of Afro-American literature.

4

KINSHIP *The Power of Association*
in Michael Harper and
Eldridge Cleaver

They were all my people.

Henry Dumas

WITH the declaration that "all of it is part of
me," Ellison virtually announces the theme of kinship, and tacitly
renounces the ex-colored man's denial. It is not kinship in the sense of
consanguinity or descent, with all its formal systems and restrictions.
Rather *kinship* means social bonding, a recognition of likenesses in
context, concern, need, liability, value. It is humanistic, a cross
between consanguinity and technical organization, not depending
on the former and not confiding in the latter (for organization by
itself only brings out the correspondence between Joe Starks in
Their Eyes Were Watching God and Brother Jack in *Invisible Man*).

Kinship has become a major option or even program of black
literature in recent years. It is the position that Cleaver's *Soul on Ice*
espouses in the final chapter, "To All Black Women, From All Black
Men"; it is the principle that explains the charm of the overlong and
relentlessly superficial *Roots*. It gives energy to Ernest Gaines's
Bloodline, to William Melvin Kelley's *A Different Drummer*, and to
John Williams's *Captain Blackman*.

Gayl Jones's *Corregidora*, Gloria Naylor's *Women of Brewster*

Place, and Ntozake Shange's *For Colored Girls Who Have Considered Suicide When the Rainbow Is Enuf* experiment technically with
kinship along feminist lines, and Alice Walker makes a tour de force
of this approach in *The Color Purple*. Kinship is the concept that
overcomes social convention and personal jealousy to make Nell
recognize and mourn the title character, Sula, in Toni Morrison's
most accomplished novel (just as the absence of kinship makes for
Pecola Breedlove's deadly breakdown in Morrison's starkest, *The
Bluest Eye*). What *Roots* would have done if Alex Haley had hon-
ored his announced plan of portraying his Schliemannesque recovery of his ancestral people, Toni Morrison translates into myth in
Song of Solomon. Thus, in myth, in military idiom (Williams, *Captain Blackman*), in the context of urban crime (Cleaver, *Soul on Ice*)
and rural naiveté (Walker, *The Color Purple*), in Mosaic wandering
(Kelley, *A Different Drummer*) and in ghetto confinement (Naylor,
Brewster Place), kinship has come to the fore.

   Why so? One is drawn at once to the idea that this flourishing
represents a response to sociopolitical nurture, with African nationalism and independence movements in the Caribbean cheering and
swelling the upsurge of black protest (and protestation) in the United States. But the Harlem Renaissance and the Garveyite movement
had clearly anticipated these conditions, without yielding a like
result. To the contrary, Claude McKay's *Home to Harlem* makes its
hero a champion of kinship whose celebration thereof in postwar
Harlem and Brooklyn soon evolves into a need to flee for his life. A
spirit for kinship may have been there, but a matrix for its realization
was to be some time coming. We may recall that the ex-colored man,
and after him Kabnis in Jean Toomer's *Cane*, also harbored such a
spirit and had it exorcised by the society.

   The necessary matrix forms, paradoxically, in the condition of
solitude. Perhaps a forecast of kinship could be argued in the tendentious naturalism Langston Hughes brought to his Simple stories. But
there is something at once formal and inarticulate in Hughes's approach, as we see in the following quotation from "Brothers":

> We're related—you and I,
> You from the West Indies,
> I from Kentucky.
> Kinsmen—you and I,
> You from Africa
> I from the U.S.A.
> Brothers—you and I.[1]

The kinship that emerged in the 1960s could not be assumed, like this, but was tempered in the crucible of public trials and private agonies. If Hughes can be seen as throwing himself in with his West Indian and African look-alikes to establish kinship, Harper rather comes to kinship after being thrown back upon himself. Self-veiling had preserved a relationship, however injurious, with the general society. In fact the inability to withstand solitude, or a too great dependence on the mere image the society returns to the self, was the unacknowledged bane of the phase of self-veiling in black literature. Janie Crawford and Jack-the-Bear definitively change that: they come to a supportable image of themselves and a plausible vision of their world. In their solitude they achieve a seminal scrutiny of themselves and of their society.

Those who come after them, as already suggested, go forward from them, and none more resolutely or complexly than Michael Harper, the poet of kinship. Harper calls his selected poems *Images of Kin*, and while he invokes blood relations in several inspired cases, his approach to kinship is a radiant one, reaching out across time, across space, even across race for a cure to the intimidation and isolation that ailed the ex-colored man, Kabnis, even Bigger Thomas and Jack-the-Bear:

---

1. *Selected Poems*, pp. 265–66. A similar approach is taken decades later by Gloria House in her poem "DIRECTION / (Political advice for young Brothers)": "You from Harlem? / Yeah? Well, coulda been Johannesburg or Birmingham, Alabama, you know. It's all the same. I'm from Fillmore. / That makes us brothers, man"; quoted by William Keorapetse Kgositsile, "Paths to the Future," in *The Black Aesthetic*, ed. Addison Gayle, Jr. (New York: Doubleday, 1971), p. 253.

> Blacks in frame houses
> call to the helicopters.
> . . . .
> This scene is about power
> terror, producing
> love and pain and pathology;
> in an army of white dust
> blacks here to *testify*
> and *testify*, and *testify*,
> and *redeem*, and *redeem*,
> in black smoke coming,
> as they wave their arms,
> as they wave their tongues.
>
> ("Song: I Want a Witness")

The idea of redemption comes as a radical new phenomenon in black literature. Perhaps Tucker Caliban's leading his people out of the house of bondage in Kelley's *A Different Drummer* prefigures it, or at least draws on the same biblical reservoir; but Kelley is only refurbishing the name of Caliban, almost casually taking off the curse imposed by Shakespeare in *The Tempest*. Harper is changing the ground and system of relationship. But he does this in a cryptic way: *redeem* is set grammatically askew as an intransitive verb, and it is left for the reader to determine what or whom the blacks are "here to . . . *redeem*," and how.

First we may note that the blacks are not to be stopped. "In black smoke coming" suggests both a frail and an invulnerable or self-healing defense, in that smoke closes up around what pierces it. Second, the waving of the arms is a form of testifying, suggesting a banner, but it also is a way of going headlong, with all that entails of danger and threat. And finally the waving of the tongues suggests, in conjunction with the hands, a natural motion that would also be unstoppable. The sequence of the zeugmatic objects, arms and tongues, entails a movement from the more to the less obvious, but also from the less to the more articulate. The parallelism of "arms" and "tongues" would lead the reader to construe *arms* in the sense of upper extremities, limbs; but even if it suggests weapons, the aim is not militaristic when the arms are *waving*. If "an army" of blacks is making an attack, its ultimate object is to achieve communication, understanding rather than mere physical mastery.

To testify, then, would merge into the power to redeem, as John the Baptist merges into Christ, expression into enactment. In like manner, the waving of arms and tongues conveys the complementary relationship of word and deed; if Harper puts deed before word, it may be again as an instance of the long reticence, the difficulty of finding a voice in black literature. We may note, too, that "wave" holds an emphatic position in the windup of the poem. It is at once dynamic and somewhat vague by itself, its form being clearer than its direction of movement. Some of its inner freight emerges, I think, by comparison with Langston Hughes's poem "Spirituals": "The waves rise / From the dead weight of the sea."[2] Harper's waves, like Hughes's, mean indestructibility, or withstanding the weight of prejudice and oppression. The black are "coming" to testify about their condition, but coming inexorably to redeem their being. And that redemption, *of black people by themselves*, comes as much from knowledge as from action, from tongues as from arms. The difference between Du Bois's sense of possession and Harper's is that with Du Bois the possession is by one (or one tenth) for all, whereas in the latter all have come to possession. All are akin.

The collective posture of "Song: I Want a Witness" might make it seem that Harper generates kinship at the expense of personality and individuality. A poem like "Brother John" proves otherwise, both preserving the category, "black man," and allowing for the integrity and variety of its members. Thus Charlie "Bird" Parker, Miles Davis, John Coltrane, and Brother John (who "plays no instrument") belong together under their differences. Thus, Miles is

2. *Selected Poems*, p. 28. The same sociopolitical-spiritual value informs Hughes's "Sea Calm": "How still. / How strangely still / The water is today. / It is not good / For water / To be so still that way" (*The Weary Blues*, p. 28).

"clean" and Bird is all "smack, booze and bitches," but each knows basically the same thing about himself: "I'm a black man; / . . . I am." With Brother John the professional prowess of being a musician becomes immaterial, and the cultural phenomenon of being a black man becomes the basis for an unadorned and unequalled cry: "I am."

> I'm a black man; I am;
> black; I am; I'm a black
> man; I am; I am;
> I'm a black man;
> I'm a black man;
> I am; I'm a black man;
> I am:
>
> *(Dear John, Dear Coltrane*, p. 4)

The involved verbal agility of the invisible man, declaring and yet not forthrightly presenting himself, hemming and hawing behind his every "I am," is simply overgone here. Brother John and, through him, the others in the poem (and by extension the poet their spokesman) seem to have accepted without essential distortion or bafflement the same condition of blackness that locks Jack-the-Bear in his manhole. If this tacit revision stands open to doubt, it seems clear that Harper is formally invoking and revising Ellison in the poem "Roland," where he writes "to Roland, to Roland, / this word from his seat / of ancestral force / on his feeding *frequency / of the high mode*" (*Images of Kin*, p. 56; italics added). Ellison's protagonist speaks on a "lower frequency" and with a tentativeness that must spring in part from his speaking only out of himself. Harper's higher frequency is not only technically but spiritually so, and this comes about because he has the added gift of "ancestral force." Kinship enhances and enlarges the individual view.

There remains, though, a subtle trap in the ground that Harper is gaining, a problematical link in the chain of kinship he is forging. It is not enough to asseverate a condition of being. The trial of realization must be passed. Harper clearly knows this. In "Eve (Rachel)" he writes:

116   **KINSHIP**

> Women bathe the wounds
> in our dark human struggle to be human:
> *This must be earned in deeds.*
>
> *(Images of Kin*, p. 12)[3]

And he directly engages with the issue. "Alice," in the fine volume
Nightmare Begins Responsibility, is another poem in the personal
vein, and one that embodies the struggle and the deed on which
"Brother John" tacitly couches itself. "Alice" begins in a condition
remote from cultivation or human contact, marked by natural
danger and personal disorientation:

> You stand waist-high in snakes
> beating the weeds for the gravebed
> a quarter mile from the nearest
> relative, an open field in Florida: lost....   (p. 96)

Only a sense of purpose makes the scene bearable; Alice is "looking
for Zora": the living woman and writer, Alice Walker, looking for her
dead forebear, Zora Neale Hurston.[4] It is an act of piety, of restoration, for no one has known (or much cared) where the deeply,
singularly gifted Hurston is buried. Alice, as woman and writer and
black person, proves to be more akin to Zora than the latter's blood
relatives, but that is in keeping with Harper's emphasis on kinship in
spirit, which is less sure but larger, when it comes, than consanguinity. Alice searches with the divining rod of the spirit, and by virtue
thereof senses where the dearly sought grave will be. The poem
proffers this phenomenon as an active communication between
generations and between persons, and not as a cold one-sided guess:

3. In *Mules and Men* Zora Neale Hurston had written: "None may wear the
crown of power without preparation. *It must be earned*" (p. 207).
4. This kind of search informs David Bradley's *Chaneysville Incident*, where
the focal action, John Washington's search for his father and his history, proves to be a
reconstitution of that father's search into his own ancestry. But Bradley uses the
familial quest with energies and resonances quite different from Harper's (see below,
chapter 7).

> and when she [Zora] speaks
> from her sunken chamber to call
> you to her side, she calls
> you her distant cousin, her sister
> come to mark her burial place
> with bright black stone.
> She has known you would do this
>
> . . . .
>
> calling her to communion.   (p. 96)

This stands as the call-and-response of time and essential unity. Alice becomes a "distant cousin," then a "sister" in a phrasing that seems to suggest kinship intensified and enhanced as distance decreases (that is, *cousin* at a distance, but *sister* up close), because the distance decreases with the will to be closer, and that will is the basis of genuine kinship.

The poet enters the poem directly on the strength of such a will:

> And for this I say your name: Alice,
> my grandmother's name, your name,
> conjured in snake-infested field
> where Zora Neale welcomed you home,
> and where I speak from now
> on higher ground of her risen
> black marker where you have written
> your name in hers, and in mine.   (p. 97)

The number of joinings in this serene and smooth passage is at last a testimony to the consummation of kinship in Harper's view. To begin with, the name Alice joins the poet's grandmother and the poem's subject, and also importantly offsets the indifference of Zora's relatives with the warmth of this family tradition. The result is that Alice is twice esteemed, for the connection with the grandmother as well as that with Zora, who is by sympathetic extension also linked with the grandmother. Again, the "conjuring" of Alice's name "in snake-infested field" is parallel to Alice's conjuring up Zora's burial place, with two corollaries: (1) Alice's deed needs to be identified and "marked" as much as Zora's burial place *and accom-*

plishment in life, or oblivion will overtake it; and (2) conjuring, the recovery of reality and value,[5] seems inseparable from danger, the snakes being part and parcel of the environment, the event. We may see, furthermore, that the poet is associated directly with Zora Neale in calling to Alice: "Where Zora Neale welcomed you home, / . . . I speak . . . now." This identification is repeated, with the poet as passive rather than self-proclaiming: "you have written / your name in hers, and in mine." But it makes little difference whether he is passive or assuming power; both end up the same, as embodying his part in the scheme of kinship.

One final joining merits special attention, and that is the joining of "sunken" in the first section of the poem with "risen" in the last. Both belong to Zora, though neither would if it were not for Alice, as donor of the "bright black stone," and the poet, as marker of Alice's gift. "Sunken" and "risen" become stages or modes of one existence, not automatically, but by virtue of the relationship Harper is substantiating. As the three figures in the poem interpenetrate, they all end up on the "higher ground" of the poet. Alice creates this higher ground as an act of piety; the ground belongs to Zora; and the poet occupies it as an act of double reverence. In this respect all are risen, all escaped from a nameless death. The "black marker" ambiguously denotes the death and the continuous life of blackness. "Alice," with its meta-physical use of the term *risen*, helps further to expound the intimations of *redeem* in "Song: I Want a Witness."

Besides the collective and personal approaches to kinship, Harper also takes an abstract historical tack. This is most evident in "High Modes: Vision as Ritual: Confirmation,"[6] a poem that founds itself on the old expression of spite and disparagement: "Black Man

---

5. Dangerous conjuring, such as we see in *The Conjure Woman*, still occurs in stories like "A Long Day in November" by Ernest Gaines; but a more positive use of conjure appears in Ishmael Reed's *Mumbo Jumbo* and Toni Morrison's *Song of Solomon*. Perhaps we should see a turning point in Janie's defiance of the conjurer employed by Joe Starks against her.

6. Harper's use of trinity titles separated by colons, in his later work, suggests analogy, affinity, kinship among the diverse elements. This poem is quoted from *History Is Your Own Heartbeat*, pp. 94–95.

Go Back to the Old Country." But Harper makes it, first, a piece of sound advice, like Greeley's "Go West, Young Man," and then shifts it back from the geographical to the cultural plane: "you went back home for the images." The images are of a basic, indeed a creative and aboriginal humanity: "the brushwork packing the mud / into the human form; and the ritual" (p. 94).

This humanity is rendered in an art steeped in nature, the pigments derived from "chocolate trees and samba / leaves." Also, it is an art where uniqueness and unity coexist, and where exclusivity is opposed, insofar as one mode, painting, readily combines with another:

> and babies
> came in whispering of one, oneness,
> otherness, forming each man in his music,
> one to one.   (p. 94)

It turns out that the going back is in memory, and has been occurring not literally but culturally as *bringing forward*. In other words, Harper has transcended the literalism of Garvey with his back-to-Africa movement. It is possible to go back to Africa, culturally, while being geographically on U.S. shores. Thus "Bird was a mode from the old country; . . . Louis Armstrong touched the old country, / And brought it back, around corners." One of the most striking manifestations of being, and bringing, back occurs in the description of Lady Day: "the grooves turned in a human face." Here ancient sculpture and modern music blend. The grooves refer to pictorial lines but also to the cut of a record. In like manner the expression "blue and green" delineates Lady Day's constitution (sad and at the mercy of the world's sophisticates), her subject matter and style (the blues, freshly rendered), and her natural environment (sky and earth).

Harper adopts the concept of modality to capture the intricacies of different forms and entities having a vital presence in one another. Every encounter among phenomena entails possible recognitions, reflections, and substitutions that are charged with evidence of a principle of unity in the face of manifest plurality. What looks like one and the same thing on two different occasions may prove to be variants of something only superficially observed. Wisdom comes from refining and rectifying observation. Thus the refrain line of "High Modes: Vision as Ritual: Confirmation" contains beneficial counsel disguised as insult: *"Black Man Go Back to the Old Country."* What that counsel yields is a new sense of self and of man:

> Africa
> the first mode, and man, modally,
> touched the land of the continent,
> modality: we are one; a man is another
> man's face, modality, in continuum,
> from man, to man, *contact-high*, to man,
> *contact-high*, to man, high modes, oneness,
> *contact-high*, man to man, *contact-high*.

> *Black Man Go Back to the Old Country....*   (p. 95)

In the long run, Harper not only exorcises the white man's curse on the black, but also the black man's curse on himself, to wit, a certain style of conjuring and its attendant credulity. Harper insists on a *creative* metamorphosis (as does Alice Walker in the Louvinie episode of *Meridian*). In "History as Apple Tree" he not only reconstitutes our sense of the practice of conjure, but also the practice of the slave illicitly increasing his food supply in dead of night.

> As a black man I steal away
> in the night to the apple tree,
> place my arm in the rich grave,
> black sachem on a family plot,
> take up a chunk of apple root.
> let it become my skeleton,
> become my own myth:
> my arm the historical branch,
> my name the bruised fruit,
> black human photograph: apple tree.
> (*Photographs: Negatives: History as Apple Tree*, no. 9)

There is a level at which a theft occurs; the speaker is deliberately taking the place and thus stealing the thunder of Roger Williams, whose name "legend conjures." There is a level at which conjure and metamorphosis take place, as the speaker inverts himself into the apple tree. But the theft is benign and reverent, and so carried out as to magnify and not diminish the victim. The metamorphosis, in turn, is chosen by and magnifies the victim, not helplessly and degradingly undergone. Besides, the speaker-as-conjurer is only doing what history and society in general do, as "legend conjures" the name and deeds of Williams. Even the latent "plot" is at once contained and self-directed, as the "black man" overthrows his subjection, even his burial, through identification with the apple tree, not through the endless cycle of conspiracy and revolt. As with the black marker in "Alice," the tree enables the speaker to attain a risen state. Everything tends toward becoming richer, more complex, surer in kinship.

Obviously the kinship Harper projects in his work stands as the antithesis of the ex-colored man's self-protectionism. Is the effect quite the antithesis of what the ex-colored man experiences, though? Is kinship the salve, the salvation, of the solitary?

Certainly a commitment to kinship gives Harper a scope and freedom of position, as well as a substance and fineness of relationship, that Johnson does not imagine, nor Wright and Ellison, for all the sweep of their works, approach. Kinship and, with it, a fuller range of psychopolitical complexity may have come into *Invisible Man* through Mary, who embodies patience, compassion, and practicality. But the inflated and drifting ambition of the invisible man will not let him operate on Mary's level. He is with his oratory what Ras is with his weaponry, a believer in grand and instant solutions. Only on this level does Ras, the creator of the riot, prevent the invisible man from going back to Mary. To go back is *physically* within his compass, but psychologically he is blocked by his persistent grandiosity. With Wright the case is even more problematical. Wright offers overpowering accumulation, without overpowering range.

But there are signs that Harper's scope and his orientation to kinship may come largely from the will. A note of harshness, an air of impatience not tempered by humor, a kind of vulnerability pitched near dark resentment and rage: these belie the grace and strength kinship would seem to connote. The metamorphosis of "The Families Album" (*Song: I Want a Witness*, p. 52) is forced and problematical: "this old house which was hers / made her crooked back a shingle, / her covered eye this fireplace oven." "Sambo's Mistakes: An Essay" (*Images of Kin*, p. 83), which is evidently inspired by A. J. Langguth's *Jesus Christs*, does not reflect the elastic irony of its source, but falls into a dehumanized, rigid violence. One is only arrested for the moment when, after a detailed account of Sambo's difficulties and disabilities, the poem comes up with its one-word litany of Sambo's "Strengths: guns." Uncomplicated by strength of principle and of heart, the strength of guns is tantamount to anarchy.

It would be worthwhile to look again at "History as Apple Tree" since, for all its eager fusion of speaker with the double subject, Roger Williams and the apple tree, that poem harbors evidence of the problematical will in Harper's work. Harper takes up the story of Roger Williams, 1603–83, maverick founder of Rhode Island. In that story, raised into myth, he finds three main points of attraction: (1) Williams's closeness to the native American Indians (though he was to serve as a sexagenarian captain of militia in King Philip's War, 1675–76); (2) Williams's liberal opposition to dogmatic authority— he was in effect read out of the Puritan congregation; and (3) the fact that Williams was found to have a living monument, with an apple tree rooted in his very skeleton.

Harper's speaker nevertheless finds a resistance to his identifying himself with Williams, apparently based on his color: "as a black man I steal away / in the night to the apple tree." But by the ambidextrous move of making himself a "black sachem," he links himself with the Indians and with Williams, who did not have much reason to concern himself with black folk. It is neat to solve such problems, but to think of them shows a degree of scrupulosity about attendant circumstances that is at odds with the impulse to identification in the speaker. Something here is reminiscent of the third section of Coleridge's "Kubla Khan," where a sudden intrusion of the first person in a state of semiecstatic, semitranscendent anticipation is accompanied by so much self-doubt and, ultimately, by self-defeat.

Like Coleridge's, Harper's speaker is striving to duplicate a mythic performance by a forebear, and indeed striving to substitute for that person. Again like Coleridge's, Harper's speaker in "History as Apple Tree" falls into a hortatory mode while making representations of an indicative state; that is, both go through with a full description of a feat they only would like to perform. There is some ambiguity about Harper's phrasing. "Let it become my skeleton, / become my own myth" could mean either "allow it" or "would that it might," but even if the phrase is construed as a stage in described action, that action is taking place very much in the private imagination, with no material correspondence, no effect.

One striking feature of "History as Apple Tree" is the speaker's orientation toward death. He may elevate himself as a sachem, but it is only to go down into a grave. While he imagines his death for the sake of his myth, only the former is within his reach. The myth stays with Roger Williams, and cannot truly become what the speaker calls "my own." Praise is due to his passion for breaking the bounds of personality and entering into myth, but it is praise heavily tempered with the pathos of guaranteed denial.

In the final analysis, "History as Apple Tree" moves as much toward introspection as toward identification.[7] It uses history to pinpoint a place and a model for the self, but at the risk of giving the self over to the grave. The poem may be counted among Harper's output on death; it is distinctive in treating the subject with a measure of detachment, and with a hint of redemptive possibility. Typically, the poems on death show a fierce resentful grief, as though death were not always in the nature of things, or as though death aggravated human pride unbearably, or as though death were somehow peculiar in black experience.

Now the matter of peculiarity raises a treacherous, double-

7. For another reading of "History as Apple Tree," the reader should consult Robert B. Stepto's "After Modernism, After Hibernation: Michael Harper, Robert Hayden, and Jay Wright," in *Chant of Saints: A Gathering of Afro-American Literature, Art, and Scholarship*, ed. Michael S. Harper and Robert B. Stepto (Urbana: University of Illinois Press, 1979), pp. 474–76.

fronted problem in dealing with all black literature. First, one may say a situation occurs only in the black sphere, and affords no point of contact or community with any other. Then again one may say a situation occurs virtually everywhere, and has no distinctive valence in the black sphere. Both views miss the vital fact that the black situation is at once like and unlike its environment; the difference is not in substance, but in degree. There are circumstances under which every person will experience what it entails to be a member of a minority group, but the black person experiences it at the drop of a glance, anywhere, anytime. That difference in degree generates a difference in quality, though that difference in quality does not transcend nature. The black community is indissolubly tied to the larger society, but with a harshly restricted tether. In this light, even the mission of kinship may indicate that things are fuller than self-veiling or solitude without being quite full in themselves.

Eldridge Cleaver's *Soul on Ice* sharply records a blind struggle for kinship. On the surface the action plays itself out in terms of female exploitation, from the first eruption of rapacity toward women when Cleaver awakens to the deprivation he has unwittingly undergone as a black person to the final plangent appeal to "all black women" to help him "build a New City on these ruins." In short, women seem to exist to compensate and to secure and to serve and to enhance (even the "idyllic" experience with the defense lawyer, Beverly Axelrod, has such a smack, both practically and emotionally). But Cleaver is not essentially exploiting women. In fact, they preoccupy and possess his mind. Where they are missing, as in "The Allegory of the Black Eunuchs," there is mere mechanism and chaos. Where they are present, there is at least relationship, however rudimentary and harsh.

Though Cleaver affects to write "from all black men," that is a null category. He has no available basis of identification with black men, and with men at large he projects only a relationship of machismo castration. In this light the book's opening discovery that privileges had been denied him is the equivalent of *conscious* castration. It is as *castratus* that he undisguisedly approaches all black women at the end.

Castration is a tacit form of feminization. In picking on women, or picking out women, Cleaver is trying to come to terms with himself. They are the ones, as victims, with whom he feels the most direct and the deepest kinship. More striking yet, they are the ones with whom he feels most kinship because they present a "cerebral image" despite victimization. Beverly Axelrod is the direct embodiment of this dual role, and *Soul on Ice* is its apologia.

Soul on Ice, then, develops from hostility toward one's own (a la Bigger Thomas in *Native Son*) through an initial, surprising knowledge of sharing with one woman, Beverly Axelrod, and beyond that to a wished-for reconciliation and collaboration with "all black women."

How, we may ask, does Beverly Axelrod, a white woman, serve as the pivot from hostility to reconciliation in Cleaver's treatment of black women, and of himself? And why is she all but jettisoned at the end? On the surface Cleaver may seem to be making arbitrary or confused maneuvers, following the outline of biographical politics perhaps, but scanting the logic of art and human growth (which he is proclaiming). A closer scrutiny brings out the fact that Cleaver is following an involved and precarious pattern of kinship. I have suggested already that Beverly Axelrod, as victim/intellect, gives substance to a condition with which Cleaver feels great affinity. But why the white woman for this purpose, and not, say, Angela Davis or Marian Anderson—why not a brilliant and powerful black woman, or a distinguished and matronly one?

It is evident that the very feature which raises the problem, namely, Beverly Axelrod's whiteness, also helps to settle it. Beverly Axelrod is not just victim/intellect, she is victim/intellect/white. That is to say, though victimized as a woman, as a white, she enjoys certain privileges and immunities that a black woman would not enjoy. By identifying with her, Cleaver gets breathing room and recovery time; he has a safety zone (as well as, perhaps, a talisman) to use in the radical battle for identity and identification. Of course there is a level at which Beverly Axelrod's whiteness is dangerous, as the helpless attraction he feels toward the white woman who occasioned Emmet Till's death would show. But Axelrod exorcises that dread, proving that Cleaver will not be lynched for going with a white woman. Only after he has gained the strength and the confidence of that relationship can he go on to the larger arena of his own blackness and his identification with "all black women." In this light his analysis of the feminine-cerebral basis of the Beatles' success must strike our attention; it is as though with the Beatles he is recapitulating Beverly Axelrod's role as intellectual female and tacitly guaranteeing his own success, or at least safety, as intellectual and public performer identified with the female.

But there is at bottom a tension between the cerebral bias in *Soul on Ice* and its emotional plangency and incantatory appeal. The text begins in quasi-solitude, and ends in would-be kinship. Both are products of analysis. It is odd to find analysis as the basis of kinship, and more so to find kinship as a basis for analysis. It is not so much kinship as the need for kinship that Cleaver portrays. One fleeting episode is telling here. The young black studs in prison ask the old Uncle Tom-like figure how it is that he hasn't died; clearly they wish to use death to terminate a kinship they cannot digest or abide.

The text has no active, substantial image for kinship. But it knows its limitations. The prayer for kinship with which the text ends has in it an important element of atonement for old injuries and neglect. If it retains the defect of all prayer, that of practical vacancy, at least it constitutes an advance over both Hurston and Ellison, who also appreciated the need for kinship. Hurston's Janie, after all, remained in a state of recapitulation, and Ellison's invisible man in a state of cryptically "speaking for" us when not dreading castration (Cleaver has come to terms with that) or pounding some hapless stranger into the sidewalk under a streetlight.

Cleaver's spontaneous and as it were piously anticipatory approach to kinship had had a precedent in Melvin B. Tolson's *Harlem Gallery* (1965). It is not crime and ignorance but an intense devotion to art that makes for the initial separation here:

> This pain is only the ghost of the pain the artist
> endures, *endures*—like everyman—alone.   (p. 30)

Not only is the artist alone, but art itself is "unique" (p. 33). The perspective of the curator somewhat palliates the severity of the artist's solitude, by introducing a functional other, but that other is focused back on the artist, their "paths coincident" (p. 39; p. 170). A collective spirit seems to enter into the poem only as the "tribe," whose "idols"—the very allusion to Bacon is ominous—give out one vociferous but vague opinion:

> The idols of the tribe, in voices as puissant as
> the rutting calls of a bull crocodile, bellow:
> "We have heroes! Celebrate *them* upon your walls!"
>
> (p. 61; cf. p. 34)

Here is all the force but also all the pathos of the herd; the reference to rutting suggests an occasional and indiscriminate discharge of blind energy. This tribe will not have any stable or significant influence.

There do occur, however, outcroppings of a more complex sense of community in *Harlem Gallery*. An undefined "we" appears as early as the second section, "Beta," and the curator seems to be a member of the group and to focus a certain radical poignancy in its situation: the group needs "a reading glass" and "a hearing aid," and "I [the curator] have both mislaid" (p. 22). The identity of the "we" is made explicit later: Harlem is meant, Harlem as the single-handed creation of black life in the United States, but also, as the presence of Dr. Obi Nkomo attests, as a tacit synecdoche for black life everywhere. But again the "I" of the curator instantly separates itself from the "we." The relationship between the two contains some element of volatility; he belongs, but he does not sustain the state of belonging:

> We have dined too long, O Harlem, with Duke Humphrey!
> In the kitchen
> the chef, I, mixes black and yellow and red
> images, leaves You at the table
> with brown bread
> and the ghost of the thing
> unsaid.   (p. 67)

The plethora of roles (Harlemite, curator, chef) reflects an almost Rinehartian elusiveness of being. The speaker has neither quite absorbed nor been quite absorbed into the basic community of interest. In fact, in an effort to effect a reconciliation of roles he goes almost at once into yet another, that of cosmopolitan historian, summing up crucial examples of expression in *European*[8] history and extrapolating from them a hope that Harlem and its artists will not be crushed out since their counterparts abroad were not.

That hope stamps the speaker as the curator of optimism and prophecy. It is at this level that the sense of community, if not the community itself, arises in *Harlem Gallery*. Like *Soul on Ice*, it is a community by anticipation. Unlike Cleaver, who is bound up as a single actor in the scene of anticipation, Tolson has the benefit of the very multiplicity of perspectives that keeps the curator from belonging unequivocally in Harlem. As a result, *Harlem Gallery* both records the actual absence of community and advances a scheme for its coming about. That scheme takes the form of a cluster of images of dawn in the poem.

The importance, or say rather the evocative potential, of the dawn image and its analogs would be difficult to overestimate. Tolson repeatedly draws on the title of Du Bois's autobiography for the phrase "dusk of dawn," and amplifies this notion to suggest the *"dusk of a people's dawn"* (p. 35), and amplifies yet further in the idea that the "voices of the voiceless" may be heard "now and then" in a manner "authentic as a people's autobiography" (p. 62). We recall that *The Souls of Black Folk* gave articulate and urgent expression to the shy, cryptic power of the people and their "sorrow songs," and we must infer that Tolson is carrying on from Du Bois, attempting on the urban scene of Harlem what his great predecessor had

---

8. The European emphasis in *Harlem Gallery* is nowhere more troublesome than in the beautiful paean to the blues that gratuitously culminates with a European reference: *"Witness to a miracle / —*I muse*— / The birth of the blues, / the flesh / made André Gide's / musique nègre!"* (p. 83). Tolson seems self-conscious about this Europeanizing of the Harlem experience when he writes: "The Zulu Club / is not the fittest place to recall / by fits and starts, / Seneca's young Nero / . . . and . . . / Aristotle's youthful Alexander!" (p. 88).

accomplished for unlettered rural folk. Continual references to "spoor" (pp. 25–34), and "chrysalis" (p. 38), and "seeds" (p. 45), and "midwife" (p. 66), and "lodestar" and "messiah" (p. 98), and "bridegroom" and "eggs" (p. 118), and even "Patmos," the isle of apocalypse (pp. 38, 116)—all reverberate with the concept of beginnings, and give variety and substance to the theme of dawn.

But it is a dawn without a day. The community that Du Bois, in *The Quest of the Silver Fleece*, had ready to fight with knowledge and arms for its existence does not really form in Tolson's hands, however much Tolson harks back to Du Bois. The people of the Harlem Gallery, from Doctor Nkomo to Black Orchid to Mister Starks (surely a mischievous swipe in passing at Joe Starks in *Their Eyes Were Watching God*) and Big Mama, stand as much apart from one another as pictures on an exhibition wall, enjoying unity of place rather than community, and that only of the sort peculiar to the *curator's* mind. Tolson seems to raise the possibility that he is dealing all along with a typical, comprehensive figure, or at least a uniform situation for many, when he sums up *Harlem Gallery* as

> paintings that chronicle
> a people's New World odyssey
> from chattel to Esquire!   (p. 173)

But here the allusion runs afoul of itself, in two ways. First, an "odyssey" to the title of Esquire, as if that were a long-lost home and kingdom, has an unworthy ring. And second, there has been multiplicity like the *Odyssey*, but without an analogous centrality. That the curator experiences a will to community is not to be denied. To find that will realized comes harder. Two reasons for this can be identified. The first is the very character of curator that the speaker adopts: to curate sidesteps participation and makes responsibility and caring formal, not personal. The second reason is that he does not seem to have found the *res ipsa* of community, but only its dawn, or spoor.

The will to community that underlies *Harlem Gallery* evidences itself again in Jay Wright's *Dimensions of History* (1976). The larger, more general canvas that Wright elects is given focus by his interest in Africa and Mesoamerica, but it still increases the difficulty of identification in a community or with a people. Compelling in its images and music, the poem employs a single speaker, an "I," to enter into a myriad of events, situations, and rites. That protean "I" cannot, however, gloss over the axiomatic discontinuity of the episodes. Nor can he refrain from falling into confessions of insufficiency and into an optative and interrogative mode to deal with his own relation to them. The poem is all purpose and desire, with attainment "in a distance" (p. 12). The verb *to assert* chimes throughout in conditions that call for more than mere assertion. The voice of the poem comes home with a poignant, almost incantatory beauty precisely where its freight is most unamenable to its purpose:

> I dream of the termination
> of these searcher's feelings
> and the day of rain, upon which
> I shall begin to build myself again.
> But here alone I sit
> with the tassel and the bell,
> holding the celebration of my people's love.   (p. 12)

The dream cannot conjure up reality, and the celebration and the people are alike absent and antagonistic to the speaker's solitude.

Some of the resistance to community or kinship in *Dimensions of History* stems from the necessity, under which the "I" operates, of first finding himself; again and again the poem swings inward: "I . . . / return and take myself in, / into myself, / unto myself" (p.75).[9] No such preoccupation enters into the most massive and the most insistent will to kinship yet seen in the Afro-American community: the protest movement that commenced in the 1950s and came to a head in the late 1960s and early 1970s. Ron Karenga, for example, bluntly denies the artist any "individuality," which he defines as "'me' in spite of everyone," and concedes "personality," that is, "'me' in relation to everyone," only with the stipulation that "no one is any

9. Jay Wright in fact quotes Martin R. Delany, the nineteenth-century black novelist, in a vein similar to the protesters: "We must MAKE an ISSUE, CREATE an EVENT, and ESTABLISH a NATIONAL POSITION FOR OURSELVES" (p. 31). But this is not a strain of great prominence in *Dimensions of History*.

more than the context to which he owes his existence."[10] And Don L. Lee, though playing the soft cop to Karenga's tough line, arrives at the same conclusion: "Creativity and individuality are the two nouns most often used to describe an artist of any kind. Black poets subscribe to both, but understand that both must not interfere with *us*, black people, as a whole. Black poets of the sixties have moved to create images that reflect a positive movement for black people."[11] And finally, LeRoi Jones, speaking as director of the short-lived Black Arts Repertory Theatre, calls for "black unity as defense against these mad white people who continue to run the world. . . . We must unify. We *must* have unity" ("blackhope," in *Home*, pp. 234, 236).

Here is kinship by exhortation. It is rhetorical and programmatic, and precarious in the sense that its strength depends upon its immediate success, and in the further sense that the more it succeeds the more it dictates to and confines those it would make free. There is a poignant paradox at the heart of willed kinship, which was necessary to, without being sufficient for, the Afro-American situation. This Malcolm X discovered and recorded; he passed from the wild destructiveness and solitude and blatant vulnerability of his youth and early life of crime to the formal, willed solidarity of the Black Muslim movement and found that wanting. What might exist beyond it to satisfy him he could not formulate. At the same time he did not let considerations of convenience, familiarity, or material loyalty prevent him from looking. Perhaps his breaking forth to seek what yet was in him and what lay beyond even the virtues of kinship should be taken as an emblem in the Afro-American scheme. A similar breaking free from a willed and "political" as opposed to an intrinsic and diffuse kinship appears in the work of Robert Hayden and Alice Walker, who articulate what Malcolm X stumbled upon, the value of intimacy.

10. Ron Karenga, "Black Cultural Nationalism," in *The Black Aesthetic*, p. 35.

11. Don L. Lee, "Toward a Definition: Black Poetry of the Sixties (After LeRoi Jones)," in *The Black Aesthetic*, p. 247. The most scathing, if also the wittiest, attack on individuality in this era comes from the pen of LeRoi Jones, in his "brief reflections on two hot shots" (*Home*, pp. 116–20).

In solitude we have seen black characters meeting themselves with lucidity and resolution; in kinship we have seen black characters meeting or wanting to meet their kind with compassion and creativity and resolution. The difficult reciprocity of meeting the whole world, not just the whole of one's world, is what writers like Robert Hayden and Alice Walker add to the black literary tradition. More basically than greater range, it is greater exposure and undefeated openness that will set these writers apart. They carry Ellison's observation that "all of it is part of me" a step further, thus yielding the apprehension: I am part of it all. In other words, Ellison's wry or reluctant acceptance of "the loved and unlovable" becomes, in Hayden and Walker, the assumption of an active, creative role in a scene of mutual belonging, a scene at once settled and emerging.

The field of blackness is enriched in Harper, but its *boundaries* stand clear. Those boundaries take on the character of a frontier in Walker and Hayden, an unpatrolled frontier in a country confident enough and honorable enough to see that whatever it attracts corresponds to and affirms what it contains. Such an adventurous sense of the self in continuity and in complicity with its context I have identified as *intimacy*. It is the polar opposite of invisibility, which after all springs in large part from a desire to avoid contact, or at least any contact whose effect cannot be guaranteed. Melville's image of "the common continent of man" suggests intimacy, but misleadingly so, for it has about it too much the smack of ideology and of an inert structure. As Octavio Paz continually indicates in *The Labyrinth of Solitude*, intimacy can be devastated by the arid victory of principles over instincts.[12] Intimacy means that the self is present vulnerably and at the same time powerfully in what it meets, becoming more itself as it better grasps and enters into what stands apart from it. In *Shadow and Act* Ellison expresses the conviction that "in the realm of the imagination all people and their ambitions and interests could meet" (p. 12). Intimacy goes further, and brings that meeting into the domain of actuality.

12. Octavio Paz, *The Labyrinth of Solitude: Life and Thought in Mexico*, trans. Lysander Kemp (New York: Grove Press, 1961), pp. 34–35, 64, 70–71, etc.

5

INTIMACY *The Interpenetration of the
One and the All in
Robert Hayden and
Alice Walker*

We are
totals, watch us, watch through yourself and become the whole
universe at once so beautiful, you will become . . .
the world,
at that incredible speed, with all the genius of a
tree.
LeRoi Jones

No one would deny that the assassination of
Malcolm X in 1965 and of Martin Luther King in 1968 cost the
national drive of Afro-Americans for free ground, for vital spiritual
space or *Lebensraum*, much of its direction and momentum. It is less
easy to see why this should have been so. King was an established
leader, a respected minister, an upholder of passive resistance. Malcolm was a rebel, an upstart leader, a firebrand. The two men
were virtual antitheses. On the face of it, losing them ought not to
have produced the same effect. Yet it was like two tornadoes on the
same site. What had been left standing after the first assassination
came down with the second.

Perhaps we need to see that King and Malcolm, as different as they were in comportment, made in essence complementary leaders. King was the master of a *general* political philosophy, with a proven tradition and technique that answered to black needs. Malcolm was the embodiment of a *black* political philosophy, with an evolutionary dynamism and a technique answerable to alterations in the external scheme and in himself. King led the way to becoming respected. Malcolm led the way to becoming authentic. King marshalled but Malcolm magnetized and generated power. When they were cut off in cruelly rapid succession, black people in America seemed to lose both structure and thrust, ground and prospect.

This despite an animated protest movement, which King had been swept up in and which Malcolm had penetrated into and transcended. Here again the surface indications may be misleading, for the protest movement remained throughout strangely dependent on the presence of the white power structure. LeRoi Jones describes the chronological sequence of essays in *Home* (1966) as the record of his becoming black, but it may be rather the way he became anti-white. Even a moving essay like "7 Principles of US Maulana Karenga & The Need for a Black Value System" retains marks of this bias. In a sense Jones may be bound by his commitment to codes and systems, whereas Malcolm clearly counted on them less and less. It is odd, then, to see Jones codifying Malcolm: "Malcolm's teachings must now be analyzed, formalized, and a structure and program issued out of them" (*Raise Race Rays Raze*, p. 145). Jones went for doctrine, Malcolm for conditioning of being. And Malcolm was the one who became surprisingly, capaciously, creatively, and independently black. He is the one who, when Jones was capitalizing on the authority of images, spoke out against the specious American "science" of images before the Harvard Law School Forum. It amounts to a terrible irony that, upon loss of the image of Malcolm's image-freedom, such a setback befell the Afro-American cause.

If we consider not the question of images—how one is seen—but rather that of vision—what one encompasses when one sees—

then the Afro-American scene becomes less bleak than the loss of
Malcolm and King leads us to expect. In vision, a quiet, deep growth
continues. King's formidable critical patience and his indomitable
attachment to the goal of black class-betterment did not come only
from courage before white society. They came from faith in the
ordinary black individual, in a drudging, trudging, but potentially
unbudging Rosa Parks. They came from an apprehension of un-
tapped power *within* the ordinary black individual, and therefore in
all blacks as a class. This is the basis of the Montgomery bus boycott
that had Rosa Parks as first violin and King as conductor.

In like manner, Malcolm X did not only brandish defiance
before white society. He flourished, unpredictably and irresistibly,
within himself. He was the power of the ordinary black individual
made manifest, in many modes. His career was fairly typical, and
fatal, until the Nation of Islam made him look *within*, to himself as a
black individual, where he had been merely looking upon himself as
an agent set against the social system. This is not to suggest that the
Nation of Islam or Black Muslims, as they are commonly called, did
not sharply set themselves against the white power structure; but
that was only the vestibule of their order. The principal part of their
business was conducted within, in dimensions of self-respect, self-
discipline, and self-development. Malcolm went as far as he could
with them and broke away because he found their inner vision had
become rigidified and their personal forms exploitive and corrupt.
On his own, he continued to gain in power and stature (1) as a further
process of self-revelation, and (2) as a matter of concentrating the
power of ordinary black individuals and, eventually, by virtue of an
act of dizzy spiritual enlargement whose practical product we were
not privileged to discover before he was cut off, of all ordinary
individuals.

The sense of powers *within* has come down from Malcolm X
and Martin Luther King into the most outstanding Afro-American
literature of recent years. They have also handed on the sense of
purpose arising *from within* and expressing an organic, vibrant

humanity rather than a formal, plastic institutionality. The result has been a simultaneous manifestation of passivity and militancy, fused in another dimension.

The work of Robert Hayden and Alice Walker best represents the new development. This holds true despite vivid differences on the surface. Hayden was through and through a gentle man; Walker is tempered to the mettle of an aristocratic woman. Hayden was a committed member of the Bahai faith; Walker thrives in a world of irony and activism. But both have come, by their contrasting routes, to a remarkable poise among conflicting lines of history and personal experience and social dictates. Whereas for most people convictions turn into a containing edifice, for Hayden and Walker convictions seem to have served as revealing barbicans, enabling them to take in more of the world, and to see further and enter more sanely and widely into it. To speak of them as both passive and militant is to recognize a sublime absence of specificity and thus of *limitation* to their passions. They are passive in the sense that they do not force a particular result upon experience. They are militant in the sense that they know experience has results and they are less than indifferent on the matter. They are for things, or goals, illustratively, not absolutely. Thus they are not possessed by things or goals, but only engaged by them, to their personal peril or enlargement. The air of immediacy and breadth that they generate in their work, their acceptance of depth along with openness of engagement, I have been calling intimacy.

It hardly needs saying that this term is invoked in the sense of whatever pertains (a) to our deepest nature and (b) to the essential relationship we bear to other people, things, systems, institutions, and the like. The Latin root of the word, *intimus* (innermost, deepest), must be kept in focus. In some quarters popular usage has led to a confusion between what is intrinsically intimate and what is putatively a material expression of intimacy. Thus sex, by euphemism or by optimism, becomes "intimacy," as gesture supplants essence, and action state. But the mechanical repetition and general uniformity of sex (ill disguised by the incidentals of the less than original manuals of recent years) give inadequate room for the abundant invention of the spirit, or for the rich singularity of experiential encounters that true intimacy generates. One further comment: the practice of calling a corner table in a restaurant, or even a basketball field house (presumably as opposed to a Big Ten football stadium, with perhaps the contrast between stadium and field *house* influencing this usage), an "intimate setting" subjects the term to propagandistic license, swelling it to a hollow thinness only short of self-destruction. In sum, the field house or restaurant constitutes sham intimacy, as the boudoir constitutes merely gestural intimacy. The works we shall be discussing effectively renounce such phenomena. This is a matter of necessity, not of choice. True intimacy has no prescribed form and affords no guarantee.

ROBERT HAYDEN: AT LARGE, AT HOME IN THE WORLD

The sense of intimacy comes out equally in Hayden's work on sports, on astronomy, and on family history, or in a meteoric piece of local journalism such as "The Crystal Cave Elegy," at which we have already taken a close look. One further remark will be in order here. "The Crystal Cave Elegy" abounds in close, not to say claustrophobic, settings: the coal mine, the cave, the home. In that respect it lends itself to intimacy for the capable spirit. "Free Fantasia: Tiger Flowers" (*Angle of Ascent*, pp. 6–7) is just the opposite, even to the extent that no more than a casual connection exists between the persons in the poem, who are drawn together briefly at a slightly déclassé boxing match. There is of course an intense involvement in the sporting event, and the sociologist Stanton Wheeler has set forth the various ways in which a spectator may "identify" with an athlete, but such involvement and identification occur within strict limits and entirely according to the spectator's needs. In other words, both the crowd conditions and the athletic setting militate against intimacy. Hayden, however, proceeds undaunted, demonstrating that intimacy inheres in the human condition, not in the circumstances under which humans meet.

The "scufflers" find Tiger Flowers's jab "righteous," implying not merely a colloquial sense of power but also a suppressed feeling for the very justice with which they play fast and loose. And the ladies are drawn out of their cautious elegance by Tiger Flowers, and betray their desire for some swift physical gesture that would turn the tables on their nameless enemies ("trick" implies they would stop short only of prostitution to gain their ends):

> Dixie odalisques,
> speeding through cutglass
> dark to see the macho angel
> trick you'd never
> turn, his bluesteel prowess
> in the ring.

Both the sports and the ladies, though coming from opposite directions, make the same use of Tiger Flowers, that is, to express what the prescriptions of their lives preclude. They meet in the phrase the speaker adopts for Tiger Flowers when the boat on which the fighter's illegal bout is taking place goes down: "elegant avenger." A sort of subdued oxymoron comes out in this phrase; elegance and the implied ferocity of vengeance are at least very much at odds. But Tiger Flowers's very name involves a crossing of boundaries, bringing the fierce and the sweet, flora and fauna, into one domain. By the same token, when the speaker finds a oneness between Tiger Flowers and Henri Rousseau's *Virgin Forest*, the stress falls on the permanence of art capturing the perishable forms of life. The point is not to repeat the oxymoron (animal : vegetable) but to advance it into acknowledgment that the power of a thing to persist in its antonym is tacit proof that that thing may be, like Flowers, deathless in the clutches of death.

> *The Virgin Forest*
> by Rousseau[1]—
> its psychedelic flowers
> towering, its deathless

---

1. Rousseau, the French primitive painter (1844–1910), has at once the efficacy of technique and the access to mystery, to sacred realms, that Hayden sees in Tiger Flowers. It is a precise and felicitous association.

> dark dream figure
> death the leopard
> claws—I choose it
> now as elegy
> for Tiger Flowers.

The very fact that the speaker *chooses* the elegy carries the relationship between Tiger Flowers and *The Virgin Forest* beyond mechanical association and the parallelism of animal and botanical. They are joined by a unifying rhythm and value.

What is tacit in Tiger Flowers, his ability to bring out suppressed images and interests, becomes explicit in Rousseau's "psychedelic flowers," and these "towering" flowers are further reflected in Tiger Flowers's elevated position in the ring *and* elevated status in his admirers' eyes. Similarly, Tiger Flowers is the "dark dream figure" of St. Antoine: he is (1) the dark-skinned figure who embodies their dreams; (2) the figure who obscurely occupies their dreams; and (3) the figure who represents their dark or unacknowledged dreams.

That this figure is being clawed by "death the leopard" might seem to make for confusion, since the leopard and the tiger should be corresponding figures. That is to say, can Tiger Flowers be present in the "dark dream figure" and in its attacker, "death the leopard," at one and the same time? The idea is possible if we recall that Tiger Flowers is both avenger and victim in himself, and for his followers both ideal and deadly threat. Rousseau's painting, as the speaker of the poem apprehends it, conveys this duality by means of the joined-and-yet-opposing characters of "dark dream figure" and "death the leopard." The speaker's choice of the painting is based on, but also *creates*, an intimacy between Tiger Flowers and *The Virgin Forest*. Within the painting the leopard and the dream figure actually come into intimacy by means of the "claw," which is both cruel and exploratory, masterly and vulnerable. And within the poem elegy becomes one with reincarnation and revelation.[2]

2. For more on the intrinsic connection between elegy and prophecy, see Michael G. Cooke, *Acts of Inclusion: Studies Bearing on an Elementary Theory of Romanticism* (New Haven: Yale University Press, 1979). The third term propounded there, satire, has a place in Hayden's poem in the lines on the "scufflers' paradise" and the "Dixie odalisques."

The poem "For a Young Artist" (*Angle of Ascent*, pp. 8-10) deals with a figure as awkward as Tiger Flowers is agile, in circumstances as squalid as Tiger Flowers's followers are elegant. But its naturalistic surface works merely as a hurdle to the transcendence its "sprawled" and "grizzled" hero seeks. "For a Young Artist" is, like "Free Fantasia," a study in the unorthodox communication, indeed the conjunction of worlds.

The ether and the pigsty, the sacred and the obscene meet in the opening frame:

> Sprawled in the pigsty,
> snouts nudging snuffling him—
> a naked old man
> with bloodstained wings.

We know he has been trying, in agony, to fly. How he came by the wings, and whether they are attached or were grown, we do not know or care. The bloodstains, like the fearful mother or the man with the yardstick near Spenser's dragon in *The Faerie Queene*, produce a sense of reality. The utter sharpness of the situation also arrests attention: an obviously unqualified old man is up against an unyielding nature, in a Wordsworthian confrontation.

But no sympathy or admiration ensues, as with the Old Cumberland Beggar or the Leech-Gatherer. Rather irony marks the case: Hayden's naked old man, his all obviously invested in his wings, has achieved intimacy with a pigsty, or it with him. Only slowly does it become apparent that he has an undeflected purpose and the uncompromising strength to avoid intimacy with a society that strives conservatively to reduce him to conventional terms and forms:

> Neither smiles nor threats,
> dumbshow nor lingua franca
> were of any use to those
> trying for clues to him.
> *They could not make him hide*
> his nakedness
> in their faded hand-me-downs.   (italics added)

Hunger, it is thought, will bring him into line, but he is not to be so easily simplified. Paradox radiates off him. He will eat only "sunflowers" and "lice" (the ethereal or the squalid), and so he totally breaks down their structure of formalities. As he presents himself as helpless and aspiring, so they present themselves as contemptuous and reverent:

> They crossed themselves and prayed
> his blessing;
> catcalled and chunked at him.

When he achieves his goal, his "angle of ascent," the poem does not show the people making any reaction. It is as if they were not there. The feat takes place "in the dark," and they may simply have gone home for the night. Or they may have become bored with their "actual angel? carney freak?" and his cumbersome striving. Whatever the case, for them he will simply have disappeared mysteriously, come morning. For the reader, too, the effect of the writing is to make the "artist" vanish from sight:

> . . . Then—
> silken rustling in the air,
> the angle of ascent
> achieved.

A sound of flight becomes a metonymy for the flier, and a mathematical abstraction (angle . . . achieved) gives proof of the flier's accomplishment. That unlocated sound and unspecified angle both instruct the reader as to the facts and leave him "in the dark" as to the actual flight, unable to experience, even vicariously, the transforming, transcendent taste of "darkness." The old man is essentially alone *with the darkness*, and *with flight*. He alone has intimacy with them.

His attainment of the angle of ascent has epochal force in black literature. After him, and perhaps also drawing on the Sea Island Negro myth of Negroes who could fly, Toni Morrison will presume on the freedom of the air in the scene that culminates *Song of*

Solomon.[3] But before him, flight was for others more privileged, and thus a reminder of failure and shame and pain; this, in fact, is the condition the old man occupies as the poem commences. Hayden may be said to have conflated two earlier scenes of aspiration to flight: Bigger Thomas's, in an early stage of *Native Son*, where the sight of planes aloft spurs him to imagine himself there; and Langston Hughes's, in the early poem "Angels Wings," where the speaker confesses that he "drug [his] wings / In the dirty mire" (*Selected Poems*, p. 25). One is sheer fantasy, the other sheer defeat. Hayden in turn has blood added to mire in "For a Young Artist," but the blood, while suggesting a harsher defeat, also signalizes a more heroic effort. In a sense Hayden also adds blood to the spectral images of Wright's protagonist. He gives substance to what was insubstantial, and sinew to what was listless.

We are left still to consider the fact that the old man experiences an assumption into the sky. Does it work in the poem? Is there anything to make it plausible, though unavailable? Some help toward an answer comes from Keats's "Ode to a Nightingale," where at the end the privileged bird makes what seems a standard flight that yet the speaker cannot follow. Following is not impossible, but improper and so denied. In the case of "For a Young Artist" a sharing is not appropriate for the society, either sneering or superstitious, that the poem depicts. They have come into an uncomfortable preintimacy with the old man at the level of brute nakedness and human aspiration, falling away inevitably at the level of transcendence where the angle of ascent is achieved. Intimacy is possible, but not guaranteed.

It is interesting to consider, though, that Hayden makes the ethereal plane available in the gemlike series "Stars" (*Angle of Ascent*, pp. 11–15). The constellation Orion and the stars Betelgeuse and Aldebaran are as removed from us as the old man achieving

3. Carlos Castaneda concludes *Tales of Power* (New York: Simon & Schuster, 1975) with just such an act of leaping from a cliff. It is supposed to be an act of crisis, defining the leaper in metaphysical terms. Castaneda does not vouchsafe an explicit outcome of the scene.

flight, but whereas his is essentially a private venture, where speech or dress or food would merely socialize him and keep him for the earth, the stars are not kept by their exaltation from being for the earth. The absence of an explicit subject in the opening poem may indicate a stunned humility, but the burden of meaning is clear: man is present to the stars.

> Stood there then[4] among
> spears and kindled shields,
> praising Orion.   (p. 11)

Not until we see "Orion" is it clear that our position is heavenly; the spears and shield, though unusual, are of our order. By the same token, it is the mention of "Orion" that brings out the menace in these objects. The human speaker does not ordinarily belong with this high intimacy, and gets away with being there only by virtue of the act or art of "praising." He has come with knowledge and reverence from a remote to an immediate intimacy, and appears to be surviving.

The sort of startled pride that marks the "Orion" poem gives way in "Betelgeuse Aldebaran" (p. 12) to a deep, insoluble astonishment: "How shall the mind keep warm / save at spectral / fires— how thrive but by the light / of paradox?" And bafflement again manifests itself in no. IV of the series, "Pulsars, blue receding," where the speaker asks of the universe, of the "Cosmic Ouija,"

> what is the
> mathematics of your message?

It is apparent that more than unforded space has given rise to a sense of incomprehension and awe. In "Betelgeuse Aldebaran" the "spectral fires" are literally dead, the ghosts of overgone life that reach us across vast tracts of space and time, but which are able to do so because of equally vast depths of original power. Likewise the "pulsars" are "dead" objects, being collapsed remnants of supernovas. The association of the color blue with the pulsars in space

---

4. "Then" seems to be the propulsion system that takes Hayden into the blue. It is, of course, both temporal and logical, implying that this makes sense in context.

further suggests the "blue door" of "The Crystal Cave Elegy," with its allusion to death. We may legitimately conclude that Hayden is seeing space and the majestic, mysterious objects of space as emblems of death. His awe is toward death as well as toward astronomical phenomena. Ultimately the poems open out upon a cosmic death, with their interrogative strain implying a failure of knowledge, but not of nerve.

Even in these poems of awe and incomprehension a sense of presence comes through. There is a willingness to be involved and exposed to spectral fires, and an implied conviction that such warmth as the mind knows will come from its exercise upon the rigorous truth, rather than from any comfortable environment.

The personality experiences two levels of temptation to duck the truth. The first is physical, involving spears and shields. But the danger they pose pales into insignificance beside the dangers of transgalactic scale in space-time, which are daunting to mind and soul—here is spiritual danger. Perhaps consolation could come from the "message," but it is "receding" (as the indecipherable depths of the universe recede). The three key terms, ouija, mathematics, and message, jostle together uncomfortably, as the middle term refuses either to blend with the other two or to remove itself so they can be reconciled.

The strength of these poems is in their poise and their lack of Saganesque presumption on the one hand and their avoidance of nihilism on the other. If there is a plaintive seeking in the question "how can the mind keep warm," there is also a potential reconciliation to "spectral fires," which are after all known to constitute what is given; and if there is frank ignorance in the question "what is . . . your message," there is also a resolution to put the question, and an implicit supposition that an answer could come.

Of course something of an answer does come in the reversal of mission that Sojourner Truth represents, in that she is earth's light sent to the stars, rather than starlight sent to the earth. Again star status and death merge, but here there is transcendence of mortality, along with evidence of the mind's capacity to make, and not just acknowledge, a star. This sort of transcendence may be referred back to the movement of self-cancellation in earlier black writing. Sojourner Truth exhibits self-abnegation, rather than self-cancellation, and ultimately lives by giving herself up so that others might live. Hayden does not urge this position on anyone, nor yet blame anyone for avoiding it. He records and honors it, and through it both relieves us of our uncomprehending subjection to the stars, with their intimation of uncontainable vastness and death, and relieves us of our uncomprehending subjection to death.

One may see grounds for analogy between "the starlight" of Betelgeuse crossing "eons of meta-space / to us" and Sojourner Truth "walking barefoot / out of slavery"; and again between the inexplicable and meaning-full pulsars and Sojourner Truth,

> ancestress,
> childless mother
>
> following the stars
> her mind a star.

The oxymoronic phrase "childless mother" suggests the pulsar's collapse upon itself and issuing of light, and makes us mindful that the term "following" conveys both the idea of imitation by adherence to a standard or way and the idea of material guidance or orientation. This poem, set at the midpoint of the series as though to hold it together, suggests on a human scale the mysteries of time ("ancestress, / childless mother"), but more importantly it identifies the stars not as astronomical masses but as ideas or bearers and generators of ideas. That is the kind of star that Sojourner Truth followed, and is. And that is the kind of star that Betelgeuse and Orion have on one level represented in the series.

In a sense then there is no purely astronomical star, as the vastness of Betelgeuse and the storminess of Orion derive from a human perspective. And Hayden says we are intimate enough with stars to create and to become them. In this vein, too, we follow them, not in space, as a hunter its prey, but in principle, as aiming for a like end. The quasi-identification of human and star is a social cliché, of course, but Hayden has reinvested it with substance, dynamism, complexity, and radiance. It becomes in his hands a fresh idea, capable of bringing its two terms into strong relief and into a vital relationship of intimacy.

Black history and Sojourner Truth do not provide the sole answer to the problematical need for warmth and a message in the "Stars" series. Hayden draws another kind of answer from "The Nine-Pointed Star" (*Angle of Ascent*, p. 15), the symbol of unity in the Bahai faith that he adhered to. The star of course represents light in the midst of darkness, and so suggests the force of the spirit in the encircling world of matter. The fact that there is one star, rather than many, conveys integrity and harmony as against multiplicity and confusion. And the nine points—drawing at once on star symbolism and on numerology—suggests the presence of truth and fulfillment in all three dimensions of the three worlds of body, intellect, and spirit. Finally, the number nine stands as the ultimate stage of the numerical series in ancient Hebrew and Greek accounting; after it unity (ten) comes again. Thus it embodies consummate development and resolution, beyond which a new beginning only is possible.

In its various manifestations I have been using the word *intimacy* to signalize Hayden's sense of a special transforming way that separate things reach for and into one another. It is worthwhile pausing to acknowledge the sheer variety and wealth of those manifestations. On the surface little appears in common between "Free Fantasia" and "For a Young Artist," or between these and the "Stars" series, or again between that series and "The Crystal Cave Elegy," or finally between the latter and the chosen "elegy" for Tiger Flowers. One must conclude that Hayden is not just recognizing intimacy but demonstrating it in his encounter with the world. Its immediacy, its versatility, its permeability are equally his. To the last, as in his *American Journal*, he gives voice to what it means to be black, but without foreordaining the possibilities of that state. In this light it is striking to see how he makes use of metamorphosis, a motif in black literature deserving of far more scrutiny than it has received.

Hayden's treatment of metamorphosis is neither Chesnutt's, which looks quasi-exploitive, nor yet Harper's, which proves asser-

tive at last. It is distinctively his own, with *both* parties to the phenomenon as it were at risk, *both* involved in a question of the nature and
limits of identity. Hayden gets inside the *experience*, while Chesnutt
and even Harper dwell largely on the *event* of metamorphosis.
Moreover, Hayden recognizes a continuum of metamorphosis, in
that customary episodes of development and change carry meta-
morphic implications.

"The Night-Blooming Cereus" (*Angle of Ascent*, pp. 24–26) is a
case in point. A sense of vigil may touch the opening statement ("And
so for nights / we waited, hoping to see / the heavy bud / break
into flower"), but the basic idiom remains true to the natural occurrence of the rare flower blooming. Seeing the bud as "Packed / tight
with its miracle" is in the same vein; that is, the "miracle" may be a
form of sentimental hyperbole. But the naturalistic sentiment leads
to troubling perceptions. The bud "swayed . . . / as though impelled / by stirrings within itself," and this intuition of another independent life unsettles the speaker. (The "as though" may be gratuitous, as there is an organic drive in the flower, a "force" sending it, as
Dylan Thomas says, "through the green fuse.") His assurance that the
bloom is coming for him is shaken. His sense of himself is thrown into
a state of indecision, "swaying" between repulsion and fascination
with the flower, because his sense *of it* cannot hold firm. One
disorientation gives rise to the other because one entity is involved
with the other. That involvement has a virtual life of its own, and
carries the speaker beyond his thrill-seeking opportunism. He begins
to experience the bloom associatively, or intuitively, as if to know its
nature, and not its spectacle in nature. He approaches animism in
taking the bud for potential "snake, / eyeless bird head, / beak that
would gape / with grotesque life-squawk." But it is animism
founded on an open desire to know, even in the face of the dreadful,
for "grotesque" means not just exceptionally ugly but, more truly,
springing from small, enclosed, unlighted places ("grotto").

His companion ("you, my dear") is unaffected by any such
animism, and remains at the stage of excited naturalism the speaker
has been seduced beyond. She—or he, for that matter—is basically
content with positive knowledge, if only of "the imminence / of

bloom." This is the naturalism of a lexicon *genus botanicum*, and we must respect it for it reasserts partial dominance over the speaker's outlook. He does not forswear his position, but he holds it with a new arch calculation, like a Noel Coward:

> we agreed
> we ought
> to celebrate the blossom,
> paint ourselves, dance
> in honor of
>
> archaic mysteries
> when it appeared.   (pp. 24-25)

The notion of using "Backster's / polygraph" to establish scientifically a "tribal sentience / in the cactus, focused / energy of will" smacks of the same Cowardesque compromise. In the same vein, "archaic mysteries," like the "antique vows" of Keats's "Ode to Psyche," suggests a sophisticated tourist indulging in a primitive rite. Painting and dancing, which in deep psychic terms would stand for evolutionary refinement of matter and the striving for growth and unity, respectively, take on the character of an affectation.

But the sophistication and scientism, postures of determinate knowledge, break down under the power of evidence. With the bud's "belling," a word that conveys its shape but also its power to send a message, the sophisticates turn into spontaneous witnesses for a mystery not archaic but eternal:

> older than human
> cries, ancient as prayers
> invoking Osiris, Krishna,
> Tezcátlipóca.   (p. 26)

In fact, not only Egypt, India, and Mesoamerica are found in one another, but they are found in modern suburban America, the land of the house plant ("a philodendron's fear") and the technological definition of truth ("Backster's polygraph"). They react with reverence before the real, humility before its depth, and, presently, stunned grief before its loss.

The essence of the night-blooming cereus is to dissolve categories, as its "Leaf-branch" and "lunar presence" show. It comes with
ceremony: note the brilliant use of the present participle in "the spike
fringe of the outer / perianth recessing / as we watched"; but it
comes at dead of night. Its shape and its smell have a "belling" effect.
Above all, its blooming is simultaneously its dying:

> Lunar presence,
> Foredoomed, already dying,
> it charged the room
> with plangency.   (p. 26)

But if one of the valences of *charged* is "to put under obligation" (as
in, "I charge you, do not fall asleep") the silence with which the poem
ends and which the flower inspires ("we spoke / in whispers
when / we spoke / at all") brings up the final paradox: plangency in
silence. It is as Hayden says: "how shall the mind ... thrive but by the
light / of paradox?" The poem, having started in prophecy, waiting
for the special coming, ends in an elegy of fulfillment, and the
speaker, who starts in intimation (snake, birdhead, beak), ends in an
intimacy of privilege and deprivation (lunar presence, already dying). The final silence reverberates with the translogical triumph of
the experience, but also with a logical sense of mourning for its loss.
Neither triumph nor loss takes precedence, though. What stands out
is the air of solemnity, in the sense that we solemnize equally a
wedding and a funeral. The unique and even exotic event has
opened up a central experience that brings an isolated couple to
solemnize their humanity across time and national boundaries. The
eternal intersects with the transitory.

Two features persist through Hayden's treatment of intimacy: it
involves great stress, and it does not last. In "The Crystal Cave
Elegy" the suggestion arises that is should not last ("open / for him,
blue door") because the stress is too great and overpowers the savor
of any future event ("I taste the / darkness yet"). In "The Night-
Blooming Cereus" it cannot last ("That belling of / tropic perfume
... / already dying"), and should not last, being "not meant for us"

and leaving a state of mourning not just for its passing but for our incapacity.

And yet it is something we expose ourselves to, as in "The Night-Blooming Cereus" or, at some social and even mortal risk on the part of the "Dixie odalisques," in "Free Fantasia: Tiger Flowers." Even so we must note that intimacy is not consciously sought, but befalls and involves Hayden's principals in these poems. The same holds true for Sojourner Truth and the nine-pointed star. Sojourner Truth does not seek to be a star, but is assumed into stardom. And the nine-pointed star is not so much a possession as a form of orientation and a symbol of aspiration. Hayden's poetry does not go about seeking intimacy, but rather shows how intimacy is met and embodied.

Actually, Hayden gives both negative and positive guidance in the matter, showing on the one hand the allure of specious forms of intimacy and on the other the veritable form and perhaps source of ultimate intimacy, light. But a curious crossover occurs, because light cannot be divorced from shadow, but makes a foil of it, while specious intimacy dwells in shadow. Which shadow is before us, at any time?

It is clear that the gorgeous, hypnotic, I-have-it-all-and-all-is-yours shadow world of "A Ballad of Remembrance" (*Angle of Ascent*, pp. 99–100) is of the wrong kind, dangerous in its allure, empty in its promises. Its basic failing lies in the fact that, as "Shadow of time, Shadow of blood" it materialistically harks back to the past, to old time and ghost's blood. The poem seems startlingly like an attack on the high style in black American manners, but is in fact a fearful evocation of blacks in hothouse mimicry of an affected style in white Southern manners, making a decor of life, and making a religion of decor ("Quadroon mermaids, Afro angels, black saints"). This shadow world offers all varieties of advice from "accommodate" to "love" to "hate," but it means none.

When things seem to merge into one another, there is no actual metamorphosis, let alone intimacy, because there are no real things, in the sense of having place and definition and function ("as well have a talon as a finger, a muzzle as a mouth, / as well have a hollow as a heart"). Here metamorphosis itself turns into moral nightmare and mayhem and zombiedom. Here the stars, far from Betelgeuse or Aldebaran, Sojourner Truth, and the nine-pointed star, amount to no more than "foil," a brilliant epithet that suggests tinsel as well as the thwarting of the good. In one of its aspects "A Ballad of Remembrance" expresses a helpless, shuddering presence-to-memory of a gorgeous shadow-world combining *Cabaret* and *Orfeu Negro*. In another, it is a cautionary remembrance, based on a restored presence of mind, a redeemed identity and choice ("I spoke / with my true voice again").

The absence of choice—choice being essential to the surrender of the known self that is intimacy—marks the world of "A Ballad of Remembrance" as spurious and degraded. By contrast, choice has ample play in "Monet's 'Waterlilies'" (*Angle of Ascent*, p. 63), where instead of a multiplicity of objects whirling in obscurity (as in "A Ballad of Remembrance") "the seen, the known / dissolve in iridescence, become / illusive flesh of light / that was not, was, forever is." Hayden is playing things off against the originative light of Genesis and the ultimate light of Revelation. There is a rendition of light that captures these for him, or puts him in mind of them, thus putting "things" in perfect perspective. He seeks out that rendition when things get worst: "as the news from Selma and Saigon / poisons the air like fallout, / I come again to see / the serene great picture that I love," Monet's "Waterlilies."

Two features stop the poem from being bald and assertive: (1) the emotional fact that the picture works for Hayden, absorbing and restoring him, and producing in us a gratuitous sympathy; and (2) the frankness and depth with which he connects that working with a universal sense of loss ("O light beheld as through refracting tears") and connects that loss with Paradise: ("Here is the aura of that world / Each of us has lost"). When he calls the waterlilies' light "the shadow of [paradisal] joy," the effect is to cinch the poem with credibility. The idea of the shadow deflates the hyperbole while preserving for the painting a lucid association with paradise.

Clearly Hayden is intimate with the painting from frequent visiting. But this is the most superficial sort of intimacy. He has found his hungers, and his solaces, in the painting. He has put his faith in it: "Here space and time exist in light / the eye like the eye of faith believes." But he has done so without idolatry, that is, without mistaking the image for the idea. Remarkable, *reliable* as it is, the painting remains a "shadow" of true light and "joy." (Hayden is one of the rare poets in this and the last century to use this word. He is more like Wordsworth than like Coleridge in associating it with a prior existence.)

"Monet's 'Waterlilies,'" reinforced by "A Ballad of Remembrance," suggests that things have a kind of Democritean existence, tumbling and chancy, but that there may supervene upon them, by a "meditative" act of choice (the saving figure of Mark van Doren in "A Ballad of Remembrance" is characterized as "meditative"), a light in which things do not shift shape or state but remain forever the same. In "Theme and Variation" (*Angle of Ascent*, p. 115), Hayden finds a figure who has experienced the world of things but who possesses the perspective of the light. He calls that figure "the stranger," a simple and still impeccable way of establishing his status in two worlds. He knows this world well enough to categorize it in terms of archaeology, botany, zoology, and anthropology: "fossil, fuchsia, mantis, man"; these are in sum the forms and stages of life. And he knows it well enough to say how it behaves: "All things alter even as I behold" (perhaps reminiscent of Blake's observation that "the eye altering alters all," in "The Mental Traveller"). What we call "reality" he calls a "striptease," with the implication of an infinite tease. Hence he prefers that other world he knows. In fact he proffers it to us, but in a curiously paradoxical form with more than a slight undertone of danger:

> There is, there is, he said, an imminence[5]
> that turns to curiosa all I know;
> that changes light to rainbow darkness
> wherein God waylays us and empowers.

---

5. One thinks at first that *immanence* might be desired here, but *imminence* carries a sense of essential unknowability *along with* a feeling of immediacy.

Imminence and *waylay* are both nervous-making terms; it is as though one might be mugged any moment by God. And the offer of "rainbow darkness" in place of light might seem a bad bargain, especially as the darkness conduces to the waylaying. The rainbow looks more promising, but imprecise, and "empowers" remains at once imprecise and grammatically elusive. In the rainbow darkness God waylays us, but empowers whom? And what power subsists or is wanted there?

To put this question is perhaps to foreclose the answer, which is either obvious or unattainable. The stranger is after all not presenting a picture but a choice: the world of things, palpable but treacherous, or the world beyond things, uncertain but intrinsically supreme and infallibly illuminated. He has in that sense no picture to present. Even the analogy of art, as in "Monet's 'Waterlilies,'" is a crutch. The eye will see more than a rainbow darkness only when it "like the eye of faith believes." Perhaps faith is an odd interest for a modern poet to espouse, at least without irony; but "the stranger," after all, is not so much pushing as positioning the speaker of the poem, by setting forth what he knows of the ways of the world, and then of the way of faith.

"Theme and Variation" boils down to a confrontation of ways. It is distinctive in that it presents a known intimacy over against a second potential intimacy, in the form of a report, where elsewhere intimacy occurs as direct encounter. It is distinctive too in bringing out the sly variety that must lead to intimacy, even when it is more available or less mystical than this "empowering." For there is a certain breath-catching appeal in the idea of an "imminence," a sudden change from "light" to "rainbow darkness," and being "way-laid" by God. Whoever can face these preliminaries is already a *Mensch*, before granting of powers. That person is already beyond the mundane, has already had an engagement, an intimacy that marks its possessor off from the ruck, even if ultimate light, or "power," cannot be assured. If it were assured, intimacy would be a state, not a revelatory encounter, and Hayden enters the long line of poets from Spenser to Shelley who have known the impossibility of that state for mortal man. Spenser's very cry to be granted "that

Sabaoths sight" confesses its impossibility, and Shelley explains it, poignantly: "Man were immortal and omnipotent, / Didst thou, serene and awful as thou art, / Keep with thy glorious train firm state within his heart."

And yet even Shelley has to temper a passion for the destination, in his case intellectual beauty, and has real difficulty reconciling himself to the long, uncertain way. What Hayden intuits (and the saints used to live by) is the fact that there is a subtle zest to the way. For other than the saints, such a position is easier to see than to live with. Even a text as steeped in religious aspiration as Baldwin's *Go Tell It on the Mountain* shows little patience with the way, giving in to instant intimacies that most resemble ancient credulities.

The concluding scene of this novel offers one of the most powerful releases of personality in black literature. It takes on special interest because the experience of release has had a long and difficult birth in black literature. *Sula* pursues it, but poignantly falls short; *Meridian* is ambiguous about it, the heroine's release being in itself obscure and for others a burdensome challenge. A classic rendition of the ensnaring passion for release comes in Ellison's "King of the Bingo Game," where the protagonist freezes to the magical electric cord that governs his wheel of chance with the promise of all the good he can imagine for himself and his wife. The release at the end of Toni Morrison's *Song of Solomon* may be the equal of Baldwin's, but clearly suffers from a kind of arbitrariness— Macon Dead's assumption into the air, even if it works according to the mechanics of his psyche and desire, literally suggests a fall into ecstatic illusion or death (comparable to the assumption of Clarence into the king's embrace in *The Radiance of the King*, by Camara Laye).

John Grimes's access to light in *Go Tell It on the Mountain* is emotionally and psychologically more plausible than that. It enjoys the benefit of falling within the protection of a social-religious convention: his neighbors confirm it and his elders vouch for it from their own experience. But it is very much like a coming out, a formal ceremony which, as it is the more heartily participated in, the more powerfully generates an aura of success. And nothing but that aura. Success is to look successful in coming out, without reference to going on.

We note that John is coming out not just religiously but also socially and physically, out of the very world that is (a) confirming his new-found prowess and (b) likely to be susceptible to it. But something self-contradictory is afoot. The sense of jubilation and epiphany is offset by continual hesitancy and insecurity. The "terrors of the night" do not leave John, nor for that matter the terrors of the day; to the end he cannot face his foster-father's severity or his mother's love, and there is an undertone of a Judas betrayal when, "to escape [his mother's] eyes, [John] kissed her"(p. 191). The summation of the novel is replete with evidence that things "never changed" (p. 185), whether at the individual or the environmental level. Gabriel Grimes, though himself guilty of fathering and aban- doning a bastard child, will still act the righteous preacher and exact revenge for the fact that John was a child brought in by Elizabeth Grimes from an outside liaison. And children will still play on "the filthy streets" (p. 180). In this ambience of filth, it is doubtful that John will stay clean. His absorption in religion is real, but not spon- taneous or deep. He wants to find out what he can feel, or believe. That once done, the Church may be said to have served its purpose.

And what prospects lie ahead? Not even John Milton's vague and curt "fresh woods, and pastures new," assumed at the end of "Lycidas." The prospect is fairly blank; John is released into a warm glow that in the nature of things turns less warm and less bright very soon. Gabriel knows whereof he speaks when he warns John that the ecstatic moment of faith "came from your mouth. . . . I want to see you live it. It's more than a notion" (p. 179). John's real advantage over the other characters is that he anticipates and tacitly chooses solitude, while it is inflicted on Florence, Gabriel's embittered and hostile sister, and on Elizabeth and Gabriel himself, in the imperfect and grating disguise of colleagueship or marriage. But there are signs, even as he goes to commence on the calling of boy preacher, that he is unlikely to "live it." His heart proves "a fearful place," and he all but prophesies his apostasy when he says to Elisha, a major force in his coming to grace: "Remember—please remember—I was saved. I was *there*" (p. 191). The moment of religious ecstasy is an interlude between solitudes; John has been "by myself down there" in the valley of despair, and seems not unlikely to find himself back there before long. Baldwin himself can be said to identify the shallowness and thinness of John's stream of self-release when he writes:

And so we search the pages of our inheritance to find the true shape of our responsibility and the terrifying dimension of our freedom.

For John is seeking escape rather than responsibility, and assurance rather than freedom. The pages of his inheritance ultimately remain closed. We are surprised to find that later Baldwin would write a short story entitled "The Death of the Prophet" about a lapsed preacher-turned-drifter by the name of Johnny.

Still, Hayden's achievement remains singular in complexity and scale, not in absolute character. We shall see that Jean Toomer, throughout *Cane*, puts his characters in at least a purblind orientation toward intimacy, though they end up, more typically, in the self-cancellation of Esther or the solitude of Dan Moore (in "Box Seat"). Intimacy does not go unimagined, but unrealized in the early half of the century. Du Bois's *Dusk of Dawn* and Sterling Brown's "Strange Legacies," from *Southern Road*, both can be said to have a system of intimacy, without intimacy itself.

A genuine anticipation of intimacy may be discerned in the conclusion of Countee Cullen's "Shroud of Color." A long Blakean poem, "The Shroud of Color" entails a visionary scouring of "earth, hell, and heaven; sinew, vein, and core," and offers various encounters with a bug taller than a tree, a mustard seed the size of a man, a rose that calls the protagonist "Coward!", Lucifer, and God. As the action whirls, the elements of the world whirl too and begin to clash—"hills, beasts, men clash, everything"—and the speaker, who had lamented his life and its racial misery, realizes under the threat of destruction that he "long[s] to live."

He lives "all sights and sounds and aspects of my race" and

comes to the revelation that "being dark, and living through the pain / Of it, is courage more than angels have" (*On These I Stand*, p. 22). His inability to die—he had tried literally to press himself into the earth—has been turned into an ability to bear life. His isolation as a black man breaks down into an identification with the plight of all black people; and that identification seems to be the herald of a new day:

> The cries of all dark people near or far
> Were billowed over me, a mighty surge
> Of suffering in which my puny grief must merge
> And lose itself; I had no further claim to urge
> For death; in shame I raised my dust-grimed head.
> . . . .
> Glad even unto tears; I laughed aloud; I turned
> Upon my back, and though the tears for you would run,
> My sight was clear; I looked and saw the rising sun.
>
> (pp. 22–23)

"The Shroud of Color" is remarkable as a dream vision induced by the narcotic of grief. But its vision of racial unity and of a new being and order of life for the individual protagonist remains untested. The work of the poem substantiates the thought that there is no other way, without making the way itself clear or concrete. The feeling of oneness or intimacy that the poem leaves us with remains at the level of resolution and prospect: "I will live persuaded by my own." All may go well, but as we look at the speaker's tear-streaked, "dust-grimed" head, we may well recall the dust-caked head of the reaper in Toomer's "Harvest Song," and the deep failure of persuasion or even communication there.

ALICE WALKER: THE CENTERING SELF

In recent years intimacy has established itself as an important if not a dominant modality in black literature. Hayden's achievement is not unaccompanied or even uncontested in excellence. What he does with intimacy in a lyrical vein Alice Walker, in *Meridian*, translates into the larger political sphere, with education, religion, social action, racial commitment, and personal love mixed in for good measure. It is Walker who illumines the inner struggle and public cost of genuine intimacy, and who unmasks the varieties of false intimacy among us. To her credit she does this without stridency, and indeed with a wry acknowledgment of the seductions of false intimacy in commercial and sexual and racial and political guises; they are Falstaff's "ginger . . . i' the mouth." And she does not squint before the fact that true intimacy in turn cannot even offer Poe's "ethereal dances" and "eternal streams." The would-be ecstatic moment of returning the land to the Indian fizzles and falls to earth. With unhurried and unexasperated resolution Walker carries us into the depths that are ours when the false bottom of forced intimacy gives beneath us, and shows us the new light of austere surprises and rewards. *Meridian* is a study of intimacy in the thick of the world, and a summons to an inimitable intimacy for a reluctant world. Both psychologically and politically it stands as one of America's most daring works of the imagination in this century.

It will be an advantage to set this novel in the context of social as well as literary preferences prevailing in the mid-1970s, when it appeared. Militancy was no longer on the sidewalks. H. Rap Brown had disappeared. Stokely Carmichael had withdrawn to Africa. And feminism had co-opted much of the firepower that women such as Nikki Giovanni and Sonia Sanchez and Audre Lorde had brought to the "black power movement." Andrew Young and Ralph Abernathy presented a new mode of leadership, not more sedate but less eruptive, less given to momentary protestations and satisfactions. The more dramatic personalities, Jesse Jackson and LeRoi Jones, for example, seemed to be taking a more analytical, expository, even philosophical stance. Under the direction of Roy Innis, CORE was renouncing integration and espousing self-determination and separatism as the road to racial equality, but no mass movement ensued; rather, Mr. Innis toured east and west African states and called for black Americans to invest in sub-Saharan Africa. Here militancy took a financial turn, very different from the volatile boycotts of the 1960s.

In a sense, militancy had gone indoors, and even into bureaucracy with Black Studies programs, affirmative action, and voter registration applying topical poultices where before a total cure had been sought throughout the society. What Walker does in *Meridian* effectively takes us through another aftermath of the massive public Civil Rights movement, wherein she penetrates not so much the new bureaucracy as the original spirit and force behind the movement. By focusing on an eccentric individual, she reminds us that the movement envisioned a fitter life for all individuals, and drew up organizations solely to that end. By focusing on a spare, astringent individual, at a time when the accoutrements of "blackness"—Afro hairdos,[6] dashikis, Swahili catch phrases—were in vogue, she reminds us that personal manners and possessions, like impersonal institutions, can smother as much as protect us. And by focusing on an individual marked with denial and defeat, and haunted by obscure images of love and justice, she reminds us of the fact that suffering need not be random and meaningless, nor a centripetal human purpose without humor, or hope, or mercy, or effect.

It is a stroke of remarkable finesse that Walker should have made her centripetal heroine an eccentric. Not to belong in any standard and comfortable way is to escape the limitation of that way. The motif of edifices, of places to occupy and identify with, sharply illustrates the case in *Meridian*. Political meeting-rooms, churches, and schools all hold out a promise of security and dignity to Meridian, if she will give herself and her convictions or instincts over in some self-diminishing way. She withstands these invitations, but oddly without clamor or assertion. She is an eccentric, as far as confining centers go; she is not an individualist, as far as the rest of society goes. To the contrary, Meridian is almost alarmingly honest in her efforts to secure human relations, and almost alarming, too, in the frankness of her personal humility. When she makes her personal edifice a sleeping bag, her life becomes unpretentious and unpro-

6. Supposed to be an authentic African style, the Afro sprang from a powerful intrariparian sense of beauty which some African states preferred to admire rather than to adopt. The Afro was banned in Tanzania.

tected, with the paradoxical effect of (a) attracting other people to her and (b) facilitating her approach to other people, most especially lucidly innocent children.

Meridian stands out as a major character in a major twentieth-century work with the force of spirit to break the dualistic division of institutionalist and individualist that George Bernard Shaw gave a modern form in *Heartbreak House*. In Boss Mangan, Shaw depicts the troglodytic form of what would become the institutional man. In Captain Shotover he depicts the tentative, wistful shoot of individualism springing paradoxically in the ground of institutionalism and growing, over the decades, into a defiant if still dependent gladiolus (the sword-plant). The fact that Boss Mangan is killed in the bombing that consummates the play's action, combined with the young and much-desired Ellie Dunn's decision to attach herself to Captain Shotover, might lead us to think that Shaw is setting up against industry and institutions, and coming out for spontaneity and individualism. But the bombing is bringing down the locus, the bastion, of spontaneity and individualism. Mangan's death will not retard institutionalism; he is a newcomer, an upstart in its scheme. By the same token, the union of Captain Shotover and Ellie Dunn is at best one of unsinewed and sterile nostalgia.

The full reverberations of the Shavian bombing in *Heartbreak House* do not come to us till more than six decades later, with Thomas Pynchon's *Gravity's Rainbow*. Pökler and Slothrop embody institutionalism and individualism, respectively, but by now the individual has an attitude of anticipation toward the effect of institutions, and that effect does not appear, as in Shaw, like a bolt from the blue, but as the painstaking and ineluctable product of a co-opted human agent. The fatal rocket comes not with sudden horror, but with slow inevitability, like the Fall in *Paradise Lost*. Only the Fall in Pynchon's work is a matter of a complex physics, and the law of physics is that thou shalt kill. Inertia brings it, more than a positive will, and it is received as though with a song, a hymn of fatal welcome. The last line of the hymn and of the novel runs: "And a Soul in ev'ry stone." Perhaps this should hark back to a primordial pantheism, but the scene is more fundamentally one of apocalypse, with unexpected pathos and with overtones of a funeral—the stone is a tombstone over the soul.[7]

The singing of hymns and the sense of ultimate forces is also associated with death in *Meridian*. But it is not associated with finality. The church scene into which Alice Walker takes Meridian uses death to focus the commemorative impulse, to express and salve grief, and to renew or inspire human solidarity and aspiration. Death is not, as in *Gravity's Rainbow*, the ultimate climax, but rather the radical challenge that confronts Meridian in politics (will she kill?), in school (the fate of the Wild Child), in personal life (will she take her child's life, or her own?), as well as here in a social-religious setting. In a sense *Meridian* makes death and institutionalism equivalent; both undo individuals *and human values*. The genius of the novel lies in its ability to set up a restorative reaction without sentimentality or evasion.

A good measure of Walker's ability to break into new ground and take command of it can be found in Marge Piercy's *Vida*, which is also a novel with a bifocal view of the revolutionary late 1960s. Like Walker, Piercy has a female protagonist who must come to terms with her old revolutionary activities and relationships and with her new life. But Vida Asch proves paradoxically conservative, clinging at once to her family and to the prolonged Movement. Moods and circumstances dictate her conduct. She does not come to a new vision and her way of life remains peculiarly passive, or at least reactive. Inflated petulance or circumscribed rebellion seem to characterize her, when she is not preoccupied with sexuality. In a sense the superficiality of her "revolution," when compared with Meridian's, is revealed in the fact that Vida dyes her hair, whereas Meridian loses hers. Meridian's experience is thoroughgoing, Vida's assumed. It is in keeping with this difference that Vida's life is passed in skulking, in spasmodic and ill-concerted activity, while Meridian's

7. In megalithic cultures, stones were taken as the dwelling-place of souls; that value seems not to operate here.

builds out into the open from her sleeping bag, and builds in power
and clarity. Vida Asch (her name suggests a confusion of life and
ashes) is smothered in the habit of revolution; Meridian Hill (her
name speaks for itself) ascends from the revolutionary cell, as from
the cell of her spiritual confusion, to lead erstwhile revolutionaries,
and children and adults in the wider social sphere, to new hope and
strength.

The opening scene of *Meridian* establishes the fact that rigid
and foolish force, on the one hand, and sanctimonious greed, on the
other, stand as the only operative values in the society. It suggests
that such a state of affairs will not suffice, but without projecting
anything like an alternative position. The novel sets out in an atmosphere of crisscrossing disgruntlements, oppositions, indecisions.
Only a sense that something new is de rigueur emerges, as the reader
is taken through various channels of ignorance and multiple layers of
illusion. What is expected, or even possible, does not have any
positive image.

The action is simple on the surface. Though it is not their "day,"
the children want to see the miraculously preserved woman, Marilene O'Shay, and so Meridian leads them, past the gun-waving,
whitewashed army tank that is bedecked with ribbons in American
red, white, and blue, and past the phalanx of rifle-bearing police,
into the circus wagon. Walker uses a double perspective on the
action, with the newcomer Truman Held and the jaundiced old
street-sweeper ("I seen rights come and I seen 'em go" p. 5) playing
off each other, to set up questions of how and whether things change,
how and whether people change, and how and whether it makes any
difference either way. Then, given the intensity and frankness of
Meridian's engagement, the question arises whether intimacy is possible or worthwhile. And finally, in view of the children's part in the
action, the opening scene prompts us to ask if intimacy can be
transmitted, and to what end.

To get at answers, we must look not only at the interplay of
deed and witness—Meridian's deed, and jointly Truman's and the
street-sweeper's witness—but also at the intricate correspondences

between Meridian's open, active, voluntary conduct and Marilene O'Shay's passive, trumped-up, hugger-mugger presence. For Walker dares to set up O'Shay as a sort of devil's-advocate counterpart to Meridian; if Meridian can withstand that, she is ipso facto established as having singular merit and virtue (or power) in our eyes. Let us look at the salient points of correspondence, or say rather obligatory association, between Meridian and Marilene (pp. 5–9):

Meridian Hill	Marilene O'Shay
a. brought home "like a coffin," Meridian says of herself: "they're used to carrying corpses"	a. "risen" from the depths of the sea, "Preserved in life-like condition"
b. Truman refers to her with the phrase "believe it or not"	b. is billed as "a wonder of the world"
c. "she thinks *she's* God"	c. "an ideal woman, a goddess"
d. "looked so burnt-out and weird"	d. "dried-up body"
e. "this weird gal"	e. "you know how childrens is, love . . . anything that's weird"
f. said to have "failed to honor not just her parents, but anyone"	f. "Obedient Daughter, Devoted Wife, Adoring Mother, *Gone Wrong*" (italics added)
g. theatricality, chosen and sustained ("they always follow me home after I perform")	g. theatricality, contrived by opportunistic widower ("red and gold circus wagon," etc.)

None of these marks is especially prepossessing, for either woman. It could be argued that Meridian puts her theatricality to the good of the children and the lessening of oppression. Or that the sweeper is as ready to believe she "ain't all there" as to charge her with thinking she can run other people's lives (the source of his arguing that she thinks "she's God"). But even such an effort to defend or exculpate Meridian gives evidence of assumed weakness in her. A true recognition of Meridian requires us also to take into account a number of elements that dissociate her from Marilene O'Shay:

Meridian Hill	Marilene O'Shay
a. "the door to Meridian's house was not locked"	a. there's a strict schedule and a fee to see the "risen" Marilene
b. the light-colored, visored cap ("she had practically no hair")	b. "her long red hair"
c. the children follow her faithfully	c. the children spot a fraud, in that there's "no salt . . . in the crevices of her eyesockets or in her hair"
d. the absence of goods, the life "in a cell"	d. had owned a washing machine, furs, and her own car, and had a full-time housekeeper-cook
e. "how can you not love somebody like that!"	e. given everything "she *thought* she wanted," but killed for infidelity and her corpse (?) exploited for cash

Both the children, in a vein of collective spontaneity, and Truman Held, as an experienced and analytical individual, attest to something in Meridian that makes for faith and love. No palpable basis for this offers itself. In fact, ordinary values seem to be overturned by Meridian: the children should "be afraid of her," while Truman is in direct encounter both "alarmed" and "bitter" toward Meridian, and rebuffed by her extreme detachment. But it is precisely in her detachment that her power may reside. She is the living antithesis to the materialism that pervades the black psyche in early twentieth-century writing. What seems like self-cancellation in her—her deathliness—is self-abnegation and an approach to self-transcendence. When she calls herself "a woman in the process of changing her mind" (p. 12), she gives a valuable clue to her position, *as long as* we do not put a teleological construction on her words. She is letting go of the known for the unknown, the limited for the limitless self. It is of great moment that her loss of health and hair constitutes, as Kimberly Benston has remarked to me, a form of hibernation. For of all the figures in the tradition of black hibernation, so cogently discussed by Robert Stepto in *From Behind the Veil*, Meridian is the only one who can be said to grow a new skin. This all but literally. Hibernation is a pure and self-conscious metaphor for "Jack-the-Bear" in Ellison's *Invisible Man*. With Meridian, the metaphor comes home to the realm of natural, involuntary experience (we may recall that Jack-the-Bear is as busy as a beaver in his hideaway world.) But Nelda Henderson, who also loses her hair progressively and irreversibly with each of her pregnancies (p. 85), enables us to see that Meridian's state is not merely physiological. Meridian's bodily decline represents a reaction to spiritual bafflement, and also gives a sign that her powers are being spent on the hidden struggle of the spirit. She experiences an ecstatic sense of continuity with nature and the universe (p. 50), but it is a *natural* occurrence, in a scheme where nature takes on uncommon dynamism and dimension. Meridian is not a transcendent or mystical figure; rather, she is one who breaks through the habitual constrictions and definitions of available knowledge.

By the same token, what seems like solitude in Meridian amounts only to a separation from specific connections, from possessive or exhaustive ties that in effect hold her away from others. She is lashed to (and by) the demands of specific events and groups and persons, that is to say, the demands of making love to Truman, of the revolutionary goal of homicide, of a violated and vulnerable Lynne Rabinowitz Held. The difference between serving these *demands* and serving the *needs* of the children lies precisely in the fact that the children's needs are not self-oriented and exclusive. They are concrete, but not specific to person or place or time. They are in that regard universal. When Meridian keeps (or finds) herself in solitude vis-à-vis amorous life, revolutionary life, or a desperately clutching personality, the effect is to keep from being cut off from a larger, more complex world. The appearance of solitude is the foundation of catholicity.

It will be necessary to come back to the question of Meridian's "solitude" or "catholicity" in light of her final departure from the other characters'—and the reader's—line of vision. But it is appropriate here to say that Meridian refuses the appearance of intimacy where the act in question does not deepen her apprehension of herself *and* her relationship to other people. Not that she never compromises herself. With Truman Held she does so, and it is noticeable that the text refers to her in disparaging animal phraseology: she becomes a "beached fish" (p. 110). She compromises herself also with her college "mentor," Mr. Raymonds (pp. 107–10), in an effort to make her way through school.[8] It is striking that the patent contrasts between the two men disappear in their common willingness to exploit her while talking up "blackness." Mr. Raymonds further embodies the exhausted, impotent character of one whose approach to *identity* goes by rote (his certificates on the wall, his clichés concerning black womanhood) and whose approach to *intimacy* means preadolescent gifts of candy and adolescent gropings and pressings at Meridian's body. The phenomena of scholarship and love grow dreary and distasteful in his person. He is all gesture, mere gesture; he reduces the vocation of teaching to gesture, as well as the impulses of passion. There is no denying that Mr. Raymonds is on a footing of "intimacy" with Meridian, but it is a furtive and sterile intimacy, the reflective counterpart to Truman's impetuous and aborted intimacy with her. (The deathliness of this kind of intimacy is brought out when Mr. George Daxter, undertaker, courts Meridian's consent from her twelfth to her fifteenth year [pp. 59–61].)

If we take into account Tommy Odds's "intimacy"—by rape—with Lynne (pp. 159–63), we can recognize a major implication of *Meridian*, namely, that a standardized *form* of intimacy such as sex

8. Perhaps her "adulterated" perseverance can be most sympathetically seen beside the swift turning aside of the ex-colored man when his dream of an education runs into some "harsh realities."

works as an impediment and even as an enemy to its intrinsic nature. Revolution here is an analog to sex. People sit around asking one another if they would kill, if they *will* kill for the revolution, treating this as the first question where it ought by its nature to be the last, the ulitmate confrontation of the capacities and failings of one's nature under the worst pressure of principle and circumstances. To adopt such killing as a policy is the *ejaculatio praecox* of politics. Truman produces the literal equivalent in love, leaving Meridian's body with an unbearable pregnancy, as she knew her conscience would have had to bear the projected killing.

Yet a third form of standardized intimacy occurring in *Meridian* is grief. Now grief above all would seem little susceptible to tampering, to artificial formation in the interest of novelty or revenge (which sex and politics so readily lend themselves to). Its occasions are clear, and binding. And yet even here Walker brings out an alarming degree of isolation and egotism, a deep dislocation of social and personal response. With an incisive revision of the McLuhan-esque theme of the global village, she notes that with modern technology making the occasions and the forms of grief (the cutting down of "Medgar Evers, John F. Kennedy, . . . Martin Luther King, . . . Viola Liuzzo") universally available, *"television became the repository of memory, and each onlooker grieved alone"* (p. 21). The word *onlooker* alone is worth reams of criticism. The basic absence of other people, the denial of public presence and mutual influence, changes the individual from sharer to onlooker. The very idiom, to watch television, interposes the medium between person and event, arrogating attention to the medium. In this sense the medium is indeed the message. The point is not only that the fullness of the human event is cheated, but the human individual is cheated of his fullness.

The episode of the Wild Child, even as it follows directly upon the assassinations passage, brings its grim story of human discontinuity into ordinary life. Meridian has tried, by refusing to kill "politically," to maintain a barrier between the momentum of political madness and the movement of personal, imaginative action; she has tried to keep that discontinuity at bay. The Wild Child's life says her task is greater than she thinks, that discontinuity will fall upon her even if she won't bring it down upon herself. The sequence from assassinations to Wild Child is structurally jarring, but only because the surface movement follows the laws of straightforward narrative, when in fact the novel operates according to abstract clues of association and is rife with psychological complexity.

Let us note the disparity between action and expectation in both episodes. What *happens* gives evidence of a total absence of principle, a pervasive randomness in social behavior. One shoots, one seduces—not for a discernible purpose or within a discernible scheme, but out of raw, random impulse. But the *reaction* to what happens, the sense of crushing and maddening trauma, tacitly presumes that life has been proceeding as more than wanton starts and turns. The episode of the Wild Child domesticates and paradoxically magnifies the lawless world of the assassination. The Wild Child's presence says life is wanton from its inception, with no responsibility, no connection, no sympathy; her pregnancy and death say that we may deplore her fate but we cannot even identify the "low-down dirty dog" who might be made to set things right.

The fact that Meridian is able to make even a rudimentary contact with the Wild Child again signalizes some socializing, some healing and freeing power in her. Almost without exception a child is involved in the crucial, seminal, cardinal episodes of the novel, as though it were working out that simplest and most uncontrollable manifestation of human presence and continuity. If Meridian's own conduct seems to give the lie to this emphasis, it is because basically Meridian is a spirit-giving mother, rather than a body-making one, and each interferes with the other. That is why she leaves her first natural child and refuses to have the second. With the Wild Child, as with the children deprived of seeing Marilene O'Shay, Meridian comes to the healing position by separating herself from the merely standard connections of the honors house at Saxon College. In this solitude of prereconciliation she lies in her room "like a corpse"; it is difficult not to see an analogy between Meridian's spontaneous behavior and the Pauline notion of dying to the *vetus homo* so that the *novus homo* can be put on.

It would be misleading to read Meridian's character hagiographically, but she is unmistakably involved in the rediscovery of the spirit, after the excess of materialism and of materialistic credulity that has marked her world. That even the Wild Child is touched by materialistic lures—"cake and colored beads and . . . cigarettes" (p. 24)—does not weaken the point. We are matter; we must begin in matter, but matter is not the be-all or end-all of our nature. In fact, Meridian comes out of her "silence" in college to recommend the destruction of matter, in the form of the president's house, and the preservation of the spirit embodied in the Sojourner tree, which has become materially less convenient with the dismantling of its carpentered platforms, and which symbolizes growth in the face of oppression, hope, harmony, and the creative tradition. When the students, enraged and thwarted at not being allowed to give the Wild Child the funeral they see fit at Saxon College, vent their passions on the Sojourner and destroy it, all that the Sojourner symbolized is invoked, and pronounced hopeless.

The destruction of the Sojourner is the ultimate act of group dynamics in *Meridian*, and significantly it displays the group undoing the good of its members. A vicious paradox appears, for the members of the group proceed in the closest concert and yet are farthest from awareness of themselves, of one another or of one another's good. They are entranced, as Meridian is entranced before approaching the Wild Child, but they are entranced to no purpose, giving all the signs of a common intimacy when really caught in the sameness of automatons.

The life of action is brought into question equally by (a) the refined young women like cross-wired maenads tearing down the Sojourner tree; and (b) the revolutionaries trying to make themselves like programmed robots, to kill on call; and (c) Tommy Odds, forcing himself on Lynne Rabinowitz like a windup toy because he cannot bear to contemplate his physical and social handicaps. *Meridian* unfolds the life of passion-as-suffering, and shows that suffering is crucial to human development. In this regard the novel weaves itself into an important thread in recent Third World writing, other examples being Wole Soyinka, *Season of Anomie*, Camara Laye, *The Radiance of the King*, Wilson Harris, *The Palace of the Peacock*, and Francis Ebejer, *Leap of Malta Dolphins*. But it must also be remembered that suffering as revelatory and redemptive is a leit-motif of the work of Nikos Kazantzakis, and important in Saul Bellow's work from *The Victim* to *Henderson the Rain King*.

In *Meridian*, Walker seems to stress the enthusiastic above the millennial aspect of the concept of suffering. That is to say, she is mainly concerned with bringing the power of divinity into the human sphere (*enthusiasm* conveys etymologically "having the god within"); correspondingly, she neglects the kind of absorption of the human into the divine sphere that marks the climactic episode in *The Radiance of the King*. Meridian's coffinlike rigidity is, for example, akin to the state of possession experienced by the chief of the Thracian Anastenarides prior to visitation by the divinity.[9] Her extreme physical reduction, to a state verging on death, is matched too by an inner draining; she seems wholly impoverished. But the other characters reveal that much is mysteriously present to her when they react with adoration rather than pity or avoidance. Even the street-sweeper's jaundiced observation that "she thinks *she's* God" (p. 8) may betray in him an envious sense of her approach to a god-related state. And we know in fact that she is anything but thinking of herself.

Nothing in the text suggests that Meridian is embarked on a mystical journey, but her adoption of the peripatetic life of poverty and chastity is reminiscent of mysticism, and her impact on the world in the state of poverty is reminiscent of Meister Eckhart's declaration that "God means absolute poverty."[10] At best, though,

9. K. J. Kakouri, *Dionysiaka: Aspects of Popular Thracian Religion of To-Day*, trans. Helen Colaclides (Athens: G. C. Eleftheroudakis, 1965), p. 105.

10. For a penetrating study of mysticism and poverty, the reader may take up Louis Dupré's *Deeper Life: A Meditation on Christian Mysticism* (New York: Cross-road Publishing, 1981).

Meridian would make a reluctant and irascible mystic. Her initial refusal to hear Lynne's story and bear Lynne's burdens must be understood as a desire to preserve a precarious detachment, but she is not dogmatic about this; she does listen, and does involve herself, even to the extent of letting the soul-crushed Truman sleep with her (p. 175) after the loss of Lynne and Truman's child. Her detachment from the principle of killing also wavers. At sight of the father demented by the loss of his son in the Civil Rights struggle, she experiences a murderous rage, and it becomes clear that she might spontaneously kill but for the fact that she spontaneously sings, or attaches herself to song. She draws away from killing again, but not before we have seen depths of emotional struggle not apparent when she was merely under peer pressure and the pressure of political theory, as opposed to the force of human identification. The capacity to know and share the experience of people she glancingly meets links Meridian with "Pa Hayden" in "The Crystal Cave Elegy." It is not a mystical capacity, but one based on sympathy and intuition, bearing toward the intensest realism.

Meridian's trances, her approximations to death, are preludes to episodes of such realism. Thus we must see the trances themselves as militating against mysticism. The text in fact goes so far as to suggest that both the triumphant confrontations with reality and the trances are theatrical. "They [the people] always follow me home after I perform" (p. 13). But the word *perform*, along with its sense of deliberately carrying out a role for public effect, also means to bring off a difficult enterprise or to bring an idea to enactment with skill and power. Meridian is one who performs, where others have failed. And yet she is without a plan of action (or script, to glance back at the question of her theatricality). In effect, by force of character Meridian corrects the mere passivity of the world of *Gravity's Rainbow*. And by dint of involvement she corrects the mere imagination of the dying world of *Pincher Martin*.

Meridian's life seeks to fuse ecstasy and justice. This is almost a distillation of her heredity: (a) of her great-grandmother Feather Mae's experience on the Sacred Serpent (repeated in her father and in her own person), and (b) of her father's insight into and attempt to live, like his alter ego, Walter Longknife, according to a "historical vision . . . as a just person" (p. 47). But she seeks to be more than a just person on a one-to-one basis (like her father giving his farm back to Longknife, a modern Cherokee, as ancestral land).[11] She seeks a just world. Ecstasy is not privilege, or even relief for her, but a burdensome, corpselike state of preparation. And justice is not the self-satisfied, shortsighted meting out of punishment for misdeeds that our society has simplistically made of it, but an intricate fitting together, with sensitivity and precision, of multiform elements habitually going athwart one another and at cross-purposes.

The slow, error-filled, even tragic manner in which Meridian comes to this position is well worth noting. Her life, in detail, is shocking enough: promiscuity, child-abandonment, abortion, disbelief in the rhetoric of "the Constitution and . . . the American Way of Life." But Meridian's life, in essence, is a fragile triumph of consciousness and choice over unconsciousness and brute obedience. When the text says that Meridian, "in the middle of her speech" on the Constitution, "stumbled and then was silent" (p. 119), it is recapitulating and rejecting the invisible man's rote performance at the degrading smoker, and at the same time signaling Meridian's dawning awareness of a possible, an integral, a necessary link between what she says and what she thinks and means. In effect, Meridian slowly gains intimacy with her true feelings, thoughts, interests, needs, capacities, and limitations by an empirical process, including the sympathetic empiricism of taking family history and national history to heart.

We need to look upon her career not as an arithmetic, but as an evolution. In the matter of her lovemaking and childbearing, for

11. If this is not a glancing allusion to Isaac McCaslin's conviction, in *The Bear*, that the social fabric can only be mended by giving land back to the Negroes who had earned it through slavery and beyond, it is certainly an entry into that discourse. Walker seems to be saying that the impulse to social justice by restitution is untimely, even unwanted. The problem is deeper than property, the solution deeper than title deeds. It is the self, not its belongings, that must change allegiance.

example, Meridian proceeds largely on a prevoluntary basis, as much an object or even victim as a participant. It is coming to consciousness that makes for the beginning of responsibility, and for her that coming to consciousness has a terrible candor and intimacy. She knows her willingness to kill her own child, and her own self, and yet retrieves her humanity without going over into Bigger Thomas's blind pit of action; she finds in herself the conviction that killing is the ultimate evil. She is seventeen years old; killing is meant to cope with unmanageable experience.

Walker had already taken up the question of motherhood and abortion in a short story that helps us to appraise Meridian's position here. In "The Abortion" (*You Can't Keep a Good Woman Down*, pp. 64–76), Imani is thinking only of her personal well-being ("I chose me" p. 70),[12] whereas Meridian is struggling through a complex of human values *as well as* trying to discover herself. Like *Meridian*, "The Abortion" has a decisive church scene/memorial service, where Imani decides to leave her husband, Clarence, because she thinks he is insensitive and unappreciative. There is an opportunistic inconsistency about Imani. Oddly, she does not sympathize with her husband's struggle in support of the first black mayor "in a small town in the South" (p. 66), while she indoctrinates her toddling daughter with anathema against the "kind of people" who "can kill a continent—people, trees, buffalo" (p. 72). Again, she does not basically wish to attend the fifth memorial service for someone she "had never seen"; in fact she wrenches the memorial toward herself, thinking of its subject as "herself . . . aborted on the eve of becoming herself," and believing that "respect, remembrance was for herself, and today herself needed rest" (pp. 73, 72). Her resentment of her husband's staying outside conducting politics with the mayor uses irreverence as a pretext. It is intrinsically based on concern for herself, whom Clarence has discommoded by (a) marrying, (b) impregnating, (c) bringing out to the service, and (d) distracting

12. By contrast, June Jordan in "Poem: From an Uprooted Condition" expresses a veritable dread of abortion: "What / is the right way the womanly expression / of the infinitive that fights / infinity / *to abort*?" (*New Days*, p. 70).

while she listens contentedly to the eulogy. In sum, Imani[13] seems relatively selfish and narrow beside Meridian, whose political and human sympathies enlarge in church.

Two things follow when Meridian knows that she can neither kill herself or her child, nor live with herself as a mother and her child as daughter: she gives up her child so that it may live better, and after the aborted relationship with Truman gives up sex so that she may live more truly and harmlessly in herself. These are stern decisions, the former out of line with traditional values,[14] the latter out of keeping with contemporary ones. But their unorthodoxy forms the basis of Meridian's honorable refusal to kill for the revolution and her amazing capacity to serve all children not as a somatic presence but as a spiritual force. It is through the most unsparing (and unexpected) intimacy with her own nature that Meridian is able, as no one else in the book is, to "belong" wherever she finds herself. She becomes intimate with others, experiencing what they experience, by way of renunciation: "she could [not] enjoy owning things others could not have" (p. 116).

Ultimately, the text suggests, to own is to destroy and to be destroyed. The great virtue Meridian attains is the willingness, or better, the will to "let . . . go" and be let go. Then, paradoxically, all things needful come to her, and she can be one with the children and with the old folk, and never a stranger, wherever she may turn. People give of themselves to her, and people come to her in search of themselves, the only limit to intimacy being set by her *on their behalf*, for to take over their lives or, alternatively, to die for them is to deny their right to live, and to die.

13. The choice of this name, especially when the husband and daughter (Clarence and Clarice) have Western names, seems purposeful, but the force of the character does not seem to chime with the purpose of the name, which LeRoi Jones, in *Raise Race Rays Raze: Essays Since 1965*, glosses this way: "IMANI (faith)—To believe with all our heart in our parents, our teachers, our leaders, our people and the righteousness and victory of our struggle" (p. 134).

14. There is about it a Dostoevskian starkness, a willingness to venture into uncharted ground; and of course the impregnation of the Wild Child is very akin to that of Stinking Lizaveta in *The Brothers Karamazov*. At least what Meridian does is preferable to Medea's course when driven to extremity, and not unlike the wife's behavior in "The Hill Wife" by Robert Frost.

The lodestar and balancing agent of *Meridian* is "peace," not in the usage concurrent with the later stages of the Civil Rights movement, but in the sense of composure of spirit in an honorable reconciliation to the environment. The text enumerates the peace that comes from natural beauty, from metasexual cuddling, from death and the cessation of connection and responsibility, and finally from confidence in a living symbol, the Sojourner tree. Each fails, and is succeeded by the next: natural beauty because the land is given and wrested away; sex because it makes usurious demands on the future to pay for its passing moments; death because it necessitates infanticide or suicide, and Meridian, long before she has to defy her revolutionary cohorts on killing to order, has opted for life; and finally the Sojourner fails Meridian as a source of peace when in torment and confusion the girls destroy even that beacon and bulwark of faith.

Even so, peace does not fail in the novel. It merely ceases to be external to Meridian. Instead of taking it in from without, she gives it off, and is never without it. What she leaves Truman at the end is peace, and she is able to leave him—he is able to bear her leaving—because of that peace. The sleeping bag he takes over from her quickly takes on copulative and uterine valences; Truman is symbolically entering Meridian, or the womb. But more deeply he enters his own space, where he has nothing but himself; that is not only enough, but enough to help others from. He is a child again, renewed, as Meridian begins and concludes helping children, rectifying life. Truman enters into Meridian's example and way of life. Here at the outset he is anxious, as she also had been, with psychosomatic symptoms of hair and weight loss. Those symptoms, we can see in retrospect, constitute a form of self-veiling that comes dangerously close to literal self-cancellation. But the probable end of experience for a Meridian is the peace that, if it does not pass understanding, is parallel to it.

Meridian faces death in the South, as the ex-colored man cannot do, and not only lives but shows others how to live better. She chooses solitude, as Bigger Thomas has no chance to do, and transforms it into catholicity. She takes the principle of kinship so deeply that she offends against its ordinary expression, leaving one child and aborting another where Harper almost goes mad at the natural death of his; but her devotion to her mother, her grandmother, her great-grandmother, and especially her father is luminous, and she not only makes the cause of all children, all weak and suffering people, her own but she mothers Lynne and Truman Held, separately, after the death of their daughter, because the necessity is there. In short, she transforms the crisis of self-veiling and even the threat of self-cancellation into intimacy, and solitude into intimacy, and kinship into a universal intimacy. She is one who can love, with deep human appreciation and understanding and protective compassion, a man whose face she sees in passing on television. She is one who can love a dead man, whose face she sees in a photograph during a memorial service long after his death. She is one who has the patience and courage to ask how she "could show her love," wanting to achieve what is "right" and not settle for what is "correct."

And yet, because that love (like "even the contemplation of murder") requires "incredible delicacy as it [requires] incredible spiritual work," and because "the historical background and present setting must be right" (p. 205), it is not actual but potential love, it is *faith* that Meridian disseminates. The ultimate intimacy she attains, or allows, is typically by renunciation, leaving Truman her cell, her sleeping bag and her role, in confidence that he too will be "free." In like manner, she achieves the greatest authority by self-effacement, divesting herself of all modesty and privacy in the telling of her story, so that reading becomes an act of intimacy for whoever enters the book. The terrible candor of the book makes this a difficult intimacy, but it is, strikingly, nowhere claustrophobic. This results in large part from the generosity Meridian exudes. She is not even possessive toward her own story. A remarkably high proportion of the text, of Meridian's text, is yielded to others, while she practices silence and abnegation. Her power is not that of being present, but of a serenely strenuous presence, in the spirit, in the minds of all she meets. The least insistent character in black American literature is the most independent, and the least orthodox the most deeply attached.

6

Jean Toomer, James Baldwin, and Ishmael Reed

> We ran through the debris in much the same way as one might run through shallow water at the beach.
>
> Ronald Fair

TRUMAN HELD's reluctance to follow in Meridian's footsteps and his forecast of daunting grief for whoever does so, even as he himself embarks upon the way, must be taken as a genuine sign of the fate of intimacy. It is rare, and as hard as it is rare. Two phenomena help us to see just how hard intimacy can be. First, Jean Toomer had adumbrated it roughly half a century before Hayden and Walker brought it to fruition; and second, other examples do not abound on the contemporary scene, though approximations can be found. It will prove valuable for our grasp of the continuing dynamism of black American literature to look more closely at Toomer's *Cane*, that storehouse of intimacy manqué, and also at James Baldwin's *If Beale Street Could Talk* and Ishmael Reed's *Mumbo Jumbo*, in both of which intimacy takes on a remarkably disturbing face.

Cane (1923) is a book essayed before its time. In it Jean Toomer sought a breakthrough to freedom and harmony with man and nature by relentlessly prying into extremes of defeat and isolation. He did not bring it off. But the style and character of the failure stamp *Cane* as the work of a writer whose genius could conquer every element of his art save his time.

· The text is written *out of* experience and observation, but it is also written *to* an idealistic conception, and the two do not accord. The matter of *Cane* is recalcitrant to the position it is patently meant to move toward. Both biographically and philosophically Toomer held to a notion of total belonging. In his life he sought to eschew being categorized as a Negro, not as a matter of racial snobbery or fecklessness, but as a way of contesting the fragmentation and constriction of humanity implied in such a categorization. In philosophy he absorbed the ideas of G. I. Gurdjieff as elaborated by P. D. Ouspensky, and came under the compatible influence of Waldo Frank and his group, with their passion for quintessential knowledge and higher slopes of consciousness. It seems apparent too that Toomer took the impress of D. H. Lawrence, who, though irritably and perhaps emulously crying down Gurdjieff and disputing Ouspensky, resembled them in espousing cosmic unity and only insisted that their system could not be counted on: "There is no way mapped out, and never will be."[1]

What Ouspensky sought to map out in *Tertium Organum* was a course of study and discipline that would lead men out of virtual sleep into self-consciousness and on to other-consciousness, world-consciousness, and ultimately cosmos-consciousness. The shifting segments of the circle Toomer uses to bridge into the second and third sections of *Cane* perhaps are meant to intimate the all-embracing circle of Ouspensky's thought.

The question arises whether Toomer had found an apt mode of conveying an all-embracing scheme, when the all cannot be made available to creatures of time but must be symbolically apprehended

---

1. Quoted in James Webb, *The Harmonious Circle: The Lives and Work of G. I. Gurdjieff, P. D. Ouspensky, and Their Followers* (New York: G. P. Putnam's Sons, 1980), p. 341.

through the medium of a moment. Toomer responds first by *exaggerating* the moment, the isolated gesture or individual or cause, but out of those circumscribed moments he makes, in *Cane*, a mosaic of infinite seeking. That primary energy of seeking, which seems to capture Toomer's characters as much as the other way about, is one of the main features separating *Cane* from a work it is usually linked to, Sherwood Anderson's *Winesburg, Ohio*. For Anderson's is a work of waiting. Seeking becomes the hallmark of *Cane*, not just at the level of character and action, but at the level of writing. As Roger Rosenblatt notes, Toomer "creates *his own* kind of solitary wanderer."[2] The writing has its own tendentious design that would be as palpable as a design in propaganda, save that propaganda knows itself and *Cane* is in effect an instrument of discovery.

What *Cane* seeks is intimacy. The natural tendency would be to ask, intimacy with what? But if we look back to *Meridian* or the poetry of Robert Hayden and ask what the central figures seek intimacy with, the result is very unprofitable. For these figures do not *seek* intimacy. They experience it, share it, suffer it, elicit it, evince it. They serve to suggest that seeking intimacy is in its way an anomaly. It differs from seeking the Holy Grail or the Northwest Passage or power or love, in that it is vested neither in a place nor a function nor a feeling, but is radically a state of relationship or being, depending on the freedom of the other. To seek intimacy then is to be fundamentally remote from it. That makes it useless to try to say what would complete the intimacy *Cane* is seeking.

And yet, out of the very hopelessness of the case, it becomes possible to say that *Cane* seeks intimacy *with anything*, as anything offers a triumph over exclusion and blankness. It is like Narcissus settling for intimacy with his own image to defeat the void. The frequency of staring and mirroring in *Cane* is itself an expression of this phenomenon.

"Bona and Paul" begins with Paul drilling and Bona staring at him. They are both teacher-trainees, and the drill, from which Bona

2. *Black Fiction* (Cambridge: Harvard University Press, 1974), p. 180.

has excused herself on a pretext of illness, is supposed to have sacramental overtones: it is the sign of order and vigor, and counts as a major part of their training in the ability to correct "the movements of sick people" (p. 134). But inevitably the drill also suggests regimentation, repetitious and monotonous action stemming from blank obedience. Faith in the corrective power of drill is hard to vindicate; the sick people "have been drilling," the text says, "all their lives," evidently without salutary effect (p. 134).

Paul's position in this scheme is badly unsettled. He has difficulty keeping in step—that is partly why Bona notices him. But he has no step of his own, and no conception of "another drummer," to invoke Thoreau's phrase. Nor can he imagine a way for the collective precision of the drill to be corrective and healing.

The drill proves an apt emblem for the action within the story, where the most personal reaction—petulance in Bona, hesitancy in Paul, the blind motion of enamored couples withdrawing from a dance floor—proves to be repetitious and limiting. Though on the level of symbol the dance and the dance hall, Crimson Gardens, are supposed to embody vitality and creativity, and to transform the mechanical workaday world into romance and transcendence, in the order of fact the dance in "Bona and Paul" is more an extension than an antithesis of the drill. Its movements are hackneyed, its repartee secondhand.

The prelude to passion is a charade of vanity and will. The heat Bona and Paul share arises from verbal challenges and social defiances; they are roles playing themselves out, not persons finding and relating to each other. The pattern of their encounter in the dance, the Dionysiac moment that should redeem him from drill and her from artificiality, is laced with the idioms of knowingness and gamesmanship.

> Paul finds her a little stiff, and his mind, wandering to Helen (silly little kid who wants every highball spoon her hands touch, for a souvenir), . . . wishes for the next dance when he and Art will exchange [partners].
> Bona knows that she must win him to herself.
> "Since when have men like you grown cold?"

"The first philosopher."
"I thought you were a poet—or a gym director."
"Hence, your failure to make love."
Bona's eyes flare. . . . She would like to tear away from him. . . .
"What do you mean?"
"Mental concepts rule you. If they were flush with mine—good. I dont
believe they are."
"How do you know, Mr. Philosopher?"
"Mostly a priori."   (pp. 150–51)

At this stage, both characters are living examples of what is
anathema to D. H. Lawrence, an external and artificial consciousness
displacing the natural blood consciousness that makes for (at least)
sexual health. The aura of *Women in Love* (1921) is palpable in the
comment about "mental concepts." But the most ominous note in
Paul's mental game with Bona is his implicit acceptance of mental
concepts *as long as they are flush with his*. It may be Lawrence as
much as Gurdjieff or Ouspensky who inspired Toomer with a reverence for wholeness, for integration with nature. But wholeness is a
standard that Paul is far from following. He is no Laurentian or
Ouspenskian hero; he has not been tentative or patient out of expectation of some great meeting and merging with another, but only out
of insistence on conformity with his conscious views, on mental
concepts that are flush with his.

It is striking, then, that as the scene continues Bona's "head . . .
strains away" from Paul while her body is flush with his (p. 151).
Passion means fragmentation and separation, without what Lawrence calls "the deepest *whole* self of man." Paul is mental where he
should be physical or holistic, and physical where he means to be
mental:

The dance takes *blood* from their *minds* and packs it, tingling, in the torsos
of their swaying *bodies*. . . . They are a *dizzy* blood clot on a gyrating floor.
They *know* that the pink-faced people have no part in what they *feel*. Their
instinct leads them . . . towards the big uniformed black man who opens and
closes the gilded exit door. . . . As the black man swings the door for them, his
eyes are *knowing*.   (pp. 151–52, italics added)

Though the language of the body and feeling and instinct now infiltrate the scene, we do not see a shift from the mental emphasis that has identified Paul and, to some extent, Bona. There is instead a state of dualism: body and mind, knowledge and feeling, instinct and convention play off each other in a disordered way. "Dizziness" suggests the disorder of the mind, and the "blood clot" the disorder of the body.

Paul's reaction to the "knowing" doorman partakes of this dualism. He is not so caught up in instinct or passion as to fail to notice the doorman. Perhaps he *expects* and so finds the knowing look. By the time he turns back to harangue the doorman, it is clear that he is acutely studying the environment because he thinks it is acutely studying, staring, at him:

He sees the Gardens purple, as if he were way off. And a spot is in the purple. The spot comes furiously towards him. Face of the black man. It leers. It smiles sweetly like a child's. Paul leaves Bona and darts back.   (p. 152)

Not just unwearied consciousness manifests itself in Paul here, on the verge of consummating his passion, but also a guilty conscience.

The "spot" may be associated with Lady MacBeth's anguished mental projection; it constitutes a reflex of the "dizzy . . . clot" that Paul had become in the grip of passion on the dance floor. The moment of apparent isolation and singularity—clot, spot—remains answerable to, and indeed insists on answering, the social context; somebody is always staring, if it is only the self.

The answer that Paul makes is intended to justify action, but it postpones action wantonly, and worse, it analyzes action with the enthusiasm and passion and lovingness that strictly belong to action itself. He turns away from Bona before she walks away from him. Actually, he turns away from himself as actor in favor of himself as explicator. Self-defense substitutes for living.

Paul's speech, Laurentian in its fervor and imagery, is an ironic prothalamion. Picking up the vocabulary of knowledge, it both enriches and confuses this theme of the story. *Know* takes on clear sexual meaning, and ontological values, in addition to its cognitive force. But it is impossible to tell whether Paul can keep the three senses of the word apart, or hold them together. The prophecy that "something beautiful is going to happen" is a weak one at best, hemmed in with obscurity (dusk is a dominant motif) and preoccupied with figures of isolation (petals instead of flowers, windows instead of houses):

I came back to tell you . . . [t]hat something beautiful is going to happen. That the Gardens are purple like a bed of roses would be at dusk. That I came into the Gardens, into life in the Gardens with one whom I did not know. That I danced with her, and did not know her. That I felt passion, contempt and passion for her whom I did not know. That I thought of her. That my thoughts were matches thrown into a dark window. And all the while the Gardens were purple like a bed of roses would be at dusk. I came back to tell you, brother, that white faces are petals of roses. That dark faces are petals of dusk. That I am going out and gather petals.[3] That I am going out and know her whom I brought here with me to these Gardens which are purple like a bed of roses would be at dusk.   (pp. 152–53)

The fact is that Paul does not know what *know* means or what it entails in commitment and consequences, any more than does Bob Stone in "Blood-Burning Moon": "He was going to see Louisa tonight, and love her. She was lovely—in her way. Nigger way. What way was that? Damned if he knew. Must know" (*Cane*, p. 60). The fact that "Bona was gone" (p. 153) when Paul went oustide to rejoin her is already adumbrated in his speech. The relationship between them has worked itself out entirely in his imagery, irrespective of his "thought." Paul is still presuming that thought, the explicit formulation of positions and purposes, will govern the matter of experience.

3. The carpe diem theme is evident here, but in a twisted and reduced form: he gathers petals, not rosebuds.

It is instructive to compare Bona and Paul's failure in the dance with the painstaking breakthrough Lawrence describes in "Frohnleichnam": "At last I can throw away world without end, and meet you / Unsheathed and naked and narrow and white / . . . / As we dance / Your eyes take all of me in as a communication; / As we dance / I see you, ah, in full! / Only to dance together in triumph of being together / . . . / Shining and touching, / Is heaven of our own, sheer with repudiation"; in *The Complete Poems of D. H. Lawrence*, ed. Vivian de Sola Pinto and F. Warren Roberts (New York: Viking Press, 1971), p. 210.

But he *says* more than he thinks, and confronts more than he thinks. His insistence on dusk suggests that, even as he proclaims his intention to the doorman, he is going into darkness, into hiding. And the way he changes the Gardens from crimson to purple *in his mind* gives a clear indication of a loss of zest in his construction of the relationship with Bona. Both colors in fact betray ambivalence: crimson may connote either shamelessness or supreme activity and vitality, and purple either penitence or passivity and lofty detachment. But in context supreme vitality and princeliness seem somewhat implausible; Paul plainly moves from (crimson) shamelessness to (purple) penitence. On this reading, Paul has not only literally but also psychologically turned away from Bona when he elects to declare himself to the black man (who may be seen as opening a psychic as well as an architectural door). If purple retains a trace of crimson chromatically, it is only as dusk retains a trace of daylight.

Paul had readily enough given over his "crimson" action for "purple" thought.[4] It is as though he finds it more important to be seen in the correct light than to be involved in a direct action. One interpretation of his choice may be racial. Paul is a "red-brown" black who moves without surface recognition or jarring among whites; Bona, neurasthenically white, is fascinated by him, but he seems to hold back protectively, ironically, and idealistically for something unblemished by the racial sting. In effect he ends up substituting the approval of the black doorman for the affection of the white girl, in a gesture that may imply male as well as race solidarity.

But we come closer to Paul's problem, and to the difficulties of *Cane*, if we see him as ultimately shying away from the very world of knowledge over which he makes such a to-do. He wants to know

4. I regard the symbolic color patterns as basically more telling and effective than the social codes of black and white races. For another view, the reader is referred to a provocative essay, "Jean Toomer and the South" by Charles T. Davis, in *Black Is the Color of the Cosmos* (New York: Garland, 1982). Special note should also be taken of "The Unity of Jean Toomer's *Cane*" by Catherine L. Innes, *CLA Journal* 15:306–22.

about Bona, or *about* himself. He does not wish knowledge frank
and direct, and pulls back from it even at the incidental level he is
offered. The doorman is a casual and probably indifferent bystander who would scarcely recognize him again except that Paul
makes such a point of thrusting himself into the other's range of
attention. (And what must this down-to-earth man have made of
Paul's highfalutin imagery and heated self-defense?) But Paul wants
the doorman to know *about* him and Bona. By extension we may
infer that he does not want to know Bona, only to know that he could
do so. In other words, he confines himself to the cognitive or specula-
tive, *safe* mode of knowledge, drawing back from its sensual or
transcendent modes, its dynamic, implicative, uncontrollable
reaches. There is something paradoxically unknowable, but not
undiscoverable, about knowledge in these ranges. That something,
like the introspective terms of his own blackness, Paul fears
exceedingly.

In a word, Paul fears what I have called intimacy, the unstinting
and unregretted encounter with the self and with the world. It is
worthwhile recalling that while he chides Bona for letting mental
concepts rule her, he is very much enamored of his own. Neither
Lawrence's unison with nature nor Gurdjieff-Ouspensky's attunement with the universe has any force in Paul's scheme, however
appealing both may have seemed to Toomer himself. Paul may have
grand thoughts ("white faces are petals of roses," "dark faces are
petals of dusk"), and he may even have the grand idea of making his
thoughts light up the world ("matches thrown in a dark window," "I
came back to tell you"); but he is above all devoted to safety. He will
be only as grand as safety allows. He tells the doorman rather than
Bona, the person dictated by logic and passion, the nature of his
grand thought.

It is ironic that Paul ends up outside, alone, in the dark: "When
he reached the spot where they had been standing, Bona was gone."
The situation is less intense than the end of "Esther," but it involves a
sort of cessation of a mode of being, an annihilation just the same.

Outside of the gaze of others, Paul hardly exists, although (but also *because*) their gaze is so threatening to him. He cannot make use of privacy and darkness as another, complementary mode of being, having different virtues from company and light. But even in his solitude, without prospect, the idea of himself as a spectacle persists. The "spot" where they were standing echoes the judgmental "spot" he had experienced in the Gardens. And of course Bona's absence constitutes a kind of judgment, a reason for feeling exposed.

Paul has protected himself with thought and finally has been seduced by thought into an unwarranted confidence in Bona and in himself. He goes for ultimate knowledge, but in such a way as to leave himself with ultimate solitude in a "spot" that does not even "leer" or "smile."

The shape of "Bona and Paul" is tripartite, with the gray formality and rigidity of the gymnasium yielding to the looser, hotter, more colorful but still formal activity of the Gardens, and that to the projected love encounter and its negatively defined character: it is not like the dancers, it is not like conventional knowledge and feeling. But in the terms of the story the pattern is meant to be triangular, with gymnasium and Gardens providing the base for an apical, transcendent movement going from confinement and negation into enlargement ("I am going out") and into illumination ("and know"). But the apex never forms. A dualistic world remains, with circumscribed, rote experience set against aspiration and intuition.

Through all the variety of *Cane*, from South to North, from canefield to classroom, from nature to citified culture and commerce, from dreamy transports to violence, we see recurring as a hallmark the triangle manqué, the dualism without apex. "Esther" offers an obvious illustration: the family store and the whorehouse are the base settings (showing the same surface contrast as the gymnasium and the Gardens, while being basically both rigid and repetitious), and Esther's vision of a redeemed life with Barlo constitutes the unreachable apex. But the void—half spiritual and half social—that remains for Paul when Bona and his fantasies evaporate on the empty sidewalk is made explicit in Esther's experience:

Like a somnambulist she wheels around and walks stiffly to the stairs. Down them. Jeers and hoots pelter bluntly upon her back. She steps out. There is no air, no street, and the town has completely disappeared.   (p. 48)[5]

Toomer deftly conveys the utter vacancy of someone who has committed, who has risked all in one act and lost. The question then arises in relation to both Esther and Paul: is their state of vacancy the product of their quest for intimacy, or the consequence of their pride? It is clear that neither Esther in relation to Barlo nor Paul in relation to Bona has left any room for reaction, let alone free action on the part of the person elected for special treatment. At the simplest level Barlo, by refusing to go with Esther, and Bona, by refusing to wait for Paul, assert a basic practical freedom. The problem of the vision their would-be partners would realize through them goes beyond that. Barlo and Bona may be incapable and even unworthy of sharing in the visions, but first and foremost they are unwilling to go along with whatever they understand of it. A kind of metaphysical justice applies here, that is, the right of each person to reject out of hand a situation or field in which another would assume control over his or her being. For it is control, not intimacy, that Paul and Esther pursue. They are victims of pride disguised as idealism. And Bona and Barlo are champions of independence in the guise of roistering and petulant flightiness.

In some respects, then, "Bona and Paul" and "Esther" serve as arenas for a clash between idealism and individuality. This clash runs through Toomer's work, and it is not surprising that he should have set "Bona and Paul," where the clash is so graphic, at the head of the ideal arrangement of *Cane*. In a prepublication letter to Waldo Frank, Toomer put down the design he saw informing his effort. "*Cane*'s design is a circle," he wrote, and went on to expatiate on the spiritual dimension:

5. One cannot but be struck with the similarity between this scene and Hester Prynne's experience on the scaffold in *The Scarlet Letter*: "She turned her eyes downward at the scarlet letter, and even touched it with her finger, to assure herself that the infant and the shame were real. Yes!—These were her realities,—all else had vanished!" The similarity between the names of the heroines requires no comment.

From the point of view of the spiritual entity behind the work, the curve really starts with Bona and Paul (awakening), plunges into Kabnis, emerges in Karintha, etc., swings upward into Theater and Box Seat, and ends (pauses) in Harvest Song.[6]

But what, we may fairly ask, does "Bona and Paul" awaken, or awaken to? And does not the pause entailed in "Harvest Song" serve to remind us that the circle is continuous and, once achieved, has neither beginning nor end? In Toomer's own iconography for the separate sections of *Cane*, no more than two segments (and these discontinuous, opposed, as it were at two and eight o'clock) are manifest. And in the individual stories the circle seems more an ideal figure than a reflection/representation of the experience at hand.

Similarly the composite effect of the stories and poems exhibits a conflict between the *condition of life* and the *consciousness of the world*. The "Harvest Song" (pp. 132–33) is supposed to stand at the culmination of the "spiritual" action, but in actuality it uses a powerful lyric consciousness to produce a paean to impotence and frustration. The speaker knows where the good resides, but lacks the means to attain it. The poem uses the central image of the harvest to suggest plenty, beneficence, fulfillment for the individual and for the community. This ideal state has evidently been prepared by a variety of laborers, though—as is characteristic of the harvest—in isolation from one another. Uncharacteristically, though, these individuals have no way of joining one another and of sharing the substance or spirit of their achievement. The individual effort that should promote the ideal state turns out, by its own insuperable individuality, to prevent it.

The speaker's case is typical. Exhausted from cradling his oats, he lacks the power to "bind" them, let alone to bind his labor to that of the other reapers. Accordingly he cannot even eat to recover strength: he breaks one grain between his teeth, and remains fam-

6. December 12, 1922, Toomer Collection, Box 3, Folder 6, No. 800. The titles are written by Toomer himself in the form recorded, that is, without the conventional punctuation.

ished. Frustrated at the level of function, he finds no recourse at the level of nature or being, for he is "a blind man who stares across the hills, seeking stack'd fields of other harvesters." The blindness, like the deafness he is soon to confess, is the perverse result of his very labors in the field: "my eyes are caked with dust." And he does not have the strength, in muscle or more importantly in will, to wash them clean:

> I fear to call. What should they hear me, and offer
> me their grain, oats, or wheat, or corn? . . . I fear
> I could not taste it. I fear knowledge of my hunger.

This is the same fear of intrinsic, as opposed to incidental, knowledge that Paul evinces. When the reaper imagines one of the other harvesters calling to him, he immediately undoes the good that might ensue: "It would be good to hear their songs . . . even though . . . the strangeness of their voices deafened me." Clearly this deafness would be in the nature of things, and not the accident of having ears "caked with dust."

Still, "Harvest Song" concludes with an address from the speaker to the other harvesters. What are we to make of this address in the context of the song's insistent privation, its melancholy verging on despair? The speaker is no less weary, his ears and eyes no less caked; the address, except in the realm of powerless desire the poem has articulated, would seem unearned and arbitrary. This difficulty diminishes if we think of the address as projected, not *actually* made. It is an address in the spirit of the speaker, and its importance lies in the change that takes place in the spirit, not of the world, but at least of the speaker. Though no one can hear his address, he is no longer in principle incommunicado; he is receptive if someone should address him, and willing to speak forth in case someone should be there.

Another oblique, nonverbal sign of progress also appears in the speaker's condition. Unable to go forward with the harvest, unable to use his voice ("My throat is dry") or to imagine that the voice of another would be anything but strange and deafening,[7] he begins in a nervous, self-consolatory way to beat his "palms, still soft, against the stubble of [his] harvesting." Without a voice, he has to make an instrument of his hands, and on the very emblem of his despair ("stubble") sends out a sound and a rhythm that might convey at least the fact that someone is there. The other harvesters do not directly hear him exhorting them to "beat [their] soft palms too"), but they will hear this stubble-drum, and may play on theirs. Thus *could* commence a communication that, while no rival to the African drums Toomer may be invoking, represents a major advance over caked eyes and parched throat. The fact that the palms are "still soft" may be less a realistic description than an emblem of retained sensitivity, artistic and human *touch*.

Given the tentative and tenuous gains against the deep privation of "Harvest Song," it is surprising that Toomer should have proffered this piece as a consummation of the circle in *Cane*. Indeed the poem seems to contain the Toomer pattern of the triangle manqué: the field with its cruel labor is one place, and the second, completing the base, would be the living quarters to which the harvesters give no thought and which presumably are cruel in their way; the apex of the triangle is the burden of the song—the unity of the harvesters and transcendence of their plight.

"Harvest Song" comes, in the standard publishing arrangement, immediately before "Bona and Paul," which seems as much a sequel as a foil to it. In only one respect does "Harvest Song" represent a clear advance over "Bona and Paul," and that is in the consciousness of the principal character. The harvester is without Paul's vanity and illusions; he has a grasp of the ideal that is founded in bitter experience and deep, sympathetic thought. But his condition is no whit improved over Paul's, for all his enhanced consciousness. And if consciousness is a state of grace, then we are faced with the difficulty

7. Here the problem of finding a voice in Afro-American literature emerges in a new dimension. The other harvesters reflect the speaker's fear that *his* voice will be counterproductive and unwelcome. The thought of breaking silence conjures up consequences that reinforce silence.

that Kabnis, who in Toomer's summary should be the harvester's antithesis, is more like his cousin-german. For Kabnis also appreciates the need to be one with the folk, the workers in the fields and the singers of sorrow songs, and he too finds communication with them impossible in fact and intolerable in essence. The harvester is the indigenous, spontaneous doubter to Kabnis's trained, artificial believer.

"Kabnis" represents consciousness as impotence and, in contrast to the Du Boisian position, as *dispossession*. The title character's consciousness indiscriminately attracts him to and cuts him off from his inner powers and dreams: "How my lips would sing for it [the South], my songs being the lips of its soul. Soul. Soul hell. There aint no such thing" (p. 158). It equally finds attraction and repulsion in the possibility of aid from external powers, divine or human. Kabnis begins to pray when he thinks lynchers are pursuing him, then cries, "hell, this aint no time for prayer" (p. 182). He experiences "a swift intuitive exchange of consciousness" with Lewis, the remarkably courageous and generous-hearted sociological researcher, and "has a sudden need to rush into the arms of this man. His eyes call, 'Brother.' And then a savage, cynical twist within him mocks his impulse and strengthens him to repulse Lewis" (pp. 191–92).

But the text scrupulously follows Kabnis's consciousness, with its swift, Byronic alternations, and ties Kabnis to Paul as well as to the harvester with the image of "a speck on a Georgia hillside," an "atom of dust in agony on a hillside" (p. 162). This could well be a description of the harvester in the field,[8] and it is strongly reminiscent of Paul's conception of himself as a grievously self-conscious and dislocated "spot." If consciousness is put at a premium in Toomer's scheme, it is consciousness of totality and unity, not of isolation. But

8. The atom recalls Democritus's philosophy, and tellingly so. But the figure in agony on the hillside also is reminiscent of Christ, in terms of suffering but not redemptive power. Further, Ouspensky's idea that we are part of a comprehensive whole, and suffer in our ignorance of that fact, may also be involved here. Alice Walker revises both Toomer's negativism and Ouspensky's intellectual methodism when Meridian finds ecstasy in the pit, overcoming a sense of being "a dot, a speck in creation" (p. 50).

besides the fact that Kabnis's consciousness fights itself, it betrays an intrinsic incapacity for totality; as Lewis declares, "Life has already told [Kabnis] more than he is capable of knowing. It has given him in excess of what he can receive" (p. 200).

What we are faced with here is of critical importance to the reading of *Cane* and Toomer. The pervasive opposition between idealism and individualism comes to a head, in that even the willing and devoted individual—Kabnis or Paul or the harvester—must from a defect of nature fail the more profoundly as he gets a better line on the ideal. As a whole *Cane* (in its conventional order) shows an increasing development of consciousness from the early to the late pieces. But it shows no development *within* the individual pieces, within the individual actors. The ideal remains as far as ever from the individual, although knowledge of it becomes more explicit and more urgent. The reader, or the occasional narrator of the separate pieces, has the only chance of growth the volume offers, but here again it means a growth of consciousness, with the real condition of things unaffected. Only Avey has the kind of extended, reflective experience that would make a matrix for growth. And she is stubbornly averse to change. That she sleeps while the narrator expounds on her need for "a larger life" and exhorts her to "build up an inner life" is symptomatic (pp. 86, 87).

Despite the fact that Toomer seemed to put "Kabnis" at the low point of the text ("plunges into Kabnis, emerges in Karintha"), he writes an exceptional imagery of sunrise into the conclusion of the story. As a rule, let us recall, there is a diminishment of color and of light as the action advances in the several pieces. But in "Kabnis" the night is called pregnant and the daybreak is presented as a birth:

The sun arises. Gold-glowing child, it steps into the sky and sends a birth-song slanting down gray dust streets and sleepy windows of the southern town. (p. 239)

This is strikingly different from the "weird dawn or some ungodly awakening" (p. 53) that occurs in "Blood-Burning Moon," and has a tonal appeal of its own. But in the larger context of the story and of

Cane, it is doubtful that anything abiding has been born. Toomer is projecting the usual insubstantial apex of the triangle whose base is made up of (a) the cabin schoolroom of Kabnis's early experience and (b) the blacksmith's shop into which he enters upon his unhappy resignation from teaching.

The repressive educational system needs little elaboration; Hanby demands attendance at church and dictates the dress, speech, and social habits of his teachers. But the blacksmith's shop is supposed to represent a redemption from Hanby's world, and its deficiencies may need to be spelled out. First, Hanby holds sway there too; he comes in and as completely and correctly assumes Kabnis's obedience as he would on his own grounds: "'You will see that it is fixed for me.'. . . And knowing that Kabnis will follow . . ." (p. 203). And second, the blacksmith's shop is very much part of the system where "th white folks get th boll; th niggers get th stalk" (p. 171). Working for nothing for Mr. Ramsay is more than a way for Halsey, the owner, to mitigate the problem Kabnis has fixing the hatchet; it also reaffirms the age-old subjection of black to white: "Yer daddy," says the indulgent Mr. Ramsay, "was a good un before y" (p. 202).

We should recall, too, that the Hole, where something special takes place between Carrie Kate and Father John, is not constituted as anything more than a safe venue "on those occasions when [Halsey] spices up the life of the small town" for himself and his friends (p. 195). Every intimation of something special—between Lewis and Carrie Kate, between Carrie Kate and Father John, between Kabnis and Lewis—is short-lived, indeed short-circuited in the story. The status of Father John bears out the pattern of defeated hope. He manages to keep alive, but he remains in a state of quasi-hibernation, with neither the activity nor the articulation of Ellison's invisible man.

The departure of Lewis from the workshop and from the story is an important index to the failure of *Cane* to sustain either individualism or idealism. Lewis is the person who consistently inspires the sense of intimacy—he is open to other people and ideas, and other people, including the practical-minded Halsey, are impelled to open themselves to him. He is a vehicle of intimacy, a personal and professional breaker-through of barriers and breaker-down of inert forms. What Kabnis says he wants, namely deep engagement and unstinting, lucid participation, Lewis enjoys by an apparent impulse of his nature. Where Kabnis shrinks from the intensity of nature, of social obligation, and of religious conviction, Lewis invites intensity. He seems to transcend the dualism that he sees paralyzing Kabnis: "'Cant hold them, can you? Master; slave. Soil; and the overarching heavens. Dusk; dawn. They fight and bastardize you'" (p. 218).

But the Toomer pattern of fading and cooling from vigorous to wan, from bright to pale, overtakes even this remarkable man. The party in the Hole, like the dance at Crimson Gardens in "Bona and Paul," affords a simulacrum of freedom to the other characters, but it proves, for Kabnis as for Paul, an irritant. For Lewis, who complicates our vision of Kabnis and who is described as Kabnis's virtual alter ego ("what a stronger Kabnis might have been" p. 189), it proves a sad revelation. He is above the fleeting intimacy of sex ("Ralph Kabnis gets satisfied that way?" p. 217), but a form for expressing his capacity for intimacy eludes him. As the party progresses, though first Stella and then Halsey confess their souls to him because "theres somethin" to him "th others aint got" (p. 219), he continues to be opposed by Kabnis, and thus continues to be a bit apart.

The indication that Kabnis and Lewis are versions of each other further leads to the inference that Kabnis expresses a latent side or at least a latent potentiality in Lewis. And indeed the weakness that has had no chance to appear in Lewis's cameo appearances earlier in the story now begins to show up in this prolonged encounter. He seems unable to keep up his side of the scene of confidence, with Stella or with Halsey; interruptions jostle him off stride, and he falls first into silence, then into discomfiture and disconnection:

Lewis finds himself completely cut out. The glowing within him subsides. It is followed by a dead chill. Kabnis, Carrie, Stella, Halsey, Cora, the old man, the cellar, and the work-shop, the southern town descend upon him. Their pain is too intense. He cannot stand it. He bolts from the table. Leaps up the stairs. Plunges through the work-shop and out into the night. (p. 226)

Lewis in fact gives special resonance to Chidi Ikonné's judgment that "Kabnis" embodies an "allegorical descent of the Negro into himself with a view to understanding and affirming the black aspect of his self."[9] Lewis is the one who brings the sense of *purpose* to the South and to the Hole, while Kabnis brings a sense of need and desperation (even his attack on Father John is a recoil from the hope, which Halsey notes, that the old man would proffer some ultimate word). But Lewis cannot stand it, and Kabnis can neither stand nor understand the situation.

Clearly anticipating a key Ellisonian motif, Toomer speaks of "Kabnis" as "plunging," and it is striking that he applies the same term to Lewis. The night Lewis plunges into is not pregnant, but blank. It is a poignant moment, for the possibility of intimacy is departing with him. The Hole may have enabled people to open up to Lewis, but it also circumscribed the degree and quality of the relationship that might ensue. Lewis is the only character in *Cane* who can boast, on both personal and professional levels, the capacity for expanded consciousness that Toomer regarded as indispensable for human fulfillment. And Lewis "cannot stand it." He illustrates an underlying problem of *Cane* as a whole, the absence of a suitable medium for *substantiating* Toomer's vision. The abrupt and unfocused solitude with which Lewis's part in the story concludes may, in fact, be used to measure the development of a capacious solitude in later Afro-American writing. Lewis, let us note, plunges upward out of the Hole, yet Ellison's Jack-the-Bear will plunge downward into his. Lewis plunges out of the story because of a fear of staying in it, but Jack-the-Bear is afraid of plunging out of history. Lewis's plunge marks an end; this stands in contrast to Jack-the-Bear's, in that the latter proves analytical, resilient, and purposive (though not decisive) in his state of trial.

I have suggested that *Cane* was a work ahead of its time. Toomer's obvious conception of intimacy as a goal, a necessity for black freedom, anticipates by many decades the development of black literature in the 1970s and 1980s. But this virtue has its defects.

9. Chidi Ikonné, *From Du Bois to Van Vechten: The Early New Negro Literature, 1903 to 1926* (Westport, Conn.: Greenwood Press, 1981), p. 136.

The environment of black experience did not furnish the most favorable matrix for Toomer's ideal, and the forms of contemporary literary output, even during the upsurge of the Harlem Renaissance, did not offer any answerable style. The fact is that the separate, staccato bursts of *Cane* put too high a demand on moments or spasms of engagement to yield lucid and permanent values. By contrast, in *The Prelude* Wordsworth painfully builds up moment on moment into what is even then a surprising revelation on Snowdon; and Tennyson, whose *In Memoriam* has about it more of Toomer's refined, melancholic, and spasmodic yearning, stubbornly sticks with the issue until relief and revelation are vouchsafed him.

Toomer's convulsive approach does not lend itself to the necessary unfolding and evolution into the fullness of being he himself espoused. We can note that in the writing of Gurdjieff and Ouspensky, who along with the new genius D. H. Lawrence had such an impact on Toomer, there is ample emphasis on the development of the individual within the realization of "Great Nature." But in his absorption with the total good Toomer makes no room for individual development. He seemed, in fact, more intent on the "terrifying and liberating" notion that it was his duty to ignore the world and "prepare [himself] in order to help God."[10]

Gurdjieff and Ouspensky, while promoting "cosmic consciousness" and "unity with the all," were also clearly promoting *themselves*, not commercially but metaphysically. Ouspensky's *Tertium Organum* actually ends with the statement that "the meaning of life is in eternal search."[11] Toomer, however, seems to have become preoccupied with the end state, and not with the search. As James

10. Quoted in James Webb, *The Harmonious Circle*; subsequent references to Webb appear in the text.

11. Ouspensky was a follower whom Gurdjieff is said to have made singular efforts to bring into his fold, and also a major figure in his own right. Gurdjieff's *All and Everything* is for the noninitiate harder reading than Ouspensky's *Tertium Organum* or *A New Model of the Universe*. But all three agree on the basic complementary relation between the individual and the all. To "work on oneself" was essential. Ouspensky favors the term *psychology*. And the commentators are emphatic about the fulfillment of the individual in the Gurdjieff-Ouspensky cosmic

Webb points out, Toomer disappeared "into the Work" (*Harmonious Circle*, p. 273). He renounced even the spasms or flashes of art that had accumulated into *Cane*, complaining of "lopsided specialists" and condemning art and literature for failing "to do anything" for their practitioners. Finally he reduced art to a "talent" for "turning out things that got reviews."[12] He would begin in 1938 to write his story "From Exile into Being," with its ominous assumption of commitment to a definite attainment. The fame he won with *Cane* gave him a momentary sense of a "higher consciousness," of the "reality of a higher experience," but he flagged in that conviction:

Writing, real writing [he concluded] . . . presupposed the possession of the very things I knew I lacked, namely self-purity, self-unification, self-development. I wasn't fit to write.   (*Harmonious Circle*, p. 275)

In short, the impatience with time and the slow uncertain search that is betrayed in every piece of *Cane* overtook Jean Toomer in his personal life,[13] where he recapitulated the tragedy of knowing about intimacy without knowing it. He left mere literature for "the world of pure being," and though he would "again see, sense, feel, understand the world from the point of view of the literary artist" (*Harmonious Circle*, p. 343), the world never after *Cane* saw him in that light.

Falling short of intimacy, *Cane* everywhere slips into its antecedents. "Kabnis" begins and ends in solitude, and it hardly matters that the initial paranoid solitude of the cabin stands in such contrast to the postexhaustion peace and openness of the final scene of

---

scheme. It should be noted that individualism was at odds with democracy for Ouspensky—that is, not every individual was eligible to develop cosmic consciousness: "a new race CONSCIOUS OF ITSELF will judge the old races." (*Tertium Organum*, rev. trans. by E. Kadloubovsky and the author [New York: Knopf, 1981], p. 278).

12. In the outline for his unfinished autobiography, Toomer Collection, Box 14, Folder 1, p. 63.

13. A. R. Orage, Toomer's principal guide in the Gurdjieff-Ouspensky school of vision, was to chide him with failing to realize that "for a long time our *chief* concern is to listen, to learn to listen, as G[urdjieff] used to say" (*Harmonious Circle*, p. 339).

dawn.[14] For the scene and its lineaments are transitory, accidental. Solitude also marks the lives of Fern and Becky, and it is the state of the speaker in "Harvest Song" as well as the speaker in "Song of the Son." In the latter case, the solitude stands out sharply against the communal import of the song. The speaker sounds like the Wordsworth of "She Dwelt among the Untrodden Ways" when he speaks of

> An everlasting song, a singing tree,
> Caroling softly souls of slavery,
> What they were, and what they are *to me*.

> (p. 21, italics added)

In all cases, we see not a solitude pregnant with the promise of development that Hurston and Wright portray, but an inert and pathetic solitude. The presence of cases of self-veiling and even self-cancellation in *Cane* is not then surprising. Esther provides the outstanding example, but John in "Theater" is her counterpart. Neither can cope in the no-man's-land of the "dictie" black person, that is, one with a marked infusion of white blood. John crushes himself inside while Esther dashes herself to despair in the chasm of her Barlo fantasy.

Cane goes further than to show, in stories like "Esther" and "Avey" and "Bona and Paul," that ideas of intimacy are illusory, and sometimes devastatingly so. It shows intimacy as frightful. In "Box Seat" Muriel quails at the prospect of intimacy, whether she is dealing with a real-life Dan Moore, her almost-lover, or with a theatrical dwarf who boldly thrusts across the confines of the stage toward her. Muriel's response reflects an uninspected impulse toward self-preservation in someone too conventional and conservative to see change as less than a threat.

Kabnis's dread of intimacy is more lucid, and comes so heavily laced with irony and aggressive pessimism that it seems all but chosen. He deliberately uproots his deepest religious susceptibility,

---

14. In some respects it resembles a postcoital condition, with all the intimations of sexuality in the Hole. But it is doubtful whether Kabnis has participated that far. The robe he dons makes him sacerdotal, and as Stella says to Lewis, Kabnis tends to "take it out in talking." For sure he does a deal of talking in the Hole.

his deepest aesthetic and social sensitivity, and his deepest human yearning. He dreads being deceived by his feelings, or exposed to unknown implications and consequences because of them. For Kabnis intimacy may entail betrayal or violation.

This is an attitude that Toomer bequeaths to black literature, and it may be his point of greatest impact on the tradition. Though we treat Sula as a boldly free person who exposes the dry rot of family ties and the dreary inertia of social custom, there is a level at which she is behaving with the dreary, rotten vindictiveness of a woman scorned. She has committed and opened herself to her "Ajax," and when she discovers that he is nothing but a traveling man named A. Jacks, it produces a virulent reaction on her mind. As with the classical Ajax and Cassandra,[15] the hero's abuse spurs Sula to memorable action, whereas she has been relatively passive, even docile, before. It does not seem unjustified to infer that the betrayal of intimacy, indeed the discovery that her intimacy with Ajax was based on illusion, has much to do with her unconventionality.

But it is James Baldwin's late novel *If Beale Street Could Talk* that gives the most graphic portrayal of the dread of intimacy. The work, a quasi-detective story on the surface, is divided into two parts, the first entitled "Troubled about My Soul," and the second, disproportionately short one, entitled "Zion." By virtue of such a structure Baldwin suggests an introspective, even a spiritual bearing in the face of an action that is heavily social, with its exposé of police malice and its outcry against the destructive misery of the black and Puerto Rican poor.

But Baldwin earns his spiritual emphasis. Virtually every significant action in the text, except the rape which is falsely attributed to Fonny, the male protagonist, arises from an engagement of souls between two people. These engagements may be hostile, as is that between Fonny and the white policeman, Bell, who feels his power and life assumptions threatened by Fonny, and who accordingly contrives to pin the rape on Fonny.

15. Needless to say, Morrison's shallow and irreverent Ajax is to be associated not with the great and tragic Telamonian, but with Ajax the Lesser.

The title of the second section, "Zion," suggesting recovery from the troubles of the soul and attainment of spiritual freedom, may be somewhat ironic. It seems evident that Fonny will be exonerated, on the grounds that (1) the damning lineup was loaded against him (he was the only black man and the culprit was very dark in hue), and (2) the victim cannot maintain her complaint, having at once lost her baby and her mind. But if we dwell a moment on this positive development, it gives rise to problems. The exoneration pivots on a technicality, and sustains itself on the destruction of another's spirit. The victim of the rape has looked into the same pit and mirror of vulnerability and violation as Fonny, and has been unable to stand it. She is the second minor character, Fonny's friend Daniel being the other, who comes too close to human cruelty, violation, and degradation. Whereas Fonny and the female narrator, Tish, prove that familiar, pedestrian life precludes ecstasy, Señora Sanchez (the rape victim) and Daniel find that the familiar preserves them from intimacy with horror.

The structure of the text, with a slow, tortured unfolding of social and spiritual distress giving way to a swift, revelatory brightness, tempts us to think of Fonny and Tish as looking into the pit of horror and, like the poet in Blake's *Marriage of Heaven and Hell*, emerging not just unscathed but with a vision of heaven.

In point of fact, though, Tish does not transcend horror, but only represses it, and the horror she knows, also connected with the white policeman, Bell, springs spontaneously from within her. As the scene occurs at the very end of "Troubled about My Soul," its shadow falls starkly into "Zion." Tish, who is portrayed as the bearer of grace and hope for the future—the novel ends with her going into childbirth—is walking home with a bagful of art supplies she has had to shoplift for Fonny to go on with his creative work. At sight of Bell walking toward her, she panics; his enmity toward herself and Fonny has been established, and she is an easy target with her stolen goods. But her reaction goes far deeper than dread of detection. The chance encounter, during which Bell is actually insinuatingly polite and oddly conciliatory, catches her with her formal defenses down and so comes home to her spirit. The evidence of a radical departure from all familiar ways is also the symbol of intimacy in the scene: she looks into Bell's eyes.

This may have been the very first time I ever really looked into a white man's eyes. It stopped me, I stood still. It was not like looking into a man's eyes. It was like nothing I knew, and—therefore—it was very powerful. It was seduction which contained the promise of rape. It was rape which promised debasement and revenge: on both sides. I wanted to get close to him, to enter into him, to open up that face and change it and destroy it, descend into the slime with him. Then, we would both be free: I could almost hear the singing.

. . . I was suddenly his: a desolation entered me which I had never felt before. I watched his eyes, his moist boyish despairing lips, and felt his sex stiffening against me.

"I ain't a bad guy," he said. "Tell your friend. You ain't got to be afraid of me."

"I'm not afraid," I said. "I'll tell him. Thanks." . . .

I never told Fonny about it. I couldn't. I blotted it out of my mind.

Baldwin has rarely written more trenchantly than here. Every phrase leaps, every phrase bites in. It is an apocalyptic scene, with all conventions of behavior, thought, and feeling briefly torn away. But it is a negative apocalypse, containing only the freedom of desolation. Baldwin draws on two of the most powerful motifs of the black tradition, freedom and singing, and discovers an association, if not an identification, with "slime" and "debasement" and revenge. The evil cop and the woman of grace are mirrored in each other's eyes, in each other's soul. The intimacy of the scene goes beyond race and beyond sociology. It also goes beyond escape, though Tish claims to have blotted it out of her mind. All she does is bottle it up in her mind. She cannot face what she has seen any more than Esther and Sula can. But where the dread of Esther and Sula stems from exposure of their fantasies, with Tish it stems from exposure of her innermost reality. The ultimate intimacy of the scene is with the self, and therein lies its ultimate dread.

In *Beale Street* intimacy-as-dread occurs on the personal level and under accidental conditions. Ishmael Reed's *Mumbo Jumbo* raises the experience of intimacy-as-dread to a national scale, with an ultraconservative Atonist Society striving in vain to contain the spirit of Jes Grew, an outbreak of happiness, unison, and love. Evidently a characterization of the innovative energy of the Harlem Renaissance, Jes Grew is an inexplicable, irresistible, and unpredictable eruption of fellow feeling, well-being, and beneficent power in direct human experience. The Atonists essentially represent Western, and more specifically WASP culture, which Reed portrays as not only repressive but repressed. The Atonist order can be traced back to the hyperorganized Urizen of Blake's prophecies, while correspondingly Jes Grew would be analogous to the ebullient figure of Orc, *but with an admixture of the creative figure* Los. Reed intimates that the Atonists represent a perversion of the true fundamental order of creation, Jes Grew, and that this perversion results not only from vain possessiveness but also from a fear of Jes Grew's creative abundance. Their "order" controls not life, but their own incapacity for living.

The action of the novel centers on an outbreak of Jes Grew in the 1920s (we may note Reed's sense of the out-of-the-blue origin of the Harlem Renaissance). The white power structure finds that it "can't . . . protective-reaction the dad-blamed thing." Statistical reports of the thousands and tens of thousands overcome by the "anti-plague" of Jes Grew, as it moves from south to north, amusingly punctuate the text. Jes Grew is taking over the country and reconstituting it. The Constitution that Ellison invoked is being transcended in Reed by a mysterious, infectious nature.

Two problems arise in this high-spirited satire. First, Jes Grew is threatening to be systemwide without being in any way systematic. In other words, while it cannot be prevented, it also cannot be sustained. And second, it has no real immediate embodiment or force the way Reed presents it, but comes as something described and feared from afar. In fact the most prominent characters are pensive and tentative, and, in the case of Earline and Berbelang, more confused and sorrowful than before Jes Grew began to spread. The separate slayings of Abdul and Berbelang by conservative

forces bode ill for any sustained realization of Jes Grew. Both problems could find a solution in PaPa LaBas. On the face of things he has
the knowledge and power to articulate the essence of Jes Grew and
to give it the permanence of a "text." He is thus able to add a sense of
conviction and propriety to what are only helpless reactions—of
submission or defiance—to Jes Grew.

But Papa LaBas is himself repressed and somewhat insular. His
importance is not reflected in his role in the text; in fact, Abdul, who
is merrily satirized and unceremoniously despatched early in the
action, plays a more crucial role than he. And Abdul's role is a
negative one. He has been entrusted with a Sacred Book that is
supposed to establish the roots of the Knights Templar, the militant
arm of the Atonist order, in ancient black lore; and it emerges that,
after translating this Book into the language of the street and failing
to find a publisher for it, he has decided to burn the Book (and the
translation is lost in the mail). These are somewhat heavy-handed
contrivances, enough so even to bring the spread of Jes Grew to a
halt. For the Book turns out to be the text of Jes Grew, which "sensed
the ashes of its writings, its litany and just withered up and died"
(p. 233).

By insisting that Jes Grew cannot survive without a central
orthodox text, Reed creates a major internal conflict in *Mumbo
Jumbo*. On the one hand Jes Grew appears as a spontaneous manifestation, an outburst of life; on the other it emerges as a matter of
faith, perhaps even credulity toward a body of language. We may
complain that Abdul does not seem a likely person to be entrusted
with the Book, or a good judge of whether it shows black people in a
desirable light; someone who cannot make that judgment until after
completing and mailing out a translation and then rereading the
original does not inspire much confidence. But the problem goes
deeper yet. *Mumbo Jumbo* itself keeps Jes Grew at arm's length. It is
not about Jes Grew, but about its opponents and its theorists. The
text itself shies away from the intimacy which its purported subject
matter promises. The Atonist opposition, who after all may be just
trying to suppress their origins in the Book that Jes Grew brings to

life, are not the only ones in dread of Jes Grew. *Mumbo Jumbo* itself evinces a measure of dread before life, cutting it off as wantonly as it does Abdul Sufi Hamid.

In effect, Reed is baffled and divided between a keen delight in the myriad independent manifestations of life and a desire for some monolithic and fail-safe authority. He is so concerned with the apocalyptic possibilities of Jes Grew that he cannot fit it to daily life, or daily life to it. This denial is maintained in the face of the eager desire of people, or at least poets (represented in Nathan Brown), to catch Jes Grew, and maintained further in the face of the text's own illustration of Jes Grew from the homeliest forms of human expressiveness: "people who put wax paper over combs and breathe through them." The advice to "Open-Up-To-Right-Here," to "your own experience," for access to Jes Grew goes directly counter to the text's insistence on the Text. Primacy is given to the word by the text of *Mumbo Jumbo*, even while its matter originates in, feeds on, and tries to identify with the primacy of fullness and freedom and joy of experience.

It is no wonder that some of the merriest scenes of *Mumbo Jumbo* have a startling, even intrusive, brevity. For merriment is more convenient than intrinsic to the text, its tool rather than its goal, which remains (in the definitive absence of the Jes Grew text and given the arbitrary manifestations of Jes Grew) obscure at best.

The arrival of the Reverend Mr. Jefferson to retrieve his "prodigal son" from the wicked life of New York City is hilarious but immaterial. The sudden influence that Erzulie, Haitian goddess of love, exerts on Earline to make her forget the rank killing of her beloved Berbelang reinforces the mystery and authority of Jes Grew, but at the cost of the plausibility of human experience. It is too easy to lug Woodrow Wilson Jefferson out of the text, too easy to set aside Earline's supposed feelings for Berbelang. At the level of personal experience and value, which Jes Grew is touted to enhance, the text gives way to the needs of an abstract, formal design and sacrifices its individual lines.

We must recognize, of course, that insofar as inconsistency puts the reader off stride and at a disadvantage, Reed may be practicing it on purpose. More, he may be doing it *of necessity*, in that he is revising our positions, reintroducing satire to a literary and social establishment so monotonous and earnest in its claims of advanced thinking and commitment to candor and freedom. But Reed does not content himself with using ridicule and parody to keep us from taking our sacred cows and shibboleths too seriously. He ends up preventing us from taking anything seriously—including his text. For the satirist must have, along with some Diogenes, some Archimedes in his makeup. In other words, he needs, along with the lonely will to demand true honesty everywhere and to expose its absence, a position from which he can employ his fulcrum to tilt the skewed world back into place.

Ostensibly that fulcrum for Reed is Jes Grew; it provides the position on which he stands and on which we must take him seriously. He undermines this position, however, like someone more given to the act than to the value of undermining. One source of the undermining of Jes Grew has already appeared in the discussion of Abdul Sufi Hamid. Another can be recognized in the late episode in which PaPa LaBas (whose name fuses the Voodoo god Legba with the French for "down below," with suggestions of the underworld and in particular of Joris Karl Huysmans's decadent novel, *La-Bas*) ceremoniously sends his acolyte, T Malice (a lesser Voodoo god),[16] for "the Book." The object is to "prove . . . that the Book is real" (p. 224). What ensues is an elaborate ritual, a "gorgeous display" that recapitulates, in Chinese box fashion, the stages of history from the degraded present to the time of pristine perfection. We see first an iron box, then a bronze box, then (as Reed outdoes the tradition) a sycamore and an ebony and an ivory box, "then silver and finally gold and then . . . empty!!" (p. 224).

It is possible to argue that Reed is mocking the clichés and encrustation of tradition, showing that the forms that sustain the tradition contain nothing, but are everything in themselves. Possibly he is making fun of the boxes, such as the invisible man's or the

16. The Haitian section of Zora Neale Hurston's *Tell My Horse* is arresting on Voodoo. The classic study of the subject is Maya Deren's *Divine Horseman: Voodoo Gods of Haiti* (New York: Chelsea House, 1970).

ex-colored man's, that dot the Afro-American literary tradition, with
the imputation that they are rhetorical vacuities. But he would appear to have chosen an odd instrument for the purpose. It is his own
nontraditional spirit of Jes Grew that ends up "empty!!" And it is his
text that ends up in self-division, as the episode of the historical
Chinese box is sharply at odds with the story of Abdul Sufi Hamid's
destroying the sole original text and the U.S. Postal Service's losing
the sole translation. The upshot is that the inspiriting vision of Jes
Grew—of a universal unity based not on tyranny or hyperrational
order but on the deepest upwelling of affection, sympathy, and
joy—simply fades away. Reed himself had ominously written, in the
prologue to *Mumbo Jumbo*: "Perhaps . . . Jes Grew will evaporate as
quickly as it appeared again broken-hearted and double-crossed"
(section 1).

None of the foregoing analysis is meant to "deconstruct"
Mumbo Jumbo or to imply doubts about Reed's importance in
Afro-American and American literature. He has a distinctive vision,
a distinctive style, and a distinctive range. That is much to say. But his
work is affected by an instinct of irresolution or at least by the
mocker's impulse to play on the moment, with the larger patterns
and principles of the situation suffering accordingly. Jes Grew allows Reed to play havoc with various pet aversions, but when the
time comes for the spirit of Jes Grew to stand on its own, and
supersede its unworthy rivals and enemies, an emptiness ensues.
Reed is subtler, more evocative than LeRoi Jones in calling for a
fresh spirit and exposing the ugliness of the mechanical contraptions
that pass for values in American society. His Atonists bear comparison with Blake's Urizen; his Jes Grew is livelier and more infectious
than anything Blake proposes for the good. Yet Reed himself seems
to resist the infection of the good, immunized perhaps by his preoccupation with outdoing the bad. That is a costly safety.

Reed, like Baldwin or Morrison (in a work such as *Sula*), seems
acutely aware of intimacy as a possibility, without really having
access to it. Perhaps we should not expect the case to be otherwise.
Intimacy, given its rigors and its indifference to the mere shibboleths

of race (even Reed implies that the Sacred Book might have joined Jes Grew and the Atonist at the root), may have come as a singular, not a regular, episode in the urgent unfolding of black literature. Recent texts may more accurately be said to pick up the stage of kinship than that of intimacy. But not with entire accuracy. For the terms of kinship have clearly developed beyond the fine work of Michael Harper. It is proper to ask: after intimacy, what? If only in rough forecast, the shape of an answer is already suggesting itself in the vigorous plenty of recent Afro-American literature.

7

*The Search for New
Meaning in Recent Black
Fiction*

> teach me to survive my
> momma
> . . . . .
> help me
> turn the face of history
> *to your face*.

June Jordan

IF mere weather betrays our most sophisti-
cated instruments, one must be gingerly in forecasting literature. The
freedom of art is tickled by the orderliness of criticism, and might be
moved to outright hilarity where the latter undertook to call art's
future turns. Still, there are signs that point to a new concern crystal-
lizing in Afro-American literature. Among the most prominent of
those signs is the following: more and more we find brought into a
decidedly modern setting the forms and values of the historical past,
including the season of slavery. At the same time, no effort is made to
approximate the historical novel, in the sense that Margaret Walker's
Jubilee or even the derivative *Roots*, by Alex Haley, is historical.
History provides an impetus rather than a matrix for current black
writing.

Two works especially typify the new development: John Edgar
Wideman's *Damballah* and David Bradley's *Chaneysville Incident*.

Perhaps the most apt term to describe what they are about would be *immersion*. This term has already acquired a history in Afro-American letters, and it is proper to indicate the influence of that history on my thinking here. Nathan Scott speaks tellingly of an intense degree of "immersion in all the concrete materialities of Negro life." H. L. Gates, Jr., goes further; he sees immersion not just as a fact but as a salient "trope" in Henry Dumas's *Jonoah and the Green Stone* and in Ralph Ellison's *Invisible Man*. Gates glosses *immersion* as a "return to a 'pre-formal' state," with a potential effect of "rebirth and regeneration."[1] In turn, Robert B. Stepto in his ground-breaking study *From Behind the Veil* carries the concept of immersion to another order of magnitude.

In Stepto's hands the local episode of "immersion" is shown to have many forms, and to occur in even the earliest Afro-American works with a kind of radical force. In other words, immersion takes on the status of a spontaneous motif in the development of Afro-American literature, and there results a "cultural immersion ritual."[2] Stepto further pairs immersion with an independent motif of ascent, so that the action of recovery in Afro-American literature is not left dependent on a mere spontaneous buoyancy (sinking followed by rising), but comes forth as a distinct, peculiar drive. He puts the case that immersion may have seen its day, and that it has been superseded in interest and force by other phenomena in Afro-American literature.

To what Stepto has so cogently set forth I would only append the comment that if immersion has run its course in one guise, it is only to recreate itself in another. For a degree of deliberateness, of willfulness even, has entered into the occurrence of immersion in

1. Nathan Scott, "The Dark and Haunted Tower of Richard Wright," in *Black Expression: Essays by and about Black Americans in the Creative Arts*, ed. Addison Gayle, Jr. (New York: Weybright & Talley, 1969), p. 298. The quotations from H. L. Gates, Jr., are taken from a commentary, as yet unpublished, on *Jonoah and the Green Stone*.

2. Robert B. Stepto, *From Behind the Veil: A Study of Afro-American Narrative* (Urbana: University of Illinois Press, 1979).

recent Afro-American writing. This is a strain of immersion that Stepto was only in a position to identify in the case of Du Bois, with his analytical, forensic, volitional engagement with the fullness of black experience. It so happens, though, that this lonely instance has suddenly acquired much company.

The new works of *re*immersion, as that may be an apt term, make no bones about their business, which is black experience. Let us pause and stress that a real difference exists between what is called "*the* black experience," which is dogmatic and political, and what is involved here, namely "black experience," which is merely axiomatic and comprehensive. In the works in question, in the bearing of black literature today, "black experience" comes to the fore, without apology, without special pleading, without threat, without inhibition from without or within.

The quality of immersion is described by Ellison in *Shadow and Act*: "The art of writing requires a constant plunging back into the shadows of the past, where time hovers ghostlike" (p. xv). In his own right Ellison is more concerned with literary than with racial-historical "plunging." His is a cautious and limited plunge,[3] though he needs yield to no one when it comes to mastery of black doings and sufferings. One is struck by the way Ellison takes considerable pains in "The World and the Jug" to distinguish himself from Richard Wright; it seems ironic that he ends up looking very much like Wright in the matter of avoiding *immersion* in the phenomena of black life. The picaresque mode of *Invisible Man* enables the protagonist to see much, but it also prevents him from absorbing let alone being absorbed into much—until his "plunge," which involves less immer-

---

3. We can fruitfully compare Ellison's stance with the one D. H. Lawrence takes in "Manifesto" (*Complete Poems*, ed. Vivian de Sola Pinto and F. Warren Roberts [New York: Viking Press, 1971], p. 266):

> Plunging as I have done, over, over the brink
> I have dropped at last headlong into nought, plunging upon
>   sheer hard extinction;
> I have come, as it were, not to know,
> died, as it were; ceased from knowing; surpassed myself.
> What can I say more, except that I know what it is to surpass myself?

sion than hibernation, that is, suspension of activity and relationship rather than complete involvement. By contrast Janie goes deeper and deeper into black life in *Their Eyes Were Watching God*: from a largely white environment during her grandmother's service to a largely black society in her first marriage and a wholly black society (but with white echoes and pretensions) in her second, and on to "De Muck," unadulterated and unadorned black society in her third. Richard Wright exceeds even Ellison's avoidance of immersion. Wright, in *Black Boy*, flees from what Ellison calls "the shadows of the past," leaving only a bleak account of his motivation:

After . . . the habit of reflection had been born in me, I used to mull over the strange absence of real kindness in Negroes, how unstable was our tenderness, how lacking in genuine passion we were, how void of great hope, how timid our joy, how bare our traditions, how hollow our memories, how lacking we were in those intangible sentiments that bind man to man and how shallow was even our despair. After I had learned other ways of life . . . I saw that what had been taken for our emotional strength was our negative confusions, our flights, our fears, our frenzy under pressure. (p. 45)

Ellison talks immersion, Wright escape; but Ellison's positive affinity for Melville and Dostoevski and Hemingway proves as much a barrier to actual black immersion[4] as Wright's dubiety and disaffection.

In *Damballah* Wideman shows all the rancor and folly and grief and confusion of black experience that put Wright off, and he shows it with candor and affection. In "Lizabeth: The Caterpillar Story," for example, a father eats the remainder of a caterpillar his baby daughter has started chewing, on the pretext that if he didn't die, neither would she. The scene is presented without revulsion and without humor. It is taken as something with the authority of human feeling and human action, and with total unconcern for any adverse opinion about blacks that it might give rise to. (We may contrast the way Reed has Abdul Sufi Hamid destroy the sacred book of Jes Grew to keep black people from being associated with obscene

4. I say this without contesting George E. Kent's observation that the author of *Invisible Man* commands "an almost godlike knowledge of Blackness" ("Ralph Ellison and Afro-American Folk and Cultural Tradition," *CLA Journal* 13:274.

rites.) But eating a caterpillar expresses more than a parental love unto death. It tells of a father's readiness to destroy whatever might endanger his child, and his willingness, where it is necessary for her protection, to go into any squalor. Though the act itself is ineffectual, the spirit behind it has a decided power, on the social as well as the symbolic level.

Wideman sets down the equivalent of the caterpillar story, again and again, defying common opinion and common etiquette. "You got to *Go there to Know where*," one of his characters proclaims (p. 104). Wideman simply takes us there and immerses us in things. In "The Watermelon Story," a wino is sitting on a stack of watermelons in front of an A & P plate-glass window when the watermelons give way under him and he is flung through the glass and has his arm "chopped off." But the wino survives and passes his time "in the Bum's Forest drinking just as much wine with one arm as he did with two" (p. 103). And this story freely modulates—because "the watermelon" is a corporate noun that includes all the fruit of that name—into the story from "slavery days" about old Rebecca and Isaac who at long last are vouchsafed a baby boy, found inside a watermelon when Isaac cracks it open with "that talking knuckle of his" (p. 105).

The story does not apologize for its miracle, but turns on the skeptical audience: "youall niggers ain't ready. . . . Youall too smarty panted" (p. 106). And it establishes its own pitch of reality with the wonderful picture of "a living breathing baby boy hid up in there smiling back at Isaac, grabbing that crusty knuckle and holding on like it was a titty" (p. 105). The phrase "smiling *back* at Isaac" fully captures Isaac's delight and belief without making an issue of them. And the image of the child "grabbing that crusty knuckle" establishes the child's instincts and health. And yet the scene is unclamorous, sure of its own knowledge, content with its own world.

Just as Wideman does not boggle at miracles, he does not scruple at disillusionment: "There's more. There's the rest goes with it so I'ma tell it all" (p. 106). The rest "was the weeping and wailing" (p. 106) and "two crinkly old people on a shuck mattress shivering

under they quilt" (p. 107), for the spirit, as inexplicably as he had
given the child, "took [it] back" (p. 106). The little boy who is being
regaled with stories of old black life finds something "cruel" in this
(p. 106), but it is neither cruel nor kind. It is "there," and enables him
to "know where." The wildness of the story in terms of miracle and
mayhem should not blind us to its relentless accommodation to
reality, indeed its wry victory over reality by virtue of such accommodation. "Accepting the lesson" has been Jack-the-Bear's greatest
difficulty; for the boy in "The Watermelon Story," who to the last
wants to think the wino's arm might have grown back (p. 107), the
trick is to get the lesson: nothing lasts, except the will to last. And
when all seems lost, what remains is "to figure out how to use what's
left" (p. 107). It seems to me that with the plate-glass window and the
baby in the melon patch Wideman spans black experience in America, urban and rural, slave and free, taking it candidly for what is
there, but knowing that something *is* there, inalienably and
incomparably.

Throughout *Damballah* Wideman is bent on getting into the
depths and hidden corners of black experience, from miracles to
madness to mayhem to malice to lust to love of freedom. Something
of his range and variety can be seen in the contrast between the first
and last pieces in the book.

The opening story centers on Orion, and radiates off two episodes where he is seen standing as it were in a world of his own. In
the first he stands in the river and mourns for the fact that he was
captured into slavery before he had learned "the fishing magic" and
"the proper words, the proper tones to please the fish" (p. 18).[5] In the
later episode Orion ends up killed as a would-be rapist for standing
in mystical absorption near his mistress, and without clothes. The

5. A recent story is apropos here. In Hong Kong a friend of mine discovered
that the Chinese use drums as part of their technique for fishing. He expressed
amazement, and offered the information that in the United States the best opinion
favors careful avoidance of casting shadows and the observance of strict silence. "You
must be right," the Chinese responded. "We've only been doing it this way for a few
thousand years."

writing is intense, but spare, like Orion, and the action clean, with an astringency that verges on harshness.

The final story is of Belle, who is twofold: (1) the old black woman who for years went around with a cage on her shoulder and in the cage bore a bell; and (2) the speaker's ancestress, Sybela, who escaped from slavery and successfully traversed five hundred miles "through hostile, dangerous territory" to establish a free family seat in Homewood.[6] But, as we learn, the modern state of the blood involves not only the new Belle's eccentricity but also crime and prison. The pure memory of Orion, standing like a monument, and the pure drive of Sybela, moving like a latter-day Aeneas, break down or scatter into angular, troubled images and actions. The very writing about Belle is denser, the structuring and unfolding of the story more crabbed and reluctant than is the case with Orion. It is as though the beginning of the accumulated story that is *Damballah* enjoyed greater lucidity of spirit and purpose, despite its pain and lack of freedom, than the end. At the end, the speaker remains caught in a search for meaning, whereas at the beginning Orion was straining to recover knowledge whose meaning he implicitly possessed and trusted.

It is as much a search for meaning as for being that inspires the trend toward reimmersion in Afro-American literature. The historian-protagonist in *The Chaneysville Incident* stands as a candid embodiment of this fact. John Washington's central act of closeting himself to study his dead father's carefully placed materials actually takes up the Afro-American motif of hibernation and makes it over into a preparation for understanding, not (as with Ellison) for action. Indeed, his "hibernation" in the quasi-sacred upstairs room contains a strong hint of his unorthodox approach, in the fact that he cannot abide *cold*. (Perhaps his instinctive reaction is aggravated by the discovery that typhus flourished in the winter [pp. 284ff.].) But as with *Damballah*, the meaning is less than clear. First, John's search into the documents during his hibernation proves fruitless, ending in the same emptiness as the Chinese-box system in *Mumbo Jumbo*.

6. Sybela appears also in Wideman's *Hiding Place*.

Then the contents of the surprise box, the hidden will of his father, Moses Washington, lead John into a series of smug missteps and finally to the symbolic act of making a box in the snow ("a frame of wood") for "the tools of [the historian's] trade" and setting fire to them. His father's name calls for a special gloss in this light; it clamorously explains itself on one level, but on another it is a source of bafflement, as neither the promised land nor the new country has any site or signposts.

The fire in the snow is likewise a rich but not an unambiguous symbol. It takes us back to the invisible man's spontaneous, pragmatic burning of the contents of his briefcase in the manhole, and adds (1) abstract and comprehensive intention, and (2) a direct sense of coping with winter or breaking the rhythm of hibernation ("I kicked a clear space in the snow" p. 450), and (3) a sense of finality, of knowing what and when to let go, and above all how to let go. But even in the act of giving over the impulse to understanding and the instruments of analytical inquiry, the protagonist seeds their recrudescence. He leaves the things that had provoked his inquiry, the resealed folio as well as the "books and pamphlets and diaries and maps . . . *for the next man who would need them*" (p. 450, italics added). And above all he dedicates his act of giving over "understanding" to the spirit of understanding: "As I struck the match it came to me how strange it would all look to someone else. . . . I wondered if that someone would understand" (p. 450). He even intensifies the dedication by giving it a personal focus, and brings it all back to himself by making that person his wife: "Not just someone; Judith. I wondered if she would understand when she saw the smoke go rising from the far side of the Hill" (p. 450).

The pressure toward understanding, let us note, precedes John's election of history as a career. It may indeed have caused it. In grade school he had discovered that ignorance equals humiliation, and that a little knowledge (outdoing Pope) comes close to being deadly, while total knowledge serves as a source of power. But the equation of understanding and power becomes less certain as the subject matter becomes larger and more complex. The only power John Washington really possesses at the end of his story is the power (admittedly not negligible) to shift the quest for understanding to Judith, and to us.

In effect Bradley has set up a circular reading of *The Chaneysville Incident*. The action ends by driving back to its beginning, to the aborted quest for knowledge of, and through, history, and to the surprise revelation of the will. Presumably, even though the "next man" cannot count on that prop, the cycle will somehow lead on to the dramatically vivid but intellectually irresolute fire in the snow and that to the thought of "someone else" who will "understand," and thus to the beginning again.

John Washington's reimmersion ends, but reimmersion must go on in perpetual resumption, at once revelatory and frustrating, at once emancipating and insufficient. The reader becomes John Washington's heir, the "next man" who however dares not burn the tools of his trade, having been enjoined to use them—that is, now, the book—in endless repetition. In this light, we might almost see Truman Held as immersing himself in Meridian's sleeping bag and then instantly making the reader *his* heir, with assurance no greater than John Washington holds out.

In the beautifully cadenced scene containing the pivotal quarrel between John and Judith Washington, the latter all but enunciates the problematical status of understanding in the new concern with reimmersion in Afro-American literature. She also places it in relation to intimacy:

"You never shared anything with me," [Judith] said. "You told me how you acted when your brother died, and I thought it was intimacy. But it was just a little piece of something you had figured out and finished with." (p. 272)

Just prior to this, Judith has charged John with keeping "a big lead vault" in his head and not letting out anything he hasn't "figured down to the last quarter inch" and "torn to pieces a thousand times." Clearly understanding is modifying not only reimmersion, but intimacy as well.

Substantially the same passion for understanding (or meaning), the same inhibition of intimacy, and the same compulsive *and tele-*

ological reimmersion as in *The Chaneysville Incident* had already appeared in two short stories, "Everyday Use" by Alice Walker (*In Love and Trouble*) and "Private Domain" by James Alan McPherson (*Hue and Cry*). The antique quilt in "Everyday Use," as Stepto has observed to me, graphically focuses the willed, detached quality of the new immersion. Dee, the daughter who "stood off under the sweet gum tree" (p. 49) while her house burned down, and who had gone "to Augusta to school" (p. 50), comes back for the heirloom when black turns fashionable. She wants it as something important to her self-image, like her new name (Wangero Leewanika Lemanjo). She wants it as something to study and display, like the pictures she is suddenly bent on making with her Polaroid ("she never takes a shot without making sure the house is included" p. 53). Dee is exposed as an opportunist, and so is McPherson's hero, Rodney, with his weekend lessons in being black. Both Walker and McPherson bring out the power of the new black movement of the late 1960s by showing how it captures and distorts two formerly proud and pretentious Afro-Americans who suddenly find it cool to pass, mirabile dictu, for black.

In a more substantial and more complex way, Gayl Jones had also wrestled with the demands of reimmersion in her first novel, *Corregidora*. The leitmotif of the text, its overt concern and fulcrum, is the matter of "making generations." Motives for so doing may be diametrically opposed: the old Portuguese seaman-slaver who gives his name to generations of women and to the book has mostly profit in mind; the women, right down to the eponymous heroine whose hysterectomy renders her incapable of "making generations," have it in mind to assure living witnesses to the progenitor's vileness. But it is the irony of war that the factions must join in one field. To this is added the irony of history: it is not enough for the Corregidora women to make generations, for they also have to hand down the reason why, with the result that the reason, the analytical and forensic spirit, gradually comes to dominate the field of action. Each generation of women has fewer children than its predecessor, until an accident leaves Ursa Corregidora childless and barren.

Imperceptibly, in other words, the fierce passion and creative malice of the first Corregidora woman has given way in her successors to a derivative, driven obedience, and a dynamic clash of spirits has turned into a vendetta with a ghost. The sameness of the sexual mission across time should not blind us to the fact that there has been a real diminution of the act, and of interest in the act, and of capacity for the act. Propaganda, or words about the mission, has taken over from the mission itself.

Corregidora espouses action, but remains a book of delay and avoidance and denial. It is at bottom a book about meaning, or attempted understanding. It continually rings changes on the idea of "pretending not to know what's meant," or not knowing and yet not asking, or being "afraid to ask more." As a result its exploitive sexual action remains strangely verbal; that is, it comes across as something that violates speech taboos more than human bodies or standards of personal integrity or moral principles. Intimacy is not at issue, though intimate things are at work. The meaning of these actions accordingly remains obscure, and the actors thwarted in two spheres. In like manner the engagement with the past proves less a matter of reimmersion than of arrest and obsession. (There is an immersion scene of sorts, but it involves the literal drowning of the runaway adolescent slave, with the cruel notation that after three days his body rose; we find no redemption here.) The meaning of the past also remains obscure. Mutt Thomas's attempt to make use of the past by adopting his grandfather's trick of eating onions and peppermints is unavailing: "I tried it but it made me sick."

Ursa Corregidora herself illustrates the basic quandary of the text, that movement seems impossible until meanings are known, and meaning seems available only through movement. The emphasis on sex results from the fact that it so readily stands as a synecdoche for movement. But sex itself is a movement toward a larger goal than the "generation" that is specified. We need to see generation as merely instrumental, the real objective being *propagation*, that is, the spreading of the word, not just the multiplication of seed.

The past, as Wilburn Williams, Jr., notes, offers "possibilities of inspiration and renewal," but it also "can exert a malignant influence on the present."[7] The Corregidora legacy is supposed to inspire a verdict but it only perpetuates itself inertially, with a faintly malignant influence. The only "verdict" that actually appears in the novel is tainted by its prevailing and reductive sexuality: "I know you got some good pussy."

In only one aspect of *Corregidora* does its obsessive and somewhat cryptic activity evolve into a measure of understanding, a measure of available meaning. That aspect is the blues. Ursa Corregidora is a blues singer whose experience of losing her baby (and her womb) at her husband's hands leads to a new style and voice for her, and to a new level of success. The blues can be taken as a subtheme of the novel. The meaning and work of the blues become all but a formal topic, receiving explicit discussion and analysis. The amplifying presence of the blues seems to give historical depth, validity, dignity, and power to Ursa's experience and to her being. And yet it is important to recognize that the same temporal alteration or denaturing that besets the Corregidora issue also infects the blues subtheme in the novel. Though at one point Ursa sings to Mutt before they make love, the blues cannot be said to break out of the condition of an isolated phenomenon of a nightclub. The novel may abound in blues-worthy incidents or situations, but its action rather deploys than absorbs the blues.

The sharpest evidence of the artificial status of the blues in *Corregidora* actually occurs where the blues tradition is supposed to be most strongly upheld, in Ursa's invention of new blues songs. Her songs are about an endless tunnel that finally closes in on a moving train "like a fist," and about a "bird woman" with eyes like "deep wells" into which a young man takes a journey that will allow no return. Right off it appears that we are dealing with the blues singer doing Freudian songs. These songs reek of literary-psychoanalytic

7. Wilburn Williams, Jr., "Covenant of Timelessness and Time," in *Chant of Saints: A Gathering of Afro-American Literature, Art, and Scholarship*, ed. Michael S. Harper and Robert B. Stepto (Urbana: University of Illinois Press, 1979), p. 77. The reader should also consult Charles T. Davis, "Robert Hayden's Use of History," in *Modern Black Poets*, ed. Donald Gibson (Englewood Cliffs, N.J.: Prentice-Hall, 1973), pp. 96–111.

metaphor; they are private songs to be enjoyed by a sophisticated audience. In other words, neither the natural communal spirit that Michael Harper and Sherley Williams identify in the blues nor yet the direct, natural idiom that Williams identifies as their hallmark can be discerned here. Jones is using the blues as a resonant storehouse, not as a living field. Ursa Corregidora's blues are at first only song and subsequently (by accident) turn into song infused with life, whereas the blues proper emerge out of life distilled into song.

We may note that *Corregidora* (1975) offers itself as a story of kinship, with a curious *serial* character. That is to say, the Corregidora women do not so much band together (though they meet in one place) as hand on to one another, generation after generation, a common enemy and a common goal. The sense of *currency* that we associate with kinship gives way to a sense of sameness over time; the purpose of "generation" is unvaried conservation. But because the conception of kinship verges on the monomaniacal, *Corregidora* operates as much in terms of solitude as of connection. Both Mutt Thomas and Tadpole McCormick, Ursa's first and second husbands, have extreme difficulty breaking down her physical reserve, and both are aware that she has withheld herself even more decisively in mental-spiritual terms.

Nor is Ursa's solitude merely temperamental. It is genuinely in the mode of solitude as a state beyond veiling and before action and association that we have identified as crucial in the development of the Afro-American literary psyche. She has a mission, however cryptic, in the making of generations, and that mission is the beginning of release, indeed redemption, from the hereditary abuse and self-denial of having fallen into the hands of the Portuguese Corregidora. But, like Bigger Thomas (the name Mutt Thomas resonates tellingly against Bigger's) and like Jack-the-Bear, Ursa (and again the name—female bear—has odd resonances) has no means of executing her mission. She is in a state of arrest, in which her solitude is *supposed to be* a form of hibernation, but which she is unable to escape.

Two instruments of escape are, however, suggested in the novel. The first is the blues. The inefficacy of this approach is apparent from the fact that the blues function as a protective arena for Ursa Corregidora; she sings in a transparent cocoon. And the second means of escape, just being essayed at the novel's close, is sexuality. But Ursa's sexual experiment, like her use of the blues, suffers from an absence of spontaneity, or from the imposition of conscious will upon nature. She frightens Mutt Thomas—with whom she is reunited—with her sudden fellatiousness, and she frightens herself. They each anticipate "hurt" from the other, rather than experiencing any sense of breakthrough or even hope. *Corregidora* ends on this restrained, faintly ominous note, which of course *Eva's Man*, Jones's second novel, will justify and amplify. More than hurt comes out there. Disaster and a sense of doom mark *Eva's Man*. The Corregidora quest for a "verdict" proves to be an obsession, a fatality, and the verdict is not moral or cultural but narrowly legal.

At various levels the preoccupation with meaning in *Corregidora* befuddles ordinary action: what does Mutt mean to do when he causes Ursa's terrible accident, and what does Jeffy mean to do when she fondles Ursa's breast, and what does Grandmama mean to do when she powders her breasts adagio in front of her daughter's husband, and what does Ursa mean when she seems to give in fellatiously to Mutt? Let us recall that Ursa Corregidora is the one who insists on meaning. The rest of the contemporary characters make at least adequate accommodations to ongoing life. She, however, needs to "generate" clarity where ambiguity, obscurity, and even downright accident prevail. Beyond impairing action, the insistence on meaning befuddles the intimacy between people and the reimmersion in the past that should guide and save. And we should note that meaning gets into the new reimmersion whether it is fated, as with the Corregidoras, or free, as with John Washington.

The distinctive thing about *Corregidora* is that it strives to incorporate the blues vitally into its system; it tries to derive meaning from the blues, if not perhaps to give meaning to the blues. In this respect the blues become a form for expressing the *principle* of reimmersion. What *Corregidora* does to the blues, Reed's *Mumbo Jumbo* does to "signifying": each takes a living, spontaneous art and fits it into a systematic formal art. It must be conceded that Jones and

Reed give their respective "folk" forms great self-consciousness and scope and weight and complexity, but they do so at the cost of natural sensitivity and swiftness and freedom. These radical forms persist, but in a manner that reverses the old French bromide, for the more they persist, the more they are altered. As Sherley Williams shows from a literary standpoint, and Kimberly Benston from a musical standpoint in his moving essay on John Coltrane ("Late Coltrane: A Re-Membering of Orpheus," in Harper and Stepto, *Chant of Saints*, pp. 413–24), the blues are still being built on today. And as H. L. Gates, Jr., shows in relation to Ishmael Reed, signifying is still being built on today. But the foundation is subordinate to the edifice it insures.

When we hear Coltrane's *Interstellar Spaces*, we are not so promptly taken back to the blues (despite Benston's elucidations) as to Hayden's planetary pieces. Both Coltrane and Hayden make us intimate with the future, rather than with the past. In like manner, the new reimmersion has designs on the future, but without the supreme capacity of a Hayden or a Coltrane to illuminate it and reveal its mystical identity with the present and the past. It is no wonder that Toni Morrison should have produced, in *Tar Baby*, a story of the avoidance of immersion ("she has forgotten her ancient properties" p. 305), or that, in the same novel, the deliberate insistence on pursuing the past on Son's part should cause him to be led by a blind woman to an islet where blind men "race . . . horses like angels all over the hills where the rain forest is, where the champion daisy trees still grow"(p. 306). The man "without human rites" ends among preternatural rites, as much without meaning in their uncanny beauty as they are without end.

It is necessary to distinguish the passion for understanding in the new reimmersion from the possession of self-knowledge and knowledge of the black situation that Du Bois initiated at the beginning of the century. For Du Bois had not abstractly and purposely set about to garner that knowledge, any more than he set out to become W. E. B. Du Bois. We know in fact the juggernaut of his nature caused him to sacrifice opportunities for influence and advancement that a dash of theater and flexibility would infallibly have brought him. *The Souls of Black Folk* is the self-proclamation of a man and of a mind, and a sort of analytical autobiography of a sensitive intellectual spirit. The study of history and the study of the sorrow-songs and the memory of studying and teaching all spring from the same source and answer the same need, to become W. E. B. Du Bois as the person he was in the circumstances dictated for him. By contrast, John Washington's historical studies in *The Chaneysville Incident* are formally undertaken and only lead to his self-discovery because Old Jack pulls on his loyalty and his dead father manipulates his historical curiosity. In like manner, it is only in this reconstituting sense that we can accommodate to the blues tradition (1) Duke Ellington's "Transblucency" and (2) the fact that Big Joe Turner, the "boss of the blues," was the veritable John the Baptist of rock and roll, with "Shake, Rattle, and Roll" and "Honey Hush."

Even as we say that Ellison's *Invisible Man* and Jones's *Corregidora* would have been impossible without the blues, or that the popular tradition of signifying was necessary to Reed's *Mumbo Jumbo*, we should remind ourselves that these later works *depart* as much as they arise from the earlier forms. To adopt the epochal distinction made by Friedrich Schiller of another body of literature, Reed and Jones stand as "sentimental" writers, whereas the blues and signifying count as "naive" phenomena. The individual authors are reflective and tendentious, because they stand separated from their ideals; the popular forms are decisive and clear, but have relatively limited amplitude and complexity.

The formal reimmersion in Afro-American literature also casts interesting sidelights on the quest for "meaning" that Martin Price sees as intrinsic to the novel in the last two centuries. Price sets up two categories of characters whose lives equally show a drive toward meaning, despite major differences in outlook and process of experience. Speaking particularly of Tolstoy, but in language that might be used as readily of Dostoevski or Flaubert or Lawrence or Faulkner or Pynchon or Bellow, Price remarks that the

central figures . . . search restlessly for a meaning in their lives. They stumble, lurch, fall into fatuous error, but eventually come to recognize that they have been too quixotically ambitious to see what lies within themselves and all about them. In contrast are those great Tolstoyan characters who cannot fully believe in life's possibilities or who have cut themselves off from all that might provide their lives with support.[8]

It is crucial to see that in both categories, those who go roundabout and self-impeded to a state of clarification and those who thwart and stifle their own chances, Price is looking at characters involved in a world of action, of ongoing personal engagements.

With the pursuit of meaning in the novels of the new reimmersion, that world of action of course remains, but it is infused with a deliberateness and specificity of inquiry into the past that would seem to make investigation a form of action. It will be easier to see how this is so if we take a moment to consider the writer who stands out as the portrayer of characters preoccupied with the past, namely William Faulkner. The element of investigation is not always present in Faulkner's characters (think of Gail Hightower in *Light in August*), but even when it is, the past does not appear large and open and many-layered. Rather, Faulkner's characters tend to be caught up in an episode or scene or event out of the past (this holds true even with Ike McCaslin in *The Bear*). They live it over, they live under its sway. It is otherwise with Bradley's characters, and Wideman's, and for that matter Morrison's. *They* are summoned by the past, sometimes, but as often they choose to search it, with a reflective, rangy, open approach. They pull away from absorption in ongoing action and circumstances, current or remembered. Conrad has described action as "consolatory," but the Afro-American inherits an action that is both belittling and obscure. Insofar as action is the "enemy of thought," to use Conrad's phrase again, it must be suspended or at least one must suspend oneself above it.

The characters in the new reimmersion move in an ambience of commitment, like Faulkner's characters, but searching the past is as much an instrument as a sign of that commitment. They lack the protection that unbreakable obsession gives to Faulkner's past-mastered characters, and they have no control over what the past

8. Martin Price, *Forms of Life: Character and Moral Imagination in the Novel* (New Haven: Yale University Press, 1983), p. xv.

will contain and, in a manner of speaking, portend for them. In compensation, however, they have a singular promise of benefits from the past.[9]

In a sense, though, within the total pattern of Afro-American literature, the new reimmersion remains problematical. Intimacy continues to elude, or to be thwarted by the irony of intending it. Even kinship, the manifestation of the black spirit that is most susceptible to the will, is called into question, as the hyperanalytical John Washington of *The Chaneysville Incident* is plainly told that he fails to be a font of brotherhood. The new historical preoccupation of Afro-American literature has, in fact, one curious resonance. Where Ellison's invisible man, a mere few decades ago, feared to plunge out of history, and so desperately clung to its surface, the new generation of writers seems to fear not to plunge *into* history. What was a source of blankness and dread has turned into a source of solace and assurance. At the same time, one partiality succeeds another. The surfaces of experience remain at odds with the depths of history, and the surfaces of history with the depths of experience.

And yet the voice of Afro-American literature is compellingly if not prophetically heard. In the final story of Wideman's *Damballah* the narrator speaks of a voice—it is Sybela's, but also his own—that "seeks to recover everything" and he harks back to Harper's "Song: I Want a Witness," and to the ever-present, ever-altering problem of finding a voice in black American literature. After the elevated silence and the sense of immanence that Walker portrays in *Meridian*, Wideman gives new voice to "everything" in the black condition.

Intimacy has been, and may be again. Reimmersion seems to take its place, while seeking to rediscover it. Michael Harper's Coltrane reappears, but not as an idol; two arrested youths in a Wideman story have the air of being "a million miles away discussing Coltrane or pussy," (*Damballah*, p. 199). But they are far from free, and seem to mark the end of the line of freedom that Sybela had laid down,

---

9. The Corregidora women show the Faulknerian narrowness of interest in a past episode, as well as Faulknerian repetitiveness and obsession in action.

except that the Supreme Court is going to take up a case that bears on theirs.

As Wideman says in the very spirit of John Coltrane, "the struggle doesn't ever end." Nor do the "connections" (p. 205). Wideman leaves the story looking ahead, to justice, but also backward to the woman who, though bound to freedom and founding it for her line, was ambivalent in her feelings:

In the quiet moments of that first morning of freedom she misses the moaning horn [that awakens the slaves] and hates the white man [who has thwarted his own father to help her escape], her lover, her liberator, her children's father sleeping beside her. (p. 197)

Sybela's story in its ultimate dimensions is the universe of Afro-American literature, ever expanding from the impacted beginnings in slavery to the guarded constellations of self-veiling, and so on to the first-magnitude forms of intimacy, and beyond. The trauma of slavery may be a receding *fons et origo*, only the ex-slave does not sleep, cannot afford that luxury. She is up with the dawn, unfolding the singular shape of her story and the unique force of her vision like new garments she must wear in lieu of the torpid comfort of bedclothes.

Primary Works of Afro-American Literature

Baldwin, James. *Another Country*. New York: Dell, 1970.
_____✓. *The Fire Next Time*. New York: Bell, 1964.
_____✓. *Go Tell It on the Mountain*. New York: Signet, 1954.
_____. *If Beale Street Could Talk*. New York: New American Library, 1975.
_____✓. *Nobody Knows My Name*. New York: Dial Press, 1961.
_____✓. *Notes of a Native Son*. New York: Bantam, 1964.
_____. *Tell Me How Long the Train's Been Gone*. New York: Dial Press, 1968.
Baraka, Amiri. *See* Jones, LeRoi.
Bontemps, Arna, ed. *American Negro Poetry*. Rev. ed. New York: Hill and Wang, 1974.
Bradley, David. *The Chaneysville Incident*. New York: Avon Books, 1981.
Brown, Sterling. *The Collected Poems*. Selected by Michael Harper. New York: Harper and Row, 1980.
_____. *Southern Road: Poems*. 1932. Reprint, with a new introduction by Sterling Stuckey. Boston: Beacon Press, 1974.
Bullins, Ed. *Five Plays*. New York: Bobbs-Merrill, 1968.
_____. *How Do You Do: A Nonsense Drama*. Mill Valley, Calif.: Illuminations Press, 1968.
Charles, Ray, and David Ritz. *Brother Ray: Ray Charles' Own Story*. New York: Warner Books, 1978.

Chesnutt, Charles. *The Conjure Woman*. 1899. Reprint. Ridgewood, N.J.: Gregg Press, 1968.

_____. *The Marrow of Tradition*. 1901. Reprint, with an introduction by Robert M. Farnsworth. Ann Arbor: University of Michigan Press, 1969.

_____. *The Short Fiction*. Edited with an introduction by Sylvia Lyons Render. Washington, D.C.: Howard University Press, 1974.

_____. *The Wife of His Youth, and Other Stories of the Color Line*. 1899. Reprint, with illustrations by Clyde O. DeLand and a new introduction by Earl Schenck Miers. Ann Arbor: University of Michigan Press, 1972.

✓Cleaver, Eldridge. *Soul on Ice*. Introduction by Maxwell Geismar. New York: McGraw Hill, 1968.

Cullen, Countee. *On These I Stand: An Anthology of the Best Poems of Countee Cullen*. New York: Harper, 1947.

_____, ed. *Caroling Dusk: An Anthology of Verse by Negro Poets*. 1927. Reprint. New York: Harper and Row, 1955.

Davis, Arthur P., and Saunders Redding, eds. *Cavalcade: Negro American Writing from 1760 to the Present*. Boston: Houghton Mifflin, 1971.

Demby, William. *Beetlecreek, a Novel*. New York: Rinehart, 1950.

_____. *The Catacombs*. Intro. by Robert Bone. New York: Perennial Library, 1970.

✓Douglass, Frederick. *Narrative of the Life of Frederick Douglass, An American Slave. Written by Himself*. 1845. Reprint. New York: New American Library, 1968.

Du Bois, W. E. B. *The Autobiography*. Edited by Herbert Aptheker. New York: International, 1968.

_____. *Dusk of Dawn: An Essay toward an Autobiography of a Race Concept*. New York: Harcourt, Brace & Co., 1940.

_____. *The Negro*. 1915. Introduction by Herbert Aptheker. Millwood, N.Y.: Kraus-Thomson, 1974.

_____. *The Quest of the Silver Fleece*. 1911. Reprint, with an introduction by Herbert Aptheker. Millwood, N.Y.: Kraus-Thomson, 1974.

_____. "Reconstruction and Its Benefits." *American Historical Review* 15 (July 1910): 781–99.

_____✓___. *The Souls of Black Folk: Essays and Sketches*. 1903. Reprint
with an introduction by Saunders Redding. Greenwich, Conn.:
Fawcett, 1961.

Dumas, Henry. *Jonoah and the Green Stone*. Arranged by Eugene B.
Redmond. New York: Random House, 1976.

Dunbar, Paul Laurence. *The Complete Poems*. Introduction to "Lyr-
ics of Lowly Life" by W. D. Howells. 1913. Reprint. New York:
Dodd, Mead, 1962.

✓Ellison, Ralph. *Invisible Man*. 1952. Reprint, with an introduction by
the author. New York: Vintage, 1982.

_____. *Shadow and Act*. New York: New American Library, 1966.

Equiano, Olaudah. *The Life of Olaudah Equiano; or, Gustavus
Vassa the African, 1789*. Reprint, with a new introduction by
Paul Edwards. London: Dawson, 1969.

Fair, Ronald L. *Hog Butcher*. New York: Harcourt, Brace and
World, 1966.

_____. *We Can't Breathe*. New York: Harper and Row, 1972.

Fauset, Jessie Redmon. *Comedy, American Style*. 1933. Reprint.
New York: Negro Universities Press, 1969.

_____. *There Is Confusion*. New York: Boni and Liveright, 1924.

✓Gaines, Ernest J. *The Autobiography of Miss Jane Pittman*. New
York: Bantam, 1972.

_____. *Bloodline*. New York: Dial Press, 1968.

✓Giovanni, Nikki. *Black Feeling, Black Talk*. 3rd ed. Detroit: Broadside Press, 1970.

_____. *My House: Poems*. New York: William Morrow, 1972.

_____. *The Women and the Men*. New York: William Morrow.
1975.

Haley, Alex. *Roots: The Saga of an American Family*. Garden City,
N.Y.: Doubleday, 1976.

✗✓Hansberry, Lorraine. *A Raisin in the Sun*. New York: Random
House, 1959.

Harper, Michael S. *Dear John, Dear Coltrane*. Pittsburgh: University
of Pittsburgh Press, 1970.

_____. *History Is Your Own Heartbeat*. Urbana: University of
Illinois Press, 1971.

_____. *Images of Kin: New and Selected Poems*. Urbana: Univer-
sity of Illinois Press, 1977.

———. *Nightmare Begins Responsibility*. Urbana: University of Illinois Press, 1975.

———. *Photographs: Negatives: History as Apple Tree*. San Francisco: Scarab Press, 1972.

———. *Song: I Want a Witness*. Pittsburgh: University of Pittsburgh Press, 1972.

Harper, Michael S., and Robert B. Stepto, eds. *Chant of Saints: A Gathering of Afro-American Literature, Art, and Scholarship*. Urbana: University of Illinois Press, 1979.

Hayden, Robert. *American Journal*. Taunton, Mass. Effendi, 1978.

———. *Angle of Ascent: New and Selected Poems*. New York: Liveright, 1975.

———. *Words in the Mourning Time; Poems*. New York: October House, 1970.

Himes, Chester. *If He Hollers, Let Him Go*. Chatham, N.J.: Chatham Booksellers, 1973.

———. *The Primitive*. New York: New American Library, 1955.

Hughes, Langston. *The Best of Simple*. Illustrations by Bernhard Nast. New York: Hill & Wang, 1961.

———. *The Big Sea*. New York: Alfred A. Knopf, 1940.

———. *Good Morning, Revolution: Uncollected Social Protest Writings*. Edited with an introduction by Faith Berry; foreword by Saunders Redding. New York: Lawrence Hill & Co., 1973.

———. "The Negro Artist and the Racial Mountain." *The Nation* 122 (23 June 1926), pp. 692–94.

———. *Not Without Laughter*. 1930. Reprint, with an introduction by Arna Bontemps. New York: Collier, 1969.

———. *Selected Poems*. New York: Vintage Books, 1974.

———. *The Weary Blues*. 1926. Reprint, with an introduction by Carl Van Vechten. New York: Alfred A. Knopf, 1945.

Hughes, Langston, and Arna Bontemps, eds. *The Book of Negro Folklore*. New York: Dodd, Mead, 1958.

———. *The Poetry of the Negro, 1760–1960*. Garden City, N.Y.: Doubleday, 1970.

Hurston, Zora Neale. *Dust Tracks on a Road: An Autobiography*. 1942. Reprint, with an introduction by Larry Neal. Philadelphia: Lippincott, 1971.

———. *Mules and Men*. 1935. Reprint, with a preface by Franz Boas, an introduction by Robert E. Hemenway, and illustrations by Miguel Covarrubias. Bloomington: Indiana University Press, 1978.

_____. *Tell My Horse*. Berkeley, Calif.: Turtle Island, 1981.

_____. *Their Eyes Were Watching God*. 1937. Reprint with a foreword by Sherley Anne Williams. Urbana: University of Illinois Press, 1977.

Johnson, James Weldon. *Along This Way*. New York: Viking, 1933.

_____. *The Autobiography of an Ex-Colored Man*. 1912. Reprinted in *Three Negro Classics*, with an introduction by John Hope Franklin. New York: Avon Books, 1965.

_____. *God's Trombones: Seven Negro Sermons in Verse*. 1927. Reprint. New York: Viking Press, 1941.

Jones, Gayl. *Corregidora*. New York: Random House, 1975.

_____. *Eva's Man*. New York: Random House, 1976.

Jones, LeRoi [Amiri Baraka]. *Black Magic: Sabotage; Target Study; Black Art: Collected Poetry, 1961–1967*. Indianapolis: Bobbs-Merrill, 1969.

_____. *Blues People: Negro Music in White America*. New York: William Morrow, 1963.

_____. *Dutchman, and The Slave; Two Plays*. New York: William Morrow, 1964.

_____. *Home: Social Essays*. New York: William Morrow, 1966.

_____. *Preface to a Twenty-Volume Suicide Note*. New York: Totem/Corinth, 1961.

_____. *Raise Race Rays Raze: Essays Since 1965*. New York: Random House, 1972.

_____. *The System of Dante's Hell*. New York: Grove Press, 1966.

Jones, LeRoi, and Larry Neal, eds. *Black Fire: An Anthology of Afro-American Writing*. New York: Morrow, 1969.

Jordan, June. *Civil Wars*. Boston: Beacon Press, 1981.

_____. *His Own Where*. New York: Crowell, 1971.

_____. *New Days: Poems of Exile and Return*. New York: Emerson Hall, 1974.

_____. *New Life: New Room*. Illustrations by Ray Cruz. New York: Crowell, 1975.

_____. *Things That I Do in the Dark: Selected Poetry*. New York: Random House, 1977.

Katz, William Loren, ed. *Five Slave Narratives: A Compendium*. New York: Arno/New York Times, 1968.

Kelley, William Melvin. *A Different Drummer*. New York: Doubleday, 1969.

———. *Dem*. Garden City, N.Y.: Doubleday, 1967.

Larsen, Nella. *Passing*. 1929. Reprint. New York: Collier Books, 1971.

———. *Quicksand*. 1928. Reprint. New York: Negro Universities Press, 1969.

Locke, Alain, ed. *The New Negro*. 1925. Reprint, with a new preface by Robert Hayden. New York: Atheneum, 1968.

Lorde, Audre, *Cables to Rage*. London: P. Bremen, 1970.

———. *The Cancer Journal*. Argyle, N.Y.: Spinsters, Ink, 1980.

———. *Chosen Poems, Old and New*. New York: Norton, 1982.

McKay, Claude. *Banana Bottom*. 1933. Reprint. New York: Harvest Books, 1961.

———. *Banjo: A Story without a Plot*. 1929. Reprint. New York: Harcourt, Brace, Jovanovich, 1957.

———. *Home to Harlem*. Chatham, N.J.: Chatham Booksellers, 1973.

———. *A Long Way from Home*. 1937. Reprint. New York: Arno Press, 1969.

McPherson, James Alan. *Elbow Room: Stories*. Boston: Little, Brown, 1977.

———. *Hue and Cry: Short Stories*. New York: Random House, 1969.

Malcolm X. *The Autobiography*. With the assistance of Alex Haley. Introduction by M. S. Handler and epilogue by Alex Haley. New York: Grove Press, 1966.

Morrison, Toni. *The Bluest Eye*. New York: Pocket Books, 1970.

———. *Song of Solomon*. New York: Alfred A. Knopf, 1977.

———. *Sula*. New York: Bantam Books, 1973.

———. *Tar Baby*. New York: New American Library, 1982.

Murray, Albert. *The Omni-Americans: New Perspectives on Black Experience and American Culture*. New York: Outerbridge & Dienstfrey, 1970.

———. *Stomping the Blues*. Produced and art-directed by Harris Lewine. New York: McGraw-Hill, 1976.

Naylor, Gloria. *The Women of Brewster Place: A Novel in Seven Stories*. New York: Viking, 1982.

Petry, Ann. *The Street*. 1946. Reprint. New York: Pyramid Books, 1961.

Reed, Ishmael. *Conjure: Selected Poems, 1963–1970*. Amherst: University of Massachusetts Press, 1972.

———. *Flight to Canada*. New York: Random House, 1976.

———. *The Free-Lance Pallbearers*. New York: Avon Books, 1977.

———. *Mumbo Jumbo*. Garden City, N.Y.: Doubleday, 1973.

———. *The Terrible Twos*. New York: St. Martin's/Marek, 1982.

———. *Yellow-Back Radio Broke-Down*. New York: Avon Books, 1977.

Sanchez, Sonia. *Home Coming; Poems*. Introduction by Don L. Lee. Detroit: Broadside Press, 1969.

———. *Love Poems*. New York: Third Press, 1973.

Shange, Ntozake. *For Colored Girls Who Have Contemplated Suicide When the Rainbow Is Enuf*. New York: Macmillan, 1977.

Thurman, Wallace. *The Blacker the Berry: A Novel of Negro Life*. New York: Macaulay, 1972.

———. *Infants of the Spring: A Novel*. Afterword by John A. Williams. Carbondale: Southern Illinois University Press, 1979.

Tolson, Melvin B. *Harlem Gallery. Book I: The Curator*. Introduction by Karl Shapiro. New York: Twayne, 1965.

Toomer, Jean. *Cane*. 1923. Reprint. New York: Harper and Row, 1969.

———. "Chapters from Earth-Being: An Unpublished Autobiography." *The Black Scholar*, January 1971, pp. 3–13.

Walker, Alice. *The Color Purple*. New York: Harcourt, Brace, Jovanovich, 1982.

———. *In Love and Trouble: Stories of Black Women*. New York: Harcourt, Brace, Jovanovich, 1973.

———. *In Search of Our Mothers' Gardens*. New York: Harcourt, Brace, Jovanovich, 1983.

———. *Meridian*. New York: Harcourt, Brace, Jovanovich, 1976.

———. *Once*. New York: Harcourt, Brace, Jovanovich, 1968.

———. *Revolutionary Petunias and Other Poems*. New York: Harcourt, Brace, Jovanovich, 1973.

———. *The Third Life of Grange Copeland*. New York: Harcourt, Brace, Jovanovich, 1970.

———. *You Can't Keep a Good Woman Down*. New York: Harcourt, Brace, Jovanovich, 1981.

Walker, David. *Appeal, in Four Articles, together with a preamble, to the coloured citizens of the world, but in particular and very expressly to those in the United States of America*. Edited with

Primary Works of Afro-American Literature

an introduction by Charles M. Wiltse. New York: Hill and
Wang, 1965.

Walker, Margaret. *Jubilee*. Boston: Houghton Mifflin, 1966.

Washington, Booker T. *Up from Slavery*. 1901. Reprint. New York:
Doubleday, 1963.

Washington, Mary Helen, ed. *Midnight Birds: Stories of Contemporary Black Women Writers*. Garden City, N.Y.: Doubleday,
1980.

Wheatley, Phillis. *The Poems*. Edited with an introduction by Julian
D. Mason, Jr. Chapel Hill: University of North Carolina Press,
1966.

Wideman, John Edgar. *Damballah*. New York: Avon Books, 1981.

———. *Hiding Place*. New York: Avon Books, 1981.

———. *Hurry Home*. New York: Harcourt, Brace & World, 1970.

Williams, John. *Captain Blackman: A Novel*. Garden City, N.Y.:
Doubleday, 1972.

———. *The Junior Bachelor Society*. New York: Doubleday, 1976.

———. *The Man Who Cried I Am*. New York: New American
Library, 1968.

———. *Sons of Darkness, Sons of Light: A Novel of Some Probability*. New York: Pocket Books, 1970.

Wilson, Harriet E. *Our Nig; or Sketches from the Life of a Free
Black*. Edited with an introduction by Henry Louis Gates, Jr.
New York: Random House, 1983.

Wright, Jay. *Dimensions of History*. Santa Cruz, Calif.: Kayak, 1976.

———. *The Homecoming Singer*. New York: Corinth Books, 1971.

Wright, Richard. *American Hunger*. Afterword by Michel Fabre.
New York: Perennial Library, 1977.

———. *Black Boy: A Record of Childhood and Youth*. New York:
Harper & Row, 1945.

———. *Black Power: A Record of Reactions in a Land of Pathos*.
New York: Harper Brothers, 1954.

———. *Native Son*. 1940. Reprint, with an introduction, "How
'Bigger' Was Born," by the author; afterword by John Reilly.
New York: Harper & Row, 1966.

———. *The Outsider*. New York: Harper & Row, 1940.

———. *Uncle Tom's Children*. New York: Harper and Brothers,
1940.

———. Untitled essay in *The God that Failed*. Edited by Richard
Howard Stafford Crossman. New York: Harper, 1949.

Index